The Real 100 Best Baseball Players of All Time ... and Why!

by Ken Shouler

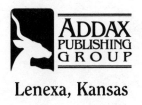

Lenexa, Kansas

Published by Addax Publishing Group
Copyright © 1998 by Ken Shouler
Edited by John Lofflin
Designed by Randy Breeden
Cover Design by Deborah Ramirez
Photos Courtesy Transcendental Graphics and AP / Wide World

For information address:
Addax Publishing Group
8643 Hauser Drive, Suite 235, Lenexa, Kansas 66215

ISBN: 1-886110-46-8

Distributed to the trade by:
Andrews McMeel Publishing
4520 Main Street, Kansas City, Missouri 64111

1 3 5 7 9 10 8 6 4 2
Printed in the United States of America

Library of Congress Cataloging-in-Publication Data

Shouler, Kenneth A.
    The real 100 best baseball players of all time— and why / by Ken Shouler.
        p.   cm.
Includes bibliographical references (p.).
ISBN 1-886110-46-8
    1. Baseball players—United States—Biography. 2. Baseball
players—Rating of—United States. I Title.
GV865.A1S514 1998
796.352'092'273—dc21
[B]   98-3347
                                                                   CIP

Table of Contents

III. The Next 25 Players

IV. The Top 25 Pitchers

Acknowledgements

I want to thank coaches, players, broadcasters, friends, family members and authors for offering their views. They include: Jim Kaat, Rick Cerone, Wade Boggs, Mike Stanton, Gene Tenace, Joe Carter, Tony Cloninger, Mel Stottlemyre, Bill Shannon, Luis Tiant, John Thorn, Mike Stanley, Joe Torre, Frank Torre, Chipper Jones and many others.

For making a substantial data base available to me, special thanks to John Thorn and Pete Palmer. Additional thanks to them for letting me make use of *Total Baseball*, the most thorough and peerless encyclopedia of baseball ever written.

Just for the love of baseball, Gordon Shouler interpreted a lot of numbers and cranked out all kinds of statistical results.

Karl Shouler worked meticulously on designing the bar graphs for the top ten players.

Thanks to Rich Garfunkel and John McCollister for their observations on baseball.

Kenneth Shouler

For My Father:

For teaching my older brothers and me by letting us hit with a fat Nellie Fox bat opposite the Brentwood lumber yard — and for always giving us a fair swing at the ball thereafter.

For My Mother:

Who bought me my first glove, autographed by Bobby Murcer, who I hoped would succeed Mickey Mantle. With a daughter and six sons, she has endured more baseball arguments and conversations than the next two people I know.

For my wife, Rose Marie, who helps me in all worthwhile things.

Foreword

Game Seven of the 1964 World Series was the first game I can remember. The Yankees — my Yankees — mounted a comeback against the Cardinals but fell short and lost. The Yankees remained my favorite team, even as their mid-sixties decline kept pace with the decline of my favorite player, Mickey Mantle.

Whether I went to Yankee Stadium or caught them on the radio or television, I kept score of the games. Looking at baseball cards and books, I would compare the statistics of the players. It was clear, even early on, that Babe Ruth was the greatest player. It was always of interest to me to find out where the others ranked.

Now it is somewhat easier to see. But baseball will challenge your ability to establish a pecking order of greats. Having gone through so many eras, each with its own offensive and defensive character, baseball stubbornly resists single interpretations of what excellence means. Pitchers from 1911 are not pitching in the same game as the hurlers from 1975 and 1998. Shortstops and second basemen can't be expected to have power statistics that outfielders do. Statistical analyses must account for these kinds of variances.

In this book I have tried to take into account the changing nature of baseball and be fair to players of all eras, while making allowances for the positions they played. In weighing players' offensive contributions, I tend to be partial to slugging average and on-base percentage. In general, I think it is also true that the great players must stand the test of time. So I have included the best five, ten and fifteen-year averages of most the top 100 players. The continuing excitement of following baseball, for me, is to see how great players like Barry Bonds, Greg Maddux, Roger Clemens, Ken Griffey, Jr., Frank Thomas and Mark McGwire will finish what they started.

Ken Shouler
White Plains, N.Y.
1998

I
The Top 25 Players

1
BABE RUTH
Pitcher/Right Field

"The Bambino" "The Sultan of Swat"
Born: 2/6/1895 Baltimore, MD, Died: 8/16/48 New York, NY
6 feet 2 inches, 215 pounds
Debut: 7/11/14, Played 22 years: 1914-1935
1914-1919, Boston (AL); 1920-1934, New York (AL);
1935, Boston (NL)

Babe Ruth's love of children, of cigars, of food and drink – in a word, his love of life – was equaled only by his greatness as a ballplayer.

Ruth is the greatest baseball player ever for many reasons. All of those reasons can be summed up by saying that he is the largest, most full-blown talent who has ever been or will ever be. When you consider that he was on a Hall of Fame course as a pitcher before he became a great home run hitter, then you are just beginning to fit the size of his talent into your lens.

It is nearly impossible to make a strong case for anyone but Ruth. His .690 slugging average is 56 points ahead of his nearest competitor, Ted Williams. His total average – derived from taking his number of bases and dividing them by his number of outs – is 1.399, 79 points ahead of Ted Williams' 1.320 and more than .170 points ahead of anyone else.

A kind of David Letterman-esque Top Ten List helps to make the case for the Babe. In keeping with Letterman's format, I will put the Top Ten reasons that Ruth is the best in reverse order. Supply your own drum roll as we approach reason number one:

TEN REASONS WHY RUTH IS THE BEST EVER

10. Ruth had 94 wins and 46 losses as a pitcher. He was the best left-hander of his time and we can reasonably infer that had he continued, he would have made the Hall of Fame as a hurler. Ruth never pitched 200 innings in a season beyond the age of 22; by 1918 the Red Sox were already giving him 300-plus at bats a year. He won 13 and lost 8 in 1918, not too shabby considering he led the American League – and all of baseball – in home runs with 11.

He won 8 more games in 1919, the same year he established an all-time Major League record with 29 homers. But his pitching opportunities dwindled after that; he would never again win more than two games in a year.

9. On the subject of pitching, Ruth's proudest record was his 29 and-two-thirds consecutive scoreless innings in World Series play, accumulated during the 1916 and 1918 Series, when he compiled a 3-0 record and an 0.87 ERA. His shutout innings record stood for 43 years, until Whitey Ford broke it in 1961. The 1918 Series, the last the haunted Red Sox ever won, was one in which Ruth had two victories.

8. At 26, Ruth became the all-time home run leader, passing Roger Connor. Finishing his career in St. Louis in 1897, Connor took 18 years to reach his total of 136 homers, while Ruth surpassed him in July of 1921, in just his third full year as a hitter.

7. Ruth's sundry famous moments rank seventh. He christened Yankee Stadium, the "House that Ruth Built," by slugging its first homer in April, 1923. He hit three homers in a World Series sweep of the Cardinals in 1928. He was the first to hit an All-Star Game homer (in 1934). His famous "called shot" drew all the attention in the 1932 Series, though Gehrig hit three homers, batted .529 and had a superior series. Playing for the Boston Braves, Ruth hit three homers in a game in 1935, his last season.

6. Ruth's comparison with Ty Cobb ranks sixth. Due to Al Stump's book and the movie "Cobb" in recent years, there has been a renaissance of interest in Cobb. Cobb was a great player, no doubt the greatest player until the Ruth era began. In heralding him as a greater player than Ruth, however, Cobb supporters make several arguments. They cite Cobb's .367 lifetime average; Ruth hit .342. But they also bring up some dubious things, like how Cobb got a greater percentage of Hall of Fame votes than Ruth, an *ad populum* argument, because it is not based on anything objective, merely on people's votes.

Three quick points (more will be made later in this section) can be made to the Cobb defenders in this debate: One is Ruth's slugging average, a gargantuan .690 compared to Cobb's respectable .513. The other was Ruth's pitching record. Cobb didn't pitch. Finally, Ruth also played on 7 World Championship winning teams; Cobb played on none.

5. Ruth had more 40 and 50-homer seasons combined than anyone who ever played. Four times he hit 50 or more homers and 6 times he hit 40 or more. Those 10 times over forty – in 17 years as an outfielder – surpass the 40-plus seasons of Ken Griffey, Jr. and Mark McGwire combined. Those modern sluggers have surpassed 40 home runs just 8 times in a combined 21 years.

4. Ruth had the most productive decade in baseball history, hitting 467 homers in the 1920s. Hornsby was second with 250.

The other decade leaders were:

1900-1909	Harry Davis	66
1910-1919	Clifford "Gavvy" Cravath	126
1920-1929	Babe Ruth	467
1930-1939	Jimmie Foxx	415
1940-1949	Ted Williams	234
1950-1959	Duke Snider	326
1960-1969	Harmon Killebrew	393
1970-1979	Willie Stargell	292
1980-1989	Mike Schmidt	313

3. Ruth hit 302 homers in a 6-year period from 1926 through 1931. That's an average of 50.3 per year. That average has never been approached over a comparable period of time.

2. Ruth has the greatest homer-per-year average ever. In his 17 years as a full-time hitter, he hit 694 homers for an average of 40.8 per year.

1a. Ruth hit a homer every 11.76 at bats, far and away the greatest ratio ever. Aaron, who finished with 755 homers, hit one every 16.7 at bats, which is 16th best on the all-time list. Give Ruth 12,364 at bats as Aaron had, with the same ratio, and he hits 1,051 homers.

1. Whenever sports radio hosts talk of great records, the knee-jerk reflex is always to bring up Joe DiMaggio's 56 straight games or Johnny Vander Meer's consecutive no-hitters. One gets the feeling that these are the only records they know.

They don't seem to know that Gehrig and Foxx knocked in 100 runs in 13 consecutive seasons or that Ted Williams had an insuperable .551 on-base percentage in 1941.

They also fail to discuss any of the aforementioned records held by Ruth. Most are not acquainted with Ruth's most benumbing statistic of all.

Ruth twice hit more home runs than any team in the league. That's no misprint. It is the most remarkable and least talked about of all the Bambino's achievements. When he hit 54 homers in 1920 and then 60 in 1927, he hit more round trippers than each and every team in the league. The St. Louis Browns hit 50 homers in 1920 to finish second in the league in team homers! Ruth hit four more than the entire Browns' team! Then he hit 60 in 1927, again beating out the Philadelphia Athletics, who finished second, hitting 56 home runs as a team. The headline is "Ruth Beats Every Team in the League." Not once, but twice. The statistic show's Ruth's utter dominance and how far ahead of his peers he was.

In each of those years, Ruth hit approximately 15 percent of the league's homers. Neither Griffey, Jr., nor McGwire accounted for even 3 percent of the league's homers in 1997.

Another way to measure Ruth's dominance is to look at his years in five, 10 and 15-year blocks. In baseball, the great players tend to maintain their greatness for five, 10, even 15-year stretches. Let's look at these five-year averages.

No one in the history of baseball has better five, 10 or 15-year averages than Ruth.

As the chart shows, for a five-year period from 1920 through 1924, Ruth averaged 38 doubles, 11 triples and 47 homers. He walked 138 times per year, far more than his 83 strikeouts per season over that time. He hit .370, had a miraculous on-base percentage of .508 and slugged .777! Here's Ruth's best-five year average versus some of the best power hitters in history.

THE BEST FIVE-YEAR AVERAGES OF
20 OF THE GREATEST HITTERS
(Players Ranked by Slugging Average)

	R	H	D	T	HR	RBI	BB	KS	AVG	OBP	SLG
B. Ruth (1920-1924)	144	182	38	11	47	132	138	83	.370	.508	.777
****
R. Hornsby (1921-1925)	123	216	41	13	29	129	70	30	.402	.472	.690
T. Williams (1941-1948*)	133	183	38	6	38	124	146	42	.362	.505	.682
L. Gehrig (1927-1931)	144	205	41	15	39	160	109	68	.354	.456	.677
J. Foxx (1932-1936)	129	196	33	8	43	144	108	96	.348	.453	.665
H. Greenberg (1935-1940)*	129	186	42	10	42	152	98	92	.327	.426	.655
J. DiMaggio (1937-1941)	121	191	34	11	34	138	62	24	.343	.409	.625
W. Mays (1954-1958)	112	191	27	13	38	103	73	60	.328	.403	.618
M. Mantle (1954-1958)	126	168	23	7	38	104	120	100	.325	.452	.618
S. Musial (1948-1952)	119	206	40	11	31	112	93	35	.349	.438	.613
H. Aaron (1967-1971)	112	197	33	8	37	119	57	65	.325	.382	.597
F. Robinson (1958-1962)	107	168	34	5	35	110	64	73	.309	.377	.583
M. Ott (1928-1932)	110	165	30	5	30	117	90	38	.322	.423	.580
M. Schmidt (1979-1983)	101	137	22	4	40	104	103	117	.275	.400	.576
T. Cobb (1909-1913)	112	210	33	17	7	95	51	**	.396	.450	.564

* doesn't count 1936, missed almost entire season due to injury
** not available, data is incomplete

ACTIVE PLAYERS

	R	H	D	T	HR	RBI	BB	KS	AVG	OBP	SLG
M. McGwire (1993-1997)	61	86	14	0	33	75	73	81	.286	.425	.667
B. Bonds (1993-1997)	114	153	28	4	40	108	123	74	.308	.446	.619
K.Griffey,Jr. (1993-1997)	102	147	26	2	41	106	72	88	.302	.393	.622
F. Thomas (1993-1997)	107	167	32	0	32	107	110	73	.330	.455	.600
J. Bagwell 1993-1997	97	158	37	2	31	109	91	95	.314	.419	.576

Notice the 87-point difference in slugging average between Ruth and his nearest five-year competitor Hornsby! Notice also the 100 and 150-point differences between Ruth and most every other great player. The dominance of his five year average runs is duplicated in his best ten and fifteen-year average (see average for all 100 individual players).

Before looking at those averages, however, look how dominant his second best five-year average is.

Ruth's Second Best 5 year Average
1926-1930

R	H	D	T	HR	RBI	BB	Ks	AVG	OBP	SLG
146	907	28	7	51	152	125	75	.350	.477	.730

Ruth's best 10 and 15-year averages follow here:

Ruth's Best 10-year Average
1920-29

R	H	D	T	HR	RBI	BB	Ks	AVG	OBP	SLG
136	173	31	8	47	133	124	80	.355	.485	.740

Best 15-year Run
1919-33

132	170	29	8	44	133	123	74	.348	.480	.713

No one in the history of the game owns numbers like Ruth's.
There is not now, never was and never will be another like him.

Lifetime Stats

G (Games)................. 2503
AB (At Bats) 8399
R (Runs) 2174
H (Hits).................. 2873
D (Doubles)............... 506
T (Triples)............... 136
HR (Home Runs) 714
HR % (Home Run Percentage) ... 8.5
RBI (Runs Batted In) 2211
BB (Base on Balls) 2056
AVG (Average) .... .342
OBP (On Base Percentage) ..... .474
SLG (Slugging Average)........ .690
K (Strike Outs) 1330
SB (Stolen Bases) 123

Pitching

W (Wins)................... 94
L (Losses) 46
PCT (Percentage)............. .671
G (Games)................. 163
GS (Games Started) 148
CG (Complete Games) 107
SHO (Shut Outs) 17
SV (Saves)................. 4
IP (Innings Pitched) 1221
H (Hits) 974
HR (Home Runs) 10
BB (Base on Balls) 441
K (Strike Outs) 488
*RATIO 10.6
ERA (Earned Run Average) 2.28

* Hits, walks and hit by pitch allowed per 9 innings

Babe Ruth vs. The Top 100 Players

The graph below shows how Babe Ruth compares to the 100 best players of all time in 14 different categories and fielding wins.

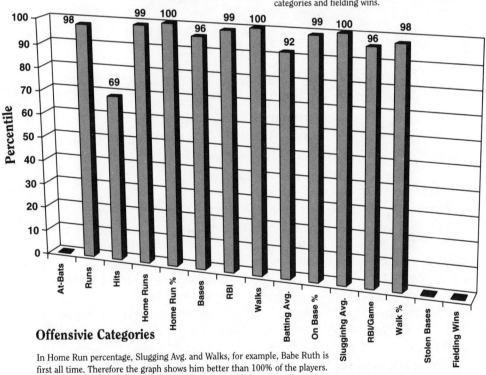

Offensivie Categories

In Home Run percentage, Slugging Avg. and Walks, for example, Babe Ruth is first all time. Therefore the graph shows him better than 100% of the players.

** Fielding wins, a statistic first devised by Palmer and Thorn and used in *Total Baseball*, measures how many games a player wins with his glove. Among the top ten players here, only Willie Mays (22nd all-time) and Honus Wagner (96th) are in the top 100 in fielding wins. A statistic based on how many runs a defensive player saves, fielding wins is adjusted for position. Interestingly, Ozzie Smith (ranked 69th in this book) is the seventh greatest fielder of all-time, winning 25 games with his glove. Second-baseman Bill Mazeroski is first, winning 38 games.

2
TED WILLIAMS
Left Field

"The Splendid Splinter: "The Thumper"
Born: 8/30/18 San Diego, CA
6 feet 3 inches, 205 pounds
Debut: 4/20/39, Played 19 years: 1939-1960 Boston (AL),
missed 1943, '44, '45 to WWII and then
missed most of '52 and '53 to Korean War

To borrow the sports vernacular of the nineties, Ted Williams was focused, utterly focused, on hitting. So focused was he at his craft that he was indifferent to legions of Boston scribes and Boston fans alike; both groups united in crying in their beer and dread over lost opportunities. Who can blame them? They have not won a World Series since 1918, the same year former President Ronald Reagan turned seven years old.

Ted Williams played from 1939 to 1960 but missed all of 1943, 1944 and 1945 to World War II. He then missed all but 43 games to the Korean War in 1952 and 1953. He thus missed 727 games – more than any other player of the time – because of military service. Despite those losses, he finished with a .483 on-base percentage, the highest all-time; second only to Ruth with a 1.32 *total average; and second to Ruth with

---

* total average is derived by dividing a players bases made (total bases + steals + walks + HBP - caught stealing) by his outs made (at bats - hits + caught stealing + grounded into double plays).

a .634 slugging average. Peruse the statistical columns that begin on page 2,269 of *Total Baseball* and record how many times you see the name "Ruth" first and "Williams" second.

Whenever Joe DiMaggio is announced as "the greatest living player" – an honor bestowed upon him after a vote by the Baseball Writers of America in 1969 – Ted Williams is the first player who comes to mind. I then think of three other living greats: Willie Mays, Hank Aaron and Stan Musial. In this book it is argued that all four were greater than DiMaggio. Mind you, the selection of DiMaggio was done by writers, a group with whom Ted Williams was rarely on the best terms.

Williams received more than his share of blame for the Red Sox not winning between 1939 and 1960. But baseball is not basketball; the best player on the diamond cannot control the outcome of the game to the same degree that the best basketball player affects what his team does. If a hitter possesses the right measures of talent and dedication, however, he can control what he does four or five times a night.

So Williams refined the "Science of Hitting" – his book by that name still rates a classic and has been read by Tony Gwynn, Wade Boggs and other great batsmen. The 6 foot 4 inch, 195-pound "Splendid Splinter" – a name given to him by Mel Allen, the late Yankees' broadcaster with the pleasing southern lilt in his voice – was simply the shrewdest hitter who ever gripped a bat. So astute was Williams' hitting that he mentally divided the 16-inch width of home plate and the strike zone from knees to shoulders into a grid of imaginary boxes. A box inside and high was a .390 sweet spot; outside and low, a .230 abyss. At the root of this grid of 77 boxes, each with its own batting average, was Williams' conviction that the first rule of hitting was to find a good pitch to hit.

Legendary stories abound about Williams' superb eyesight and reflexes. Some of these – like the one about how he could smell foul tips or see the spin on the ball – are most likely apocryphal. But it is no exaggeration that he became excellent at most anything he put his mind to – like fishing and piloting.

He hit .406 in 1941 and then won another batting title 17 years later, at the age of 40. The year before that, 1957, he hit .388. He won seven batting titles in all. Less known but more impressive, he won seven of eight slugging titles between 1941 and 1951. The one he didn't win (again, not counting the 1943, 1944 and 1945 seasons that he missed due to his military service) was in 1950 when he slugged .647 but had only 334 at bats.

Listen to baseball conversations and you'll notice that a mention of slugging average rarely arises. Fans, and even writers, seem not to know what it signifies. Despite the general ignorance about slugging average, it is a far better measure of a hitter than batting average. While batting average only tells us what percentage of the time a batter gets a hit, slugging average – calculated by dividing a players' total bases by his at-bats – tells us whether he hit mostly singles or hit for power. A .500 slugging average is a very good one and usually indicates that a hitter has good power.

Ted Williams slugged more than .700 twice, the second time in 1957, when he was 39 years old. He slugged .731 that year, not to mention hitting .388 and finishing with an ungodly on-base percentage of .528. The first time he slugged over .700 was 1941, the first of his two Triple Crown seasons. Everyone knows that Williams hit .406 in 1941, the last person ever to do so. What few people know is Williams' 1941 season is simply one of the greatest offensive seasons ever posted.

In the *Hidden Game of Baseball*, one of the most ambitious books of statistical derivations ever compiled, Williams' 1941 season was rated the fourth-best offensive season of all-time, behind Ruth's 1921, 1920 and 1923 campaigns. Interestingly, Joe DiMaggio's 1941 season was ranked 99th, far behind eight of Williams' best seasons. Nonetheless, the .406 hitter – and league leader in home runs, slugging average, on-base percentage and runs – lost the MVP Award to DiMaggio, who hit in 56 straight games but batted only .357 (49 points less than Williams) and slugged .643 (92 points less than Williams). Many voters must have been mesmerized by DiMaggio's streak that year; he received 291 points in the MVP voting to Williams' 254.

Twelve times in his career Williams slugged .600 or better. After the age of 33, however, he never got more than 420 at-bats in a season. Whenever he had 450 or more at-bats, he finished with more than 100 runs batted in. In fact, he knocked in between 113 and 159 runs in each of his first eight seasons. He broke this streak by getting only 97 runs batted in (in 334 at-bats) in 1950 and then knocked in 126 in 1951. To go with six batting titles, Williams led the league in on-base percentage a staggering 12 times and in slugging eight times.

With the Yankees winning all the pennants, it was destined that Williams' talents would be underappreciated. If the MVP voting in 1941 seemed like larceny, then the voting in 1942 is a bigger theft than the Lufthansa job.

Ted Williams not only won the Triple Crown in 1942, he coasted to the finish line. He hit 36 home runs, 9 more than the runner-up. He had 137 RBI, 23 more than DiMaggio in second place and his .356 average was 25 points better than his teammate Johnny Pesky. Those figures were good enough for the Triple Crown in both leagues.

Williams also led the league in runs (141), total bases (338), base on balls (145), on-base percentage (.499) and slugging (.649), 135 points ahead of runner-up Charlie Keller. His total average was an obscene 1.394, miles ahead of Keller, who finished second at 1.038. Despite this awesome display, on Nov. 3, 1942, the writers awarded Yankees second baseman Joe Gordon the MVP. He beat Williams by 21 votes (270 to 249). Gordon hit 18 homers, batted in 103 runs and hit .322. He led the league in only three categories: most times grounded into double plays (22), most errors at his position (28) and most strikeouts (95).

Williams got his first MVP in 1946. If the writers had troubled themselves with the facts, it should have been his third. He led the league in four offensive categories, including a .667 slugging average. If fairness and objectivity had ruled, Williams would have won his fourth MVP in 1947. Instead, he was edged out for the third time in a controversial vote.

In 1947 he won his second Triple Crown and again it was not enough for the writers. Joe DiMaggio won the MVP by a single point over Williams. Williams received 201 points in the voting and was left completely off a Boston writer's ballot, when even a 10th-place vote would have given Williams the needed two points to get the award. Here are the 1947 seasons of Williams and DiMaggio:

	Runs	Hits	HR	RBI	Average	On Base %	Slugging Average	Total
Williams	125	181	32	114	.343	.499	.634	1.391
DiMaggio	97	168	20	97	.315	.391	.522	.918

The Greek philosopher Socrates said that he didn't like democracy because democracy was "government by the many". He thought citizens were ruled by passions and bias, and he thought they acted randomly when you might expect them to act reasonably. The American League MVP voting in 1941, 1942 and 1947 proved Socrates' point. You cannot trust "the many" to decide on the basis of reason and evidence. Their biases and rooting interests get in the way and cloud their views.

After all these years Babe Ruth and Ted Williams remain numbers one and two.

Best 5-year Average
1941-48 (missed 43, 44, 45)

R	H	D	T	HR	RBI	BB	K	AVG	OBP	SLG
133	183	38	6	38	124	146	42	.362	.505	.682

Best 10-year Average
1941-55 (not including 43, 44, 45, 52, 53)

118	163	32	4	35	118	135	38	.350	.495	.659

Best 15-year Average
1939-58

113	162	33	5	33	112	124	42	.345	.483	.643

Lifetime Totals

G	2,292
AB	7,706
R	1,798
H	2,654
D	525
T	71
HR	521
HR %	6.8
RBI	1,839
BB	2,019
K	709
AVG	.344
OBP	.483
SLG	.634

Ted Williams vs. The Top 100 Players

The graph below shows how Ted Williams compares to the 100 best players of all time in 14 different categories and fielding wins.

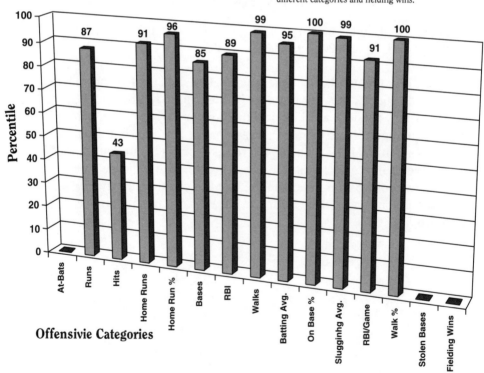

3
LOU GEHRIG
First Base

"The Iron Horse"
Born: 6/19/03 New York, NY, Died: 6/2/41 Riverdale, NY
6 feet, 200 pounds
Debut: 6/15/23, Played 17 years: 1923-1939 New York (AL),
played only 8 games in 1939 due to illness, in 1923
he played 13 games and in '24 he played 10 games

The greatest first baseman who ever lived, and the greatest RBI-machine the game ever saw, Lou Gehrig was accustomed to being second. In the 1932 World Series, when the Yankees swept the Cubs, Gehrig hit three homers and batted .529, only to be overshadowed by Ruth and his "called shot" in game three. Earlier that year, on June 3, Gehrig hit four homers in a game against the A's in Philadelphia's Shibe Park. On that same day, John McGraw resigned his managerial post with the New York Giants. His resignation got front page billing in the *New York Times* the next day and dominated radio reports around the country.

Gehrig even came in second in death. On Sept. 6, 1995, 54 years after Gehrig died, Cal Ripken Jr. passed his streak of 2,130 consecutive games. "There's not much we have in common besides the streak," Ripken said, having looked at Gehrig's records. It was a recognition by one great ballplayer that a man to whom he was bound in history was an even greater ballplayer.

Just how great was Lou Gehrig?

Make up a list of the greatest first basemen who ever lived and Gehrig is on top of that list. My generation saw Willie McCovey and Harmon Killebrew. The current one has watched Mark McGwire and Frank Thomas. There are still people alive who saw George Sisler and Jimmie Foxx. Stan Musial (who played 1,016 of his 3,026 games at first) came after. Gehrig is irrefutably greater than all of them.

The numbers don't lie. For his career, the "Iron Horse" - the name of a locomotive depicted in cigar and other advertisements in the early 1900s – averaged .92 runs batted in per game, higher than Ruth (.88), Foxx (.83) and Williams (.80). He drove in 100 runs 13 years in a row. Gehrig had the even temperament ideally suited to such constancy. "The ballplayer who loses his head, who can't keep his cool, is worse than no ballplayer at all," he once said, describing his steadiness, one of his most important baseball tools.

Gehrig was not knocking in a mere 101 or 105 runs per season. His totals between 1926 and 1938 require a double-take. In those 13 years he knocked in 1,912 runs – an average of 147 a season. He reached 175 in 1927 to break Ruth's major league record of 170 set in 1921. He "fell off" to 142 in 1928, to lead the league a second straight year, the year the Yankees swamped the Cardinals in their second straight series sweep. In 1930 and 1931, Gehrig went positively nuts, posting totals of 174 and then 184 runs batted in to break his own American League record. The Cubs' stocky outfielder Hack Wilson had knocked in a record 190 in 1930. But Wilson would never achieve Gehrig's year-in, year-out consistency.

"Larrupin' Lou" would again lead the league in 1934, plating 165 Yankees in Ruth's last year with the team. It was his fifth and last RBI crown. But he still had two more 150-plus seasons up his powerful sleeves, posting 152 and 159 in 1936 and 1937.

In 1936 Gehrig was the leading run producer on a Yankees' jugger-naut that won 102 and lost 51, winning the pennant by 18 games over Detroit. That squad is notable in several respects.

The 1936 Yankees scored 1,065 runs, still a major league record for a team. The figure rounds off to seven runs per game. 1936 was also the begin-ning of a run of four consecutive World Series victories for the Yankees. Until that time, no team had ever won even three Series in a row. In their run of four titles, the Yankees would barely be challenged. They won pennants by margins of 19, 13, 11 and then 17 games over Detroit and Boston. In the four World Series, they punished the opposition, winning 16 games and losing 3, including sweeps of the Cubs and the Reds in 1938 and 1939.

1936 was notable in still another way. It was the rookie year for Joe DiMaggio. With DiMaggio, the Yankees had five players who produced

100 or more runs batted in that season. No team has ever equaled the feat. The five who produced 100 runs were: Gehrig, 152; DiMaggio, 125; second baseman Tony Lazzeri, 109; right fielder George Selkirk, 107; and catcher Bill Dickey, 107. The Yankees hit .300 as a team. Surprisingly, they did not lead the league in hitting. That honor fell to Cleveland, which hit .304 but finished in fifth place. Detroit also hit .300 that season. The hitting exploits of any one team are less astounding when you consider that the entire league averaged .289!

Gehrig enjoyed two more stellar seasons in 1937 and 1938. Then, in the spring of 1939, both his streak of 13 100-plus RBI seasons and his streak of 2,130 games, met a full and sudden stop. On May 2, 1939, Gehrig waited for his manager Joe McCarthy in the lobby of the Book-Cadillac hotel in Detroit. The Yankees had a game that afternoon at Briggs Stadium. Gehrig, who had faltered in spring training was hitting just .143 after 8 games. He met McCarthy and the two went up to the manager's room. McCarthy knew what was coming. "I'm benching myself, Joe," Gehrig said. McCarthy paused and asked why. "For the good of the team, Joe. Nobody has to tell me how bad I've been and how much of a drawback I've been to the club." McCarthy suggested that he rest for a week.

Then he told McCarthy about something pitcher Johnny Murphy had said. McCarthy grew angry. But Gehrig explained that in the ninth inning of the previous game, Murphy fielded a grounder between the mound and first and then had to wait for Gehrig to cover. What should have been a simple play was too close for comfort and on the way off the field Murphy said "nice play, Lou." "I knew then it was time to get out," said Gehrig.

As Ray Robinson recounts in his book *Iron Horse*, Gehrig delivered the lineup card to home plate. Then the announcement came over the public address: "Dahlgren at first." 11,379 people were silent but then gave Gehrig a two-minute ovation. "Come on," said Dahlgren to Gehrig. "You better get out there. You've put me in a terrible spot." Gehrig told him to "get on out there, Babe, and knock in some runs."

In the seventh inning Dahlgren tried to persuade Gehrig again.

Gehrig said the team was "doing fine." So was Dahlgren. He had knocked in three runs in a 22-2 New York victory. Ever ready with a line to lighten the moment, Lefty Gomez approached Gehrig. "Hey, Lou, it took them 15 years to get you out of the ballgame. Sometimes they get me out in 15 minutes."

On June 12 Gehrig checked into the Mayo Clinic in Rochester, Minnesota The news eight days later was ominous. Dr. Harold Harbein reported that Gehrig was suffering from amyotrophic lateral sclerosis, a kind of infantile paralysis. His career was over. He was 35 when he played his last game and had turned 36 on June 19. His career, which debuted on June 15, 1923, stopped just short of 16 years.

After the illness was diagnosed, Gehrig received and accepted an offer from Mayor Fiorello LaGuardia to work as a parole commissioner for the City of New York. The mayor thought Gehrig would be an inspiration for youngsters in trouble.

In a scene rooted in baseball lore, Gehrig made an emotional farewell address at Yankee Stadium on July 4, 1939. The Yankees had quickly arranged a Gehrig Appreciation Day with the Senators in town for a doubleheader. Over 62,000 fans came out to pay tribute. Joe Dugan, Waite Hoyt, Tony Lazzeri, Bob Meusel, Herb Pennock, Mark Koenig, and Earl Combs represented Murderer's Row of 1927. Ruth showed up, late as usual. He hadn't spoken to Gehrig in years.

Gehrig was at first too moved to speak, but a chant of "We want Gehrig," "We Want Gehrig" poured out from the three tiers of the stadium. Gehrig advanced to the microphone, wiping his eyes with a handkerchief. McCarthy, thinking Gehrig might fall, whispered to Dahlgren, "catch him if he starts to go down." Then Gehrig began. "Fans, for the past two weeks you have been reading about a bad break I got. Yet today I consider myself the luckiest man on the face of the earth. I have been in ball parks for seventeen years and I have never received anything but kindness and encouragement from you fans..." For several more minutes he went on, praising the Yankees' owners and managers Miller Huggins and Joe McCarthy. He praised the grounds keepers for their gifts, his parents for providing him an education, his wife for being a "tower of strength and courage." He ended by saying, "I might have had a bad break, but I have an awful lot to live for. Thank you."

At the close of his speech, the crowd roared and Ruth went over to his teammate and wrapped his burly arms around his neck.

He died on June 2, 1941, less than 18 years after his promising debut. Gehrig was buried in Valhalla, N. Y.

His career stands as a model of consistency. In his own list of the top 20 hitters of all time, Ted Williams, who began playing the same year Gehrig retired, selected Gehrig as the second greatest hitter of all time. Williams excluded himself althogether and put Ruth first.

Gehrig's slugging average was .632. His on-base percentage of .447 was fifth best ever, behind only Williams, Ruth, John McGraw and Billy Hamilton. Also a great clutch performer, Gehrig hit .361 and slugged .731 in 119 World Series at-bats. He played in seven World Series and the Yankees won six, five of them sweeps. He was an essential part of two Yankees' dynasties, the 1920s edition with Ruth, Lazerri and "Murderer's Row" and the Bronx Bombers of the 1930s.

His ten and fifteen year runs are better than everyone's with the exception of Ruth and Williams. He was only second on the Yankees for many years because of the character and achievements of Ruth.

Best 5-Year Average (1927-1931)

R	H	D	T	HR	RBI	AVG	OBP	SLG
144	205	41	15	39	160	.354	.456	.677

Best 10-year Average 1927-1936

| 142 | 202 | 39 | 12 | 39 | 153 | .350 | .455 | .660 |

Best 15-year Average 1924-1938 (played only 10 games, batted 12 times in 1924)

| 125 | 180 | 35 | 11 | 33 | 132 | .341 | .446 | .634 |

Lifetime Totals

G	2,164
AB	8,001
R	1,888
H	2,721
D	534
T	163
HR	493
HR %	6.2
RBI	1,995
BB	1,508
K	790
AVG	.340
OBP	.447
SLG	.632
SB	102

Lou Gehrig vs. The Top 100 Players

The graph below shows how Lou Gehrig compares to the 100 best players of all time in 14 different categories and fielding wins.

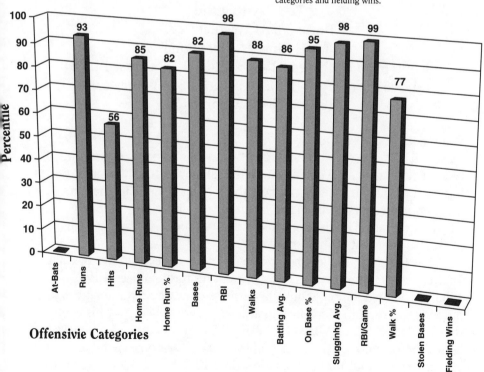

4
WILLIE MAYS
Center Field

"The Say Hey Kid"
Born: 5/6/31 Westfield, AL
5 feet 11 inches, 180 pounds
Debut: 5/25/51, Played 22 years: 1951-1973 (missed 1953)
1951-1957, New York (NL); 1958-1972, San Francisco (NL);
1972-1973, New York (NL)

When Barry Bonds hit his 300th home run toward the end of the 1996 season, it was cause for celebration. Hitting 300 homers and stealing 300 bases is no mean achievement. But after acknowledging how great Bonds has been for San Francisco, my next thought was, "only 360 homers more and he equals Willie Mays." As great as Ken Griffey, Jr., Barry Bonds and Frank Thomas are, the burden of proof is on them. Each must stand the test of time that Mays has.

The lesson is plain. Baseball excellence isn't achieved in five or even 10 great years. After missing 274 games to military service in 1952 and 1953, Mays, then 23, set about the business of ravaging National League pitching. Starting in 1954, he will always be remembered for his over-the-shoulder catch off Vic Wertz in the 1954 World Series, Mays played between 151 and 162 games each of the next 13 seasons. He twice topped 50 homers and four other times went over 40. By the time the 1965 season was over, Mays, having played just 13 full seasons, had 505 home runs – an average of 39 per year.

That assessment doesn't even include his fielding prowess. By 1965, he was already the best outfielder in the Major Leagues. He had led the league in stolen bases four consecutive years and triples three other times, something no power hitter had ever done. Like New York Giants' manager Leo Durocher once said of his young outfielder, Mays could hit, hit for power, throw, run and catch. If there was something he couldn't do, no one had found it.

Fifties newsreels of Mays' heyday show a guy with a broad grin and a juiced step every time he played the game. In the early 1950s it was not unusual for Mays to play a doubleheader at the Polo Grounds and then head to Harlem to play stick ball with the kids. In major league parks he played with smarts, rarely throwing to the wrong base or wasting an out on the bases.

Mays' scurrying style of running brought to mind Jackie Robinson's derring-do on the paths. Fans in the fifties recall how fast Mays scampered from first to third. Mays had a habit of running while looking over his shoulder to see where the ball was. Rounding second he might grab the shortstop's shirt and hope to get third base on an interference call.

His year-to-year totals show his consistency and his lifetime marks reveal a simply astounding bottom line. He scored 100 runs or more 12 years in a row and was still averaging 101 runs per year after his 19th season. Each of 10 straight years he amassed between 176 and 208 hits, most impressive for a power hitter. He hit 35 or more homers 11 times. When it came to knocking in runs he was reliable: he is one of only 9 players in baseball history to knock in 100 runs in 10 or more seasons. And despite several "decline years" played between his 40th and 42nd birthdays, his lifetime average stayed above .300.

Like Williams, Mays is often compared with another great New York center fielder, Joe DiMaggio. He also drew frequent comparisons to Hank Aaron, Mickey Mantle and Roberto Clemente, three other great outfielders of his time. When comparing him to DiMaggio it cannot be overlooked that DiMaggio retired after 13 years, while Mays went on to play 22 seasons. DiMaggio played his last game before his 37th birthday. Mays was still hitting homers and knocking in runs well past that age.

In Mays' first 11 seasons he had five years in a row, and six altogether, where he recorded more than 400 putouts; DiMaggio did it only three times in 13 years. Mays made 88 errors in his first 13 years; DiMaggio, 105. DiMaggio's fielding average was .978; Mays, .981. Cut both players off at 13 years and Dimaggio had 153 assists to Mays' 149, counting 1952, a year that Mays played only 34 games. DiMaggio took part in 30 outfield double plays in his career, while Mays took part in 43 over the same period. So ample evidence exists that Mays – who won 11 Gold Gloves – enjoyed an edge in the field. No wonder Dodgers' executive Fresco Thompson said that Willie Mays' glove is, "where triples go to die."

Then the home run totals must be dealt with: DiMaggio finished with 361; Mays, 660. Mays hit more homers in his best 10-year period (1954-1963, when he hit 383) than Dimaggio did in his entire career, and Mays slugged .597 doing it. It is generally acknowledged that Mays was faster on the base paths and the proof is in the stolen bases totals: Mays stole 338 bases to DiMaggio's 30. DiMaggio's team won more often, but that team continued to win right after he retired, taking 11 pennants and six World Championships in the next 13 years.

Here are the totals for DiMaggio's 13-year career and Mays' first 13 full seasons:

	G	AB	R	H	2B	3B	HR	RBI	SB	AVG	SLG	HR%
Mays	2071	7467	1480	2351	373	114	501	1379	272	.315	.598	6.8
DiMaggio	1736	6821	1390	2214	389	131	361	1537	30	.325	.579	5.3

DiMaggio leads in RBI and batting average. But Mays leads in the all-important slugging categories, home runs and slugging average. Then add longevity, because Mays played nine years longer and was a productive player for more than half of them. If some argument concludes DiMaggio is superior to Mays, I'd like to see how that conclusion is reached.

Mays versus Aaron is a more difficult matter, almost too close to call. Forced to choose between them, the edge goes to Mays. The latest buzz seems to be that the only difference between Mays and Aaron is that Mays played with abundant flash and Aaron didn't. I heard several sports radio hosts in New York taking this angle and Joe Torre, who played eight years with Aaron, said essentially the same thing in a conversation we had last year. I believe that flash is one difference in their games. But I don't believe it is the only difference.

Evidence abounds that Mays was a far better outfielder than Hank Aaron. According to the sabermetric measurements done by Palmer and Thorn in *Total Baseball*, Mays rates near the top of all the outfielders who ever played in the categories of fielding runs, fielding runs by position and fielding wins. The only center fielders consistently found ahead of Mays in the *Total Baseball* lists are Tris Speaker and Richie Ashburn. By all evidence a consistent outfielder, Aaron does not even appear on these lists of the best outfielders.

Mays was, by all accounts, a better runner, too. What Aaron has over Mays, and over most every other power hitter who ever lived, is an ability to hit for power longer. Mays last hit 30 homers in 1966, when he was 35. But Aaron's power hitting defied age. He not only hit 44 homers at the age of 35, but hit 38, 47, 34 and 40 in the following four years – for an average of 40.4 homers between his 35th and 39th birthdays! No doubt his quick, compact swing helped him in this regard. His slugging average ranged between .514 and .669 during that time. This makes the call even tougher.

But the 274 games Mays lost to military service in 1952 and 1953 were followed with years of 41 and 51 homers. Aaron slugged .555 and Mays .557. But Aaron had 12,364 at-bats and to see where he stands at Mays' total of 10,881 at bats, you must cut him off after 1972 and eliminate his last four seasons, "decline years" in which he slugged .643, .491, .355 and .369. His slugging average without those years is .566, a slight edge over Mays.

Roberto Clemente was a great percentage hitter and terrific outfielder with a deadly throwing arm for nearly two decades. He won 12 Gold Gloves. But while the contest between Clemente and Mays on defense is a close call, Mays wins hands down over Clemente at the plate. Clemente hit .317 to Mays' .302 but that's his last edge.

Mays slugged .557; Clemente, .475. Mays hit 660 homers to Clemente's 240. Both of those are huge gaps. Need we go further? Mays had 100 runs batted in 10 times, while Clemente did it only twice. Anyone who saw the 1971 World Series knows just how great and how dominant a player Clemente could be. But while the speed and fielding comparison come close, there is no comparison between the two as hitters.

In his early years, Mays was compared to Mickey Mantle more often than he was to anyone else. If you take Mantle's peak years, 1956 and 1961, it is clear that those peaks are higher than Mays' best years. But what's even more clear when you gaze at the statistical ledger is that Mantle's career had many holes in it. In 18 years, Mantle knocked in 100 runs only four times. Like Mantle once said, "you have to look at the bottom line and Willie's bottom line was way better than mine." Mantle turned 33 on October 20, 1964. He had just finished his last good season, a season in which he hit 35 homers, knocked in 111 runs and led the Yankees past Baltimore and Chicago during the last days of the season. He hit 3 homers against the Cardinals in the World Series. But that was it. He would never hit 25 homers again.

By comparison, Mays was showing no signs of decline, hitting 47, 52 and 37 homers between the ages of 33 and 35. He passed Mantle in homers during the 1965 season when he hit 52 to Mantle's 19. And that was it. While Mantle may have been the fastest man in baseball in the first half of the 1950s, injuries to his legs robbed him of much of his explosive speed. Mays' speed stayed with him and he was appreciably better than Mantle in the outfield.

Mays was simply an awesome combination of consistency, power and speed. Ten times between 1954 and 1966 he had 100 or more RBI. In 22 seasons, he slugged under .500 only 6 times. All those who think power hitters must strike out a great deal should look at Mays' performance. Mays didn't strike out 100 times in a year until 1971, his 21st season, when he was 40 years old.

It's hard to think of a position player who did everything as well as Mays. Griffey, Jr., and Bonds are in the ballpark, but I'm not sure that they will stay in the ballpark long enough to achieve the kind of bottom line that Mays did.

New York Times writer Red Smith said, "you could get a fat lip in any New York saloon by arguing who was better, Duke Snider, Mantle or Mays. One point was beyond argument, though. Willie Mays was by all odds the most exciting."

Best 5-year Average:
1954-1958

R	H	D	T	HR	RBI	AVG	OBP	SLG
115	191	27	13	38	103	.328	.403	.618

Best 10-year Average:
1954-1963

| 118 | 188 | 31 | 10 | 38 | 109 | .320 | .394 | .611 |

Best 15-year Average:
1954-1968

| 112 | 177 | 28 | 8 | 38 | 104 | .311 | .387 | .586 |

Lifetime Totals

G	2,992	RBI	1,903
Ab	10,881	BB	1,464
R	2,062	SO	1,526
H	3,283	AVG	302
D	523	OBP	387
T	140	SLG	557
HR	660	SB	338
HR %	6.1	CS	103

Willie Mays vs. The Top 100 Players

The graph below shows how Willie Mays compares to the 100 best players of all time in 14 different categories and fielding wins.

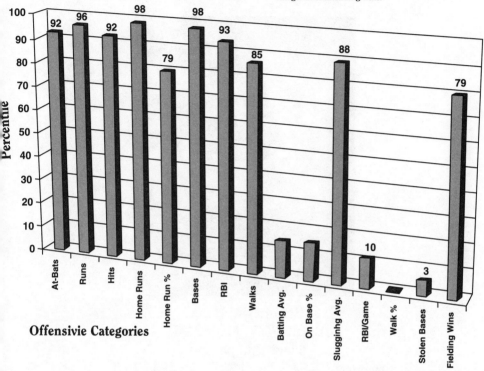

Offensivie Categories

5
HANK AARON
Right Field

"Hammerin' Hank"
Born: 2/5/54 Mobile, AL
6 feet, 180 pounds
Debut: 4/13/34, Played 23 years: 1954-1976
1954-1965, Milwaukee (NL); 1966-1974, Atlanta;
1975-1976, Milwaukee (AL)

Hank Aaron's teammate Joe Adcock once said that "trying to slip a pitch past Aaron is like trying to slip a sunrise past a rooster." Because his formative years were spent in Milwaukee, a great baseball town but a small media market, Hank Aaron's smooth skills went largely unnoticed. He ran down fly balls in right field, stole bases and swung the bat with an effortless, fluid grace. Because his stroke was so quick and compact you got the idea he was invulnerable at the plate. His home runs resulted from the rolling over of his powerful wrists.

"Hammerin' Hank" will forever be synonymous with the home run, smacking his record 715th on an April evening in Atlanta in 1974. He finished with 755 lifetime. But in homers per at bat, he is only 16th among all those who ever played.

His real virtue was constancy. In near anonymity, he performed year in and year out. He clobbered a mind boggling 645 homers in the 17 years from 1957 through 1973, for an average of 38 per year! No one in the history of baseball, save Ruth – who hit 666 in a 15-year span from 1919 through 1933 – put up such a gaudy average over so long a period. "I don't want them to forget Babe Ruth," he said during the home run chase. "I just want them to remember me."

Anyone who was awake couldn't help but remember Hank. Hank Aaron could do it all, so it doesn't matter whether the world was watching or not. As time marched on, it was just the sheer weight of Aaron's consistency that overwhelmed you. He didn't hit homers in groups of 50, but 15 times he hit more than 30, 11 times more than 35 and eight times 40 or more. He knocked in more than 100 runs 11 times. Two other times, years when he belted 44 and 40 homers, he finished with 97 and 96 RBI. He hit 245 homers after the age of 35 and had his best year at 37. In that 1971 season he hit 47 homers, knocked in 118 runs and slugged .669. Fifteen times he scored 100 runs or more.

People who don't rate Aaron high on their list haven't happened within a mile of a record book. Sure, his 755 homers owe to his having 3,968 more at-bats than Ruth. But he should also be credited for playing so well for so long. Aaron, Mays, Mantle and Frank Robinson are the greatest outfielders of their time. And while Mays deserves the nod over Aaron, Aaron played better for a longer period than Mays, just as he played better for a longer period than Mantle and Robinson.

Aaron also helped the Braves to a World Championship, hitting .393 and clobbering three homers in the 1957 series to beat the Yankees. The following year the Yankees came back from a three games to one deficit and beat the Braves. Aaron hit .333 in that series.

Aaron's walks (61 per year) and his on base percentage (.377) are low for a great hitter. But so are his 60 strikeouts per year. These three totals remind us that Aaron was a "contact power hitter." Three times he had 200 or more hits. Four other times he had 190-plus. These are unusual totals for a home run hitter, because home run hitters usually have bigger swings. Aaron had a short stroke, ideal for average hitting, but also had the power to hit homers and finish with 1,477 extra base hits.

No one got so little credit, for so long, from so many, as Henry Aaron did. He didn't hit 500 foot homers in New York or appear in the World Series nearly ever fall like Mantle did. He didn't run with his limbs flying in every direction and his cap flying off on both coasts like Mays did. So before hitting home runs number 700, 714 and 715, he hadn't received the same buildup. Then his 715th clout brought a storm of attention his way. You might say he had it coming. For many years no one had given him what he deserved. Despite the detractors whose hate mail wished him ill, he chased after Ruth's legend with quiet dignity.

Like Lou Gehrig, Aaron possessed a steadiness of character that served him well. "Making the majors is not as hard as staying there," he said the year he passed Ruth's 714. "It's like being married. The hardest part is to stay married."

He played his last two years, 1975 and 1976, in Milwaukee. He hit his final 22 homers there as a designated hitter. "If I strike out with the bases loaded and two outs, I won't be able to redeem myself with a big play in the outfield," he said, explaining why he didn't like being a DH.

Here are his best 5-year, 10-year and 15-year averages.

Best 5-year Average
1957-1961

R	H	D	T	HR	RBI	AVG	OBP	SLG
112	197	33	8	37	119	.325	.382	.597

Best 10-year Average
1956-1965

113	195	33	7	36	113	.324	.384	.579

Best 15-year Average
1957-1971

103	183	31	4	38	113	.313	.383	.577

Lifetime totals

G	3,298	RBI	2,297
AB	12,364	BB	1,402
R	2,174	K	1,383
H	3,771	AVG	.305
D	624	OBP	.377
T	98	SLG	.555
HR	755	SB	240
HR %	6.1	CS	73

Hank Aaron vs. The Top 100 Players

The graph below shows how Hank Aaron compares to the 100 best players of all time in 14 different categories and fielding wins.

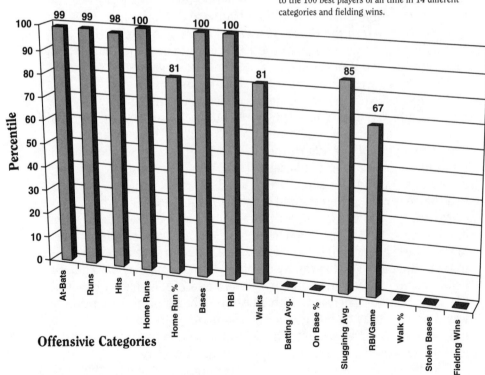

6
TY COBB
Center Field

"The Georgia Peach"
Born: 12/18/1886 Narrows, GA, Died: 7/17/61 Atlanta, GA
6 feet 1 inch, 175 pounds
Debut: 8/30/05, Played 24 years: 1905-1928
1905-1926, Detroit; 1927-1928, Philadelphia (AL)

"Ty Cobb lived on the field as if it was his last day," Branch Rickey once said. Alone with his biographer, Al Stump, not long before he died, Cobb explained that people didn't understand about his life. "Give 'em the word," he told Stump. "I had to fight all my life to survive. They were all against me...tried every dirty trick to cut me down. But I beat the bastards and left them in the ditch. Make sure the book says that..."

Cobb's mode was attack and he is the first hitter on this list not to hit home runs. But most of the years in which he played – from 1905 to 1928 – were years when home runs weren't plentiful. Cobb was living proof you can slug without hitting homers.

Cobb led the league in slugging average eight times. Try to find five sluggers in history who led the circuit in slugging that many times. You cannot. Here's a list, including all the members of the 500-home run club:

Slugging Average Chart
Number of Times Leading the League in Slugging Average

Babe Ruth	13 times	Reggie Jackson	3 times
Ted Williams	9 times	Willie McCovey	3 times
Rogers Hornsby	9 times	Dick Allen	3 times
Ty Cobb	8 times	Lou Gehrig	2 times
Honus Wagner	6 times	Duke Snider	2 times
Stan Musial	6 times	Ernie Banks	1 time
Willie Mays	5 times	Harmon Killebrew	1 time
Jimmie Foxx	5 times	Mel Ott	1 time
Mike Schmidt	5 times	Willie Stargell	1 time
Hank Aaron	4 times	Hank Greenberg	1 time
Mickey Mantle	4 times	Juan Gonzalez	1 time
Frank Robinson	4 times	Jeff Bagwell	1 time
Barry Bonds	3 times	Frank Thomas	1 time
Mark McGwire	3 times	Ken Griffey, Jr.	1 time

Only three players ever won more slugging titles than Cobb. He was surely one of the greatest players – and sluggers – the game has ever known.

Cobb was fueled by a depth of desire that people have been trying to figure out for a long time. There are several reasons for his passions and I will return to them shortly. It's clear he had desire from the outset.

In Al Stump's biography *Cobb*, a story is told about sportswriter Grantland Rice. Then working with the *Atlanta Journal Constitution* and on his way to national renown, Rice tells a story about getting *Western Union* telegrams from Anniston, Alabama about a young phenom. The person sending the wires signed off as "James Jackson, news-tipster." The letter read, "Tyrus Raymond Cobb, the dashing young star from Royston, has just started playing ball with Anniston. He is a terrific hitter and faster than a deer. At the age of 17 (spring, 1904) he is undoubtedly a phenom." Since the telegram interrupted his poker game, he tore it up and returned to the table. He wrote back, "after this, the mails are good enough for Cobb." Rice had never heard of him.

But communique's kept arriving at the office. "Keep your eye on Cobb, he is the finest hitter I've ever seen..." "Watch Cobb of Anniston, he is sure to be a sensation." "Have you seen Ty Cobb play ball yet? He is the fastest mover in the game." "Cobb had three hits yesterday, made two great catches." "A sure big leaguer in the making." Rice received more than a dozen such notices a month – letters, postcards, wires, sent by "interested fans," and "faithful readers" and signed by Jackson, Brown,

Kelly, Jones, Smith and Stewart. The handwriting showed a variety of slants and styles, so Rice didn't suspect fraud. Finally, he wrote a "blind," column, singing the praises of a ballplayer named Cobb, a "new wonder boy" and "darling of the fans" that he had never seen. He hoped that would stop the steady flow of mail. But notices continued to arrive form Tennessee, Alabama and Georgia.

In 1951, at a General Electric Co. banquet honoring Cobb's sixty-fifth birthday, the source of the letters was revealed. Cobb confessed to the 71-year-old Rice that he had written all the notices carrying a steady stream of praise. Rice was at first furious. "That was a sneaky thing to do, Cobb," Rice fumed. "Why did you do it to me?" "I was in a hurry, Granny," answered Cobb. Rice forgave him and their friendship was renewed.

The story shows Cobb's unquenchable desire to be noticed and make a name for himself. It wasn't long before he delivered on his written boasts. He won a batting title in his first full-season, hitting .350 at the age of 20 in 1907. He then won the batting title the next eight years in a row. He missed winning it in 1916, hitting .371 and then won the next three in a row. So, in a 13-year period, he led the league in hitting 12 times.

He led the league in hits eight times, 10 times surpassing 200 hits in a season. He never led the league in walks but did lead in on-base per-centage six times and runs five times. Suffice it to say there is a load of bold ink in *Total Baseball*, for all the 58 times he led the league in one category or another.

Questions arise about how to compare Cobb to post-1920 sluggers like Ruth and Gehrig, Foxx and Williams, Musial and Mays, Aaron and Schmidt. But there are no questions when comparing him to players of the pre-1920 era. He is flat out the best player that baseball produced until Babe Ruth came along.

Cobb took all that was available to him in the early game. He just took everything. Home runs weren't plentiful but triples were. So were singles and walks and stolen bases. Few players could take bases like Cobb. To be sure, Cobb competed against an abundance of great players. Honus Wagner was regarded by some as the game's best all-around play-er. Not only could he hit and run but he could field any position on the diamond, leading John McGraw to say, "I'll take him over anyone. He can do everything." Forget opinion. The record – average, slugging, stealing, scoring – shows he wasn't nearly Cobb's equal.

The greatest second baseman and one of the great all-around hitters, was Napoleon Lajoie. Playing with the Philadelphia A's and then with Cleveland, Lajoie, player-manager at the age of 29, presented a perennial challenge to Cobb for hits and batting titles. Lajoie hit .422 in 1901, which is still a league record. Tris Speaker, whose Hall of Fame plaque identifies him as "the greatest center fielder of his day," played more shallow in center field than anyone else and still was able to get under long flies. Twice he threw out 35 runners in a season. He was no slouch at the plate, either, hitting .344 and holding the major league record with 793 doubles.

But Cobb was a step ahead of them all. Cobb's peers thought his impact on the game was greater than anyone from his time. He led the league in hits eight times and was always on-base, leading the league in on base percentage six times. Once on base, he stole 892 bases, leading the league 6 times and successful on an amazing 83 percent of his steal attempts.

Cobb hit only 117 home runs but he had 1,019 doubles and triples. Add to that the 3,170 singles he collected.

Cobb's game lost much of its thunder when Ruth started slugging. Ruth changed the game and this bothered Cobb deeply. The best he could do was muster left-handed, jealous compliments about Ruth, like "he ran pretty good for a fat man." Ruth outperformed Cobb in head-to-head competition and Ruth's teams won the World Series. In 22 years, Cobb's Tigers never won.

But it is no shame finishing behind Ruth. Cobb was fighting from the outset. Near the end of Cobb's life, Stump asked him, "why did you fight so hard in baseball, Ty?" A fierce look came over Cobb's face. "I did it for my father, who was an exalted man. They killed him when he was still young. They blew his head off the same week I became a major leaguer. He never got to see me play. Not one game, not an inning. But I knew he was watching me...and I never let him down. Never."

Cobb's father, W.C., was killed when Ty was 18, gunned down at the window of his own Royston, Georgia home. Ty's mother, Amanda, fired the shotgun when she heard a noise at the window and suspected a burglar.

If it's true that this added to Cobb's motivation, then it's no wonder he played with such fury. But an external event, even a violent event like the sudden death of his father, didn't account for his entire motivation. He was driven to excel years before his father's death. "Baseball is not unlike a war," he once said. "And when you get down to it, we batters are the heavy artillery."

Best 5-Year Average
1909-1913

R	H	D	T	HR	RBI	AVG.	OBP	SLG
112	210	33	17	7	95	.396	.450	.564

Best 10-year Average
1910-1919

| 105 | 195 | 31 | 16 | 5 | 83 | .387 | .459 | .542 |

Best 15-year Average
1908-1922

| 104 | 194 | 33 | 15 | 5 | 87 | .380 | .446 | .535 |

Lifetime Totals

G 3,035
AB 11,434
R 2,246
H 4,189
D 724
T 295
HR 117
HR % 1.0
RBI. 1,937
BB 1,249
K. . . . . 357 (incomplete figures)
AVG. 366
OBP. 433
SLG. 512
SB. 892
CS . . . . 178 (incomplete figures)

Ty Cobb vs. The Top 100 Players

The graph below shows how Ty Cobb compares to the 100 best players of all time in 14 different categories and fielding wins.

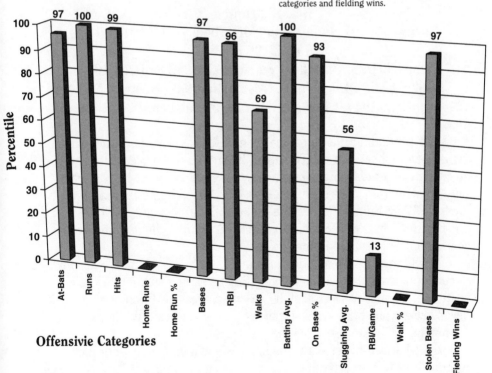

Ty Cobb vs. The Top 100 Players — Percentile by Offensive Categories: At-Bats 97, Runs 100, Hits 99, Bases 97, RBI 96, Walks 69, Batting Avg. 100, On Base % 93, Slugging Avg. 56, RBI/Game 13, Stolen Bases 97

JIMMIE FOXX
First Base

"Beast" "Double X"
Born: 10/22/07 Sudlersville, MD, Died: 7/21/76 Miami, FL
6 feet, 195 pounds
Debut: 5/1/25, Played 20 years: 1925-1945 (missed 1943)
1925-1935, Philadelphia (AL); 1936-1942, Boston (AL);
1943-1944, Chicago (NL); 1945 Philadephia (NL)

Jimmie Foxx could hit a ball as hard and as far as anyone. "When Neil Armstrong first set foot on the moon, he and all the space scientists were puzzled by an unidentifiable white object," Hall of Famer Lefty Gomez said. "I knew immediately what it was. That was a home run ball hit off me in 1937 by Jimmie Foxx." The homer in question landed where no one hit them: in the third deck at Yankee Stadium. The drive busted a chair about 550 feet from home plate.

Ted Williams was Foxx' teammate in 1939, the last year Foxx lead the circuit in homers. He recalls Foxx hitting an upper-deck job in the left-center field stands in Detroit that was the longest he'd ever seen. "I never saw anyone hit a baseball harder than Foxx," said Williams. Said a teammate, "He wasn't scouted, he was trapped."

A right-handed hitter with huge biceps and a vicious, all-out hack, Jimmie Foxx was an unfailingly consistent run producer. Like Gehrig, he knocked in 100 or more runs 13 years in a row. That's just the start. Foxx also owns the major league record with 30 or more homers in 12 consecutive years. To Foxx belongs the fourth highest slugging average in baseball history (.609), the highest of any right-handed hitter. Foxx' career was written about less than any of the top 10 players here. His nickname, "The Beast," attests both to his size and lumberjack arms and to the savage way he attacked a ball.

He began his career as a catcher in 1925, but by 1929, the 22-year-old was the steady first baseman for the Philadelphia A's. From 1929 through 1940 he assaulted American League pitching. In 1929 the A's, with Lefty Grove and Al Simmons, won 104 games and took the American League pennant by 16 games over the second place Yankees, despite Ruth and Gehrig finishing first and second in home runs. But Philadelphia was the only team in the league with an ERA of four runs per game and Grove and Earnshaw won 44 games between them. Philadelphia then won the Series easily, beating the Cubs four games to one.

In 1930, Foxx improved to 37 homers and 156 runs batted in, losing out to Gehrig who finished with 174. Again the A's won the pennant easily, posting 102 wins and beating Washington by eight games and the Yankees by 16. The Yankees hit .309 as a team and scored 1,062 runs, but Grove and Earnshaw combined for 50 wins, while the Yankees' staff surrendered nearly five runs a game. This time the A's dealt the Cards a four games to two defeat. The team had all the pieces of a dynasty, especially pitching and power.

When the A's finished 107 and 45 in 1931, it must have seemed to Gehrig and Ruth, now 36, that they would never take a another pennant. New York won 94 games but still finished 13 games behind the A's. The first crack in the A's armor was a seven-game loss to the Cardinals in the Series.

In 1932, Foxx had his best season by far. He pounded out 58 homers, knocked in 169 runs and slugged .749, leading the league in four categories. Foxx would have won the Triple Crown, but Dale Alexander who hit .367 but only got 400 at bats, was awarded the title over Foxx, who hit .364. Despite Grove's 25 wins and despite Foxx and Simmons finishing one and two in runs batted in, New York returned the favor, winning 107 games and finishing 13 paces ahead of Philadelphia. The Yankees swept the Cubs in the 1932 Series and for all intents and purposes the A's fire, which burned hot but quick, was already doused.

It would be another 40 years before the A's, then the 1972 Oakland A's, would win another pennant. But across his career Foxx just kept right on hitting homers and producing runs. He won his second consecutive MVP in 1933 – this time taking the Triple Crown with 48 homers, 163 runs batted in and a .356 average. He also slugged .703, his second straight year slugging above .700. "Double-XX"' third MVP came in 1938 when he hit 50 homers a second time. He also collected his personal best in runs batted in with 175 and slugged .704, both league-leading totals. Foxx hit his 500th homer in 1940.

Best 5-year Average
1932-1936

R	H	D	T	HR	RBI	AVG	OBP	SLG
129	196	33	8	43	144	.348	.453	.665

Best 10-year Average
1930-1939

124	185	32	9	42	140	.336	.439	.653

Best 15-year Average
1927-1941

111	167	29	8	35	116	.331	.429	.628

Totals

G	 2,317	RBI	 1,922
AB	 8,134	BB	 1,452
R	 1,751	K	 1,311
H	 2,646	AVG	325
D	 458	OBP	428
T	 125	SLG	609
HR	 534	SB	 87
HR %	. . . . . 6.6	CS	 72

Jimmie Foxx vs. The Top 100 Players

The graph below shows how Jimmie Foxx compares to the 100 best players of all time in 14 different categories and fielding wins.

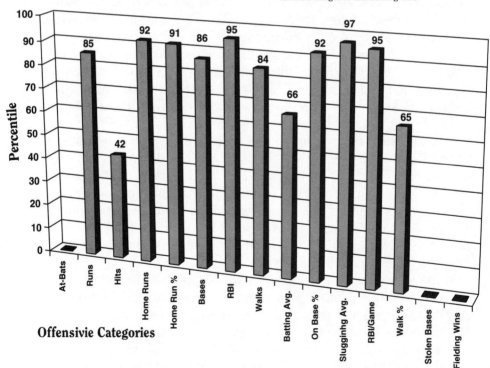

Offensivie Categories

8
STAN MUSIAL
Left Field/First Base

"Stan the Man"
Born: 11/21/20 Donora, PA
6 feet, 175 pounds
Debut: 9/1/41, Played 22 years:
1941-1963 (missed 1945) St. Louis (NL)

"The secret of hitting is physical relaxation, mental concentration and don't hit the fly ball to center," Stan Musial once said. There's more to those words than at first appears. The concentration was evident in the way he attacked the ball. When the pitch came in, Musial uncoiled, his thin, 6-foot, 175-pound frame rotating into the pitch with maximum mechanical advantage. Someone once said Musial at the plate looked like a kid peeking around a corner.

Stan Musial was such a great player, so why does he not receive more acclaim? Musial was the National League bookend to Ted Williams for about 20 years. Just as Williams won the majority of batting and slugging titles in the American League, Musial won the majority in the senior circuit. Stan Musial won seven batting titles and six slugging percentage titles between 1943 and 1957. He was the class of the National League at a time when the American League was winning most of the World Series and most of the All-Star games.

His sweet swing produced 3,630 hits. "What's the best way to pitch to Stan Musial," Joe Garagiola responded to someone's query. He couldn't think of a way to answer and gave up. "That's easy. Walk him and try to pick him off first," he finally offered.

Musial's offensive distinctions are better suited to 10 pages of an accountant's ledger than to one Cooperstown plaque. He didn't fail to hit .300 until he was 38 years old and at age 41 he hit .330. He is also just one of nine players ever to record 100 runs batted in 10 times.

Author Bill James wrote, "Look at his career totals of doubles and triples and they'll remind you of something that was accepted while he was active and has been largely forgotten since: Stan Musial was one player that always left the batter's box on a dead run."

When he retired in 1963, he was the National League leader in hits, doubles and RBI. His lifetime average was .331 and his slugging average was .559. The best measure of the man was his outrageous consistency. Find another player whose best 15-year run includes 2,947 hits – nearly 200 per year! Then check if that player also slugged .595 for those years, as Musial did, or just hit singles.

Musial hit 475 homers. He never hit 40 in a season, but in his best run of years, 1948 through 1957, he hit 320 homers, averaging 32 while knocking between 21 and 39 each year. Musial slugged .600 or better six times.

By the time Musial came along, the Cardinals had finished the "Gas House Gang" era that won two World Series in the early thirties. But in the forties they were at it again. In 1942 Mort Cooper won 22 games and Johnny Beazley 21. The outfield of Musial, Terry Moore and Enos Slaughter was coming together, with Slaughter leading the team (.318 and 98 runs batted in) and Musial hitting .315. The team won 106, lost 48 and dumped the Yankees in five Series games.

In 1943, Musial, now 22, had his coming-out party. He took MVP honors, leading the league in six offensive categories, including hits (220), doubles (48), triples (20), average (.357), on-base percentage (.425) and slugging (.562). But now the Yankees returned the favor, winning the series in five games.

In 1944, with many of the game's stars at war, the Cardinals met the St. Louis Browns in the World Series and won in six games. Stan Musial had his best World Series to date, hitting .304. He missed 1945 due to World War II but returned to play in one of the most memorable World Series in 1946.

The Series matched the game's best two hitters, Williams and Musial. But that anticipated showdown fizzled when Musial hit .222 and an injured Ted Williams batted .200. The Series will always be memorable for Enos Slaughter's "Mad Dash" home, all the way from first, on an eighth-inning single to left center by Harry Walker. Slaughter just kept on coming, scoring when Red Sox shortstop Johnny Pesky double-clutched before firing home. The Cardinals held on to win their third Series in five years.

The feat capped an unbelievable year for Slaughter, who led the league with 130 RBIs. Musial won his second MVP, leading the league in six offensive categories, including batting (.365) and slugging (.587). As great as Musial's 1946 season was, it was nothing compared to his achievement in 1948, one of the greatest years ever by a hitter.

Musial utterly dominated the league in 1948, leading in eight offensive categories. He reached his personal high in homers with 39, but also led the league in runs, doubles, triples, runs batted in, average (.376), on-base percentage (.450) and slugging (.702). The slugging average was the highest in the National League for 46 years, until Jeff Bagwell slugged .750 in the strike shortened 1994 season! Musial captured his third and last MVP award. He was soon making $75,000 a year, the highest salary in the National League.

But four more batting titles were still in store for "The Man." It wasn't easy winning batting titles in the 1950s, not with Musial past 30 and Mays and Aaron just beginning. Nonetheless, Musial won batting crowns in 1950, 1951, 1952 and 1957. He worked tirelessly on that stylish swing even at the end of his career. His work inspired others. In his own struggle to hit the curve ball, the late Curt Flood said, "Musial also helped, mainly by working as hard as he did on his own perfect swing. If this immortal felt the need for frequent extra practice, how could I hope to prosper on less effort?"

At the 1962 All-Star Game President John F. Kennedy walked over to Musial. "A couple of years ago they told me I was too young to be president and you were too old to be playing baseball," the President said. "But we fooled them, and we're still fooling them." When Musial retired after the following season, he had played 22 years with the Cardinals and posted 1,377 extra base hits.

On the occasion of his retirement, Commissioner Ford Frick said, "Here stands baseball's perfect warrior. Here stands baseball's perfect knight." Less than 40 years after his retirement, the Man from Donora, Pennsylvania seems all but forgotten. Where is the talk about Stan Musial when the greats of the game are mentioned? Musial would rate the all-time best left fielder if not for Ted Williams playing there. As it stands, he was a hitting, run-producing and slugging machine.

He is undeniably in the top 10 of all-time.

Best 5-year Average
1948-1952

R	H	D	T	HR	RBI	Avg	Obp	Slg
119	206	40	11	31	112	.349	.438	.613

Best 10-year Average
1948-1957

111	196	40	9	31	112	.339	.427	.597

15-year Average
1943-1958 (missed 1945)

109	197	41	10	26	104	.349	.434	.595

Lifetime Totals

```
G ....... 3,026
AB .... 10,972
R ....... 1,949
H ....... 3,630
D ........ 725
T ......... 177
H ........ 475
HR % ..... 4.3
RBI ..... 1,951
K ...... 1,599
BB ....... 696
AVG ...... 331
OBP ...... 418
SLG ...... 559
SB ........ 78
```

Stan Musial vs. The Top 100 Players

The graph below shows how Stan Musial compares to the 100 best players of all time in 14 different categories and fielding wins.

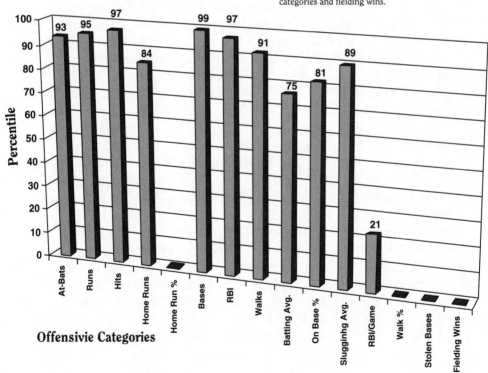

9
ROGERS HORNSBY
Second Base

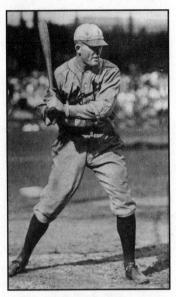

"The Rajah"
Born: 4/27/1896 Winters, TX, Died: 1/5/63 Chicago, IL
5 feet 11 inches, 175 pounds
Debut: 9/10/15, Played 23 years: 1915-1937
1915-1926, St. Louis (NL); 1927, New York (NL);
1928, Boston (NL); 1929-1932, Chicaco (NL);
1933, St. Louis (NL); 1934-1937, St. Louis (AL)

"Every time I stepped up to the plate with a bat in my hands I felt sorry for them," Rogers Hornsby once said about pitchers. His record shows why. There is no question that Rogers Hornsby was one the greatest hitters of his time, certainly the greatest right-handed hitter of his time. He was also the National League's preeminent hitter his entire career. Add one more title: Hornsby was by far the greatest second baseman who ever lived.

He hit for power and performed feats that no one before him or since has achieved. Only Babe Ruth was more consistent than Rogers Hornsby in the 1920s. Hornsby finished his career with a lifetime average of .358, second best of all-time, a well-known fact. Less known, but more impressive, is his run of years between 1921 and 1925 when he averaged .402 for a five-year period. This run included his 1924 season, where he compiled a .424 average, the highest ever.

Hornsby was so committed to hitting that he refused to see movies for fear that they would compromise his batting eye. There's the well-worn story about the time in 1927 when Hornsby, then playing for the Giants, waited out a full count while the Dodgers' pitcher, Jim Eliott, and catcher Hank DeBerry squawked about every pitch. Finally pitcher Jim Eliott threw the ball down the middle and Hornsby hit it into the right field seats. As Hornsby circled the bases, umpire Cy Prirman walked toward the mound and yelled to Eliott, "Mr. Hornsby will let you know when the ball is over the plate."

Like everyone else in the 1920s, Hornsby was overshadowed by the achievements of Babe Ruth. Nonetheless, he finished second in the decade in homers with 250 (Ruth had 467) and second in RBI to Ruth with 1,153 (Ruth had 1,331). He led the league in slugging nine times, second only to Ruth's 13 league-leading slugging totals.

Hornsby also led the senior circuit in batting seven times and in on-base percentage eight times. It must have been especially meaningful for Hornsby, as the Cardinals player-manager in the 1926 World Series, when the Cards beat the Yankees in game seven after Grover Cleveland Alexander stopped the favored Yankees' last ditch rally.

The Cardinals had won their first World Series and Hornsby, the 30-year old manager of the club, had contributed not only by piloting the team, but also by hitting .317 that season, for him a kind of "off-season" in which he hit 11 homers and knocked in 93 runs.

Hornsby was traded to the Giants before the 1927 season, but the deal was stalled because Hornsby, as a manager with St. Louis, had owned more than 1,000 shares of the Cardinals' stock. League rules prohibited shareholders of one team signing a contract with another. Hornsby and St. Louis owner Sam Breadon couldn't agree on a price to be paid, with Breadon offering $80,000 for the stock and Hornsby demanding $140,000. Finally NL President John Heydler got the other clubs in the league to put up the difference.

Hornsby still had three more great seasons left. In 1927 he had his sixth 200-hit season, belting 26 homers, knocking in 125 and hitting .361. The following year he was traded to the Boston Braves. It was his third team in three years and he excelled on all of them. He hit 21 homers, knocked in 94 and led the league in hitting for his seventh and last time, batting .387. He had also been named manager of the Braves in May of 1928. But this Braves' team won 50 and lost 103, with Hornsby's share of the damage being 39-83 (.320). He was dismissed and traded to the Chicago Cubs, continuing his tour of National League cities.

In Chicago, he had a stellar season, hitting 39 homers, batting in 149 runs and leading the league in slugging for the ninth time in 13 years with a mark of .679. The Cubs also had Hack Wilson, who hit 39 homers and led the league in RBI with 159. The two of them led Chicago to a 98-54 record and the National League pennant. The Philadelphia A's overwhelmed them in the World Series, however, four games to one.

In September of 1930, Hornsby was named manager of the Cubs, his third managerial post. He would manage his fourth team, the St. Louis Browns, in July 1933, after being released by the Cardinals. As a player, you know where you stood with Hornsby as a manager. "I treat all players alike," said the Browns' manager. "I can't have two sets of rules." Sportswriter Lee Allen went further: "Hornsby was frank to the point of being cruel and as subtle as a belch." He played with the Browns through 1937, ending his career as a part-time second baseman and pinch hitter at the age of 41. He had hit his 300th homer with the Browns three years before. He managed the Browns and the Reds in 1952, then managed his last year with Cincinnati in 1953. Alas, one of the greatest hitters who ever lived couldn't pass on his knowledge to his troops. His lifetime record in 15 years as a manager was 701 and 812, though he did win that memorable World Series over the Yankees and "Murderer's Row."

Besides his .358 lifetime average, "the Rajah" finished with two most valuable player awards and was the leading National League home run hitter at the time of his retirement.

Hornsby was made batting coach for the New York Mets in 1962. The team finished 40 and 120 and it must have been like purgatory for Hornsby, who had dedicated his entire waking life to baseball and now had to watch the poorest team he had ever seen. Hornsby didn't smoke, drink or even stay up late. He looked at a newspaper only to see the box scores. While coaching the Mets, he once told writer Robert Lipsyte, "Baseball is my life; the only thing I can know and talk about, my only interest."

He died on January 5, 1963, before the 1963 season commenced. He was 66 years old. More than 60 years after he played his last game, his reputation is still intact. He remains, irrefutably, the greatest second baseman of all time.

Runs

Best 5-Year Average
1921-1925

R	H	D	T	HR	RBI	AVG	OBP	SLG
123	216	41	13	29	129	.402	.472	.690

Best 10-Year Average
1920-1929

| 111 | 209 | 41 | 12 | 25 | 115 | .382 | .457 | .626 |

Best 15-Year Average
1917-1931

| 87 | 179 | 34 | 10 | 19 | 97 | .365 | .438 | .593 |

Lifetime Totals

G 2,259
AB 8,173
R 1,579
H 2,930
D 541
T 169
HR 301
HR% 3.7
RBI . . . 1,584
BB . . . 1,038
K 679
AVG 358
OBP 434
SLG 577
SB 135
CS . . . . . . 64 (incomplete figure)

Rogers Hornsby vs. The Top 100 Players

The graph below shows how Rogers Hornsby compares to the 100 best players of all time in 14 different categories and fielding wins.

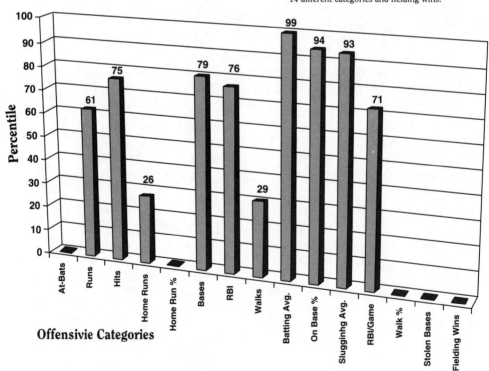

10
HONUS WAGNER
Shortstop

"The Flying Dutchman"
Born: 2/24/1874 Chartiers, PA, Died: 12/6/55 Carnegie, PA
5 feet 11 inches, 200 pounds
Debut: 7/19/1897, Played 21 years: 1897-1917
1897-1899, Louisville (NL); 1900-1917, Pittsburgh

It was said of Honus Wagner that his arms were so long he could tie his shoes without bending. Barrel-chested and long of limb, he was also long on baseball skill. The hulking, 5-foot-11-inch, 200-pound shortstop was bow-legged and appeared ill-equipped to handle the most demanding position on the diamond. Appearances deceive, because handle shortstop he did.

In his career he played everywhere but catcher. Said manager John McGraw: "Honus was first on my list, not just because he was first at shortstop, but because he could have been first at any position. I never saw such a versatile player."

Little doubt was raised about his prowess at the plate, either. For 16 straight years (between 1898 and 1913) he hit .300 or better, winning the National League batting title eight times, all between 1900 and 1911. Little doubt was raised about something else, either. When he died on Dec. 6, 1955, he was the greatest shortstop who had ever played. At that time he held

National League records for games, 2,792; hitting .300 the most times, 17; hits, 3,415; and runs, 1,736. He also had 722 stolen bases and thus came his name "the Flying Dutchman," a sobriquet given to him by fans for his quickness in the field and speed on the bases. Now, about 125 years after he was born, there is still little doubt who was the greatest shortstop of all-time. No shortstops knock in 100 runs nine times, lead the league in slugging six times or hit .327 lifetime. None except Wagner, that is. Couple that with his fielding and aggressive base running and Wagner was a great all-around player.

When he started sandlot ball as a teenager, he was already making his living as a barber. His first professional experience came with a Steubenville, Ohio club in 1895. One story goes that Ed Barrow, who operated a Paterson, New Jersey franchise in the Atlantic League, made a trip to scout Honus' brother Al Wagner. On the way he spotted a large, ungainly and rawboned kid in dungarees who was picking up rocks and scaling them in a river near railroad tracks. So Barrow forgot Al and ended up singing Honus, the big kid in the dungarees. "We had a league limit of $100 a month for players," Barrow said later, "but I offered Wagner $125."

Wagner was eventually purchased from Peterson by the Louisville Colonels for $2,100. He played outfield, second, first and third with Louisville. When Louisville disbanded in 1899, he joined Pittsburgh. He made shortstop his primary position in 1903, his seventh year. By that time Honus had the necessary seasoning for the long haul. One time he said to a Giant who hit a homer, "nice hit." But opposing players didn't want praise. "Go to hell," the hitter told Wagner. "I liked that remark," Wagner later admitted to *New York Times* columnist Arthur Daley. "He was the first major leaguer ever to speak to me."

Wagner played in the first World Series ever, in 1903. He played poorly, hitting only .222, and Pittsburgh lost in eight games (the Series was then a best of nine affair) to the Boston Pilgrims.

He resolved the same poor showing would not happen the next time he reached the Series. In 1909 the Series between Pittsburgh and Detroit caused a great stir. It was billed as a matchup of the game's greatest players, Ty Cobb and Honus Wagner. The 34-year-old Wagner had won his seventh batting title that season, hitting .339. Cobb, just 23, had won his third of nine consecutive batting crowns, hitting .377. As great as Wagner's year had been, Cobb's was better. Cobb led the league in seven other offensive categories that season: slugging, .517; hits, 216; homers, 9; home run percentage, 1.6; runs, 116; runs batted in, 107; and stolen bases, 76.

Cobb was acutely aware of the rivalry and had another reason to show up the Dutchman. Detroit had been drubbed in the last two World Series by the Chicago Cubs – in a sweep in 1907 and in five games in 1908 – and Cobb didn't play well. The contrast between the two players' temperaments couldn't have been sharper. Wagner was kind, agreeable, humble; Cobb, mercurial and prone to violent outbursts.

The tone was set early as Cobb got on first and hollered to Wagner at short. "Watch out krauthead, I'm coming down; I'll cut you to pieces." Wagner returned fire, "Come on ahead then." When Cobb slid into second, Wagner tagged him in the face, splitting his lip.

Pittsburgh won the series, with Wagner knocking in two runs in the seventh game. Though knocking in six runs, Cobb wasn't nearly the factor Wagner was, hitting just .231 for the Series and stealing two bases. Wagner hit .333 and stole six bases – the Pirates stole 18 – and the Pirates romped in the seventh game, 8-0.

Thereafter Wagner's play was steady. Though he would earn only two more batting distinctions – a batting title (.334) in 1911 and an RBI-crown in 1912 (102) – Wagner further cemented his defensive reputation, posting league-leading fielding averages in four consecutive years between 1912 and 1915. Remarkably, Wagner was still a regular shortstop in 1916, when he was 42 years old!

The following year he was named manager of the Pirates. He also played in 74 games, most at first and third.

He managed just five games that season, finishing with a record of 1-4, as the Pirates finished the season in eighth place with 103 losses.

It is more than 80 years since he played his last game and his numbers are unblemished. He is seventh in hits with 3,418, seventh in doubles with 643, third in triples with 252 and eighth in stolen bases with 722.

He is also immortalized in another fashion. The Honus Wagner T-206 baseball card is regarded as the most sought after prize of collectors. The price of the card was driven up by either or both of two reasons, says Wagner's biographer William Hageman. One, it is said that Wagner wanted the cards recalled after finding the packs included chewing tobacco, which he didn't want children to have. Two, Wagner wanted more money from the card makers, couldn't get it and told them to stop distributing. Either explanation is believable. Barry Halper, who owns the largest collection of baseball memorabilia in the world, estimates the card's value to be near $1 million.

When Pirates owner Barney Dreyfuss once offered to double his salary to keep him from jumping to another team, Wagner declined, saying, "I'm not worth it." His top salary was reported at about $10,000 near the end of his career. It never seemed to bother Wagner that he was born too early for the big money. He played in an era when, to use his words, "A glass of beer was only a nickel."

Wagner's reputation after his death was secure. In 1936 he was one of the first five players elected to the Hall of Fame, along with immortal Ty Cobb, Babe Ruth, Christy Mathewson and Walter Johnson.

Best 5-year Average
1900-1904

R	H	D	T	HR	RBI	AVG	OBP	SLG
101	185	37	16	4	99	.354	.408	.513

Best 10-year Average
1900-1909

| 101 | 185 | 37 | 15 | 5 | 96 | .352 | .410 | .508 |

Best 15-year Average
1898-1912

| 97 | 182 | 36 | 14 | 6 | 96 | .342 | .400 | .494 |

Lifetime Totals

G 2,792
AB 10,430
R 1,736
H 3,415
D 640
T 252
HR. 101
HR % 1.0
RBI 1,732
BB. 963
K. 327
(totals incomplete)
AVG 327
OBP 391
SLG 466
SB. 722

Honus Wagner vs. The Top 100 Players

The graph below shows how Honus Wagner compares to the 100 best players of all time in 14 different categories and fielding wins.

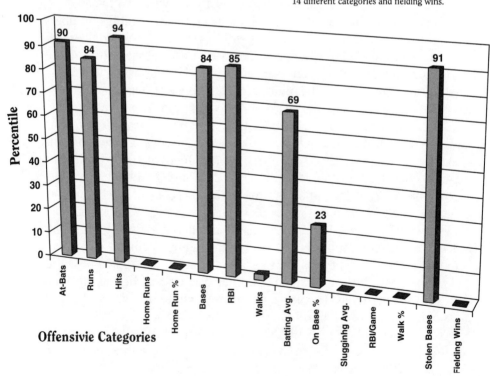

11
JOE DiMAGGIO
Center Field

"Joltin' Joe" "The Yankee Clipper"
Born: 11/25/14 Martinez, CA
6 feet 2 inches, 193 pounds
Debut: 5/3/36, Played 13 seasons:
1936-1951 (missed 1943-45) New York (AL)

Explaining why he played so hard every game, Joe DiMaggio once said, "There is always some kid who may be seeing me for the first or last time. I owe him my best." After Babe Ruth, no baseball player's life has passed over into American mythology quite like Joe DiMaggio's. This fact is at once fascinating and frustrating. It is fascinating because as great as his baseball achievements were, his reputation always seemed larger than those achievements. It is frustrating, too, because so many people, even those who never saw him play a game, cannot get past the DiMaggio legend to even attempt an objective analysis of his career.

Few ballplayers enjoyed more instant success than Joseph Paul DiMaggio. He came to the Yankees in 1936, a year they won the first of four consecutive World Championships. The Yankees had all the pieces – a team that led the league in runs, home runs and earned run average. Lou Gehrig busted 49 homers and drove in 152. He was one of five Yankees, including DiMaggio, to knock in more than 100. The team won

102 and lost 51 games and the second place Tigers disappeared from the rear view mirror, 19-and-a-half games behind.

DiMaggio was not just a contributor on this post-Ruth juggernaut in the making. In his first season the twenty-one year old was already the second best hitter on the team, not a mean feat on a team that included Lou Gehrig, Bill Dickey, Tony Lazzeri and George Selkirk. The Yankees handled the Giants four games to two in the Series with DiMaggio hitting .346.

The next year, 1937, DiMaggio had his best season ever. He hit 46 home runs, the only time he hit 40 or more, and he had a personal best 167 RBI. Gehrig added 159 runs batted in and Dickey chipped in 133. DiMaggio's slugging average, .673, was also his highest, as were his 151 runs scored. He led the league in runs, homers and runs batted in.

Over the winter DiMaggio sought a $40,000 contract from the Yankees, a $25,000 raise over his 1937 deal. Yankee owner Ed Barrow said, "Young man, do you realize that Lou Gehrig only makes $43,000 a year after 13 years?" DiMaggio replied, "In that case Mr. Barrow, Mr. Gehrig is a very underpaid ballplayer."

DiMaggio was on his way. He knocked in more than 100 runs in each of his first seven years. He assumed the leadership role on the Yankees after Gehrig's sudden illness in early 1939 and death in 1941. That was the year of DiMaggio's streak.

On the day Gehrig died, June 2, DiMaggio extended his streak to 24 games. Five more and he would tie the Yankees' club record of 29 held by Roger Peckinpaugh and Earle Combs. After that came the American League record of 41 straight games held by George Sisler. Then the major league mark of 44 owned by Willie Keeler. DiMaggio needed several breaks to keep the streak going.

He broke the Yankees' record with a bad-hop single on June 17 against Chicago. In the 36th game he needed an eighth inning safety to keep alive the streak. Bob Moncrief of the St. Louis Browns pitched to DiMaggio rather than walk him and DiMaggio got the hit. In the eighth inning of the 38th game Henrich got permission from manager Joe McCarthy to bunt so that he would not rap into a double play and deny a hitless DiMaggio another at bat.

The strategy worked and DiMaggio doubled off Eldon Auker. In the 39th game Johnny Babich, the A's pitcher who delighted in beating the Yankees, said he would stop DiMaggio at 39. He walked him on four pitches and ran the count to 3-0 DiMaggio's second time up. McCarthy spotted what was happening and gave DiMaggio the green light and DiMaggio lined a blue streak between Babich' legs for a hit.

On July 2, he broke Keeler's record with a homer, but only after a favorable call from official scorer Dan Daniel of the *New York World-Telegram* the day before. DiMaggio hit a tough hopper to third and Jim Tabor, the Boston third baseman, hurried and threw the ball past first. Ordinarily a tough scorer, Daniel ruled it a hit. "Damn you, DiMaggio," Daniel was heard to yell in the press box. "I gave you a hit this time, but everything has to be clean from now on." DiMaggio had no other hits that game. The hitting streak ended in Cleveland on July 17. He faced Jim Bagby, Jr., and went 0-3 with a walk. Cleveland third baseman Ken Keltner made a backhand grab to throw him out from foul territory in the first inning.

On August 29 later that season, the Yankees were now far ahead of second-place Boston – on their way to beating them by 17 games in the standings. DiMaggio's closest pal, Lefty Gomez, told DiMaggio to go with him to stop by Selkirk's room at Washington's Hotel Shoreham, where they were staying. When DiMaggio walked into the room 40 men – teammates and sportscasters – raised champagne glasses for a toast. Gomez presented DiMaggio with a silver cigar humidor which had been ordered from Tiffany's. On the cover was a likeness of DiMaggio swinging, with the number 56 on one side and the number 91 on the other, which was the total number of hits he had during the streak. The inscription read: "Presented to Joe DiMaggio by his fellow players on the New York Yankees to express their admiration for his consecutive-game hitting record, 1941."

The two obstacles DiMaggio faced in his career were significant. One was the Second World War and the other was the size of Yankee Stadium. World War II stopped his string of seven 100-RBI seasons in 1943. He missed all of 1943, 1944 and 1945 to the War, and when he returned to play in 1946, he was not the same player. His average fell under .300 for the first time in 1946 and his runs batted in also dipped below 100. In 1947 he climbed to .315 and the Yankees reached the Series again, their seventh Series since DiMaggio joined the team 12 years before. In a thrilling series that featured some of the most memorable moments in baseball history, the Yankees won in seven games.

DiMaggio hit just .231 in the Series, but he hit two homers and one he didn't hit is far more remembered than the ones he did. In game six, the Yankees were trailing 8-5 in the sixth inning when they got two men on with two out against Brooklyn reliever Joe Hatten. DiMaggio belted one toward the bullpen gate, 415 feet away in left center. But Al Gionfriddo was playing deep and backpedaled furiously. He reached and made a one-handed catch with his back against the bullpen gate. The Yankees scored another run in the ninth but Brooklyn held on to win and even the series at three games apiece.

The catch showed why DiMaggio didn't hit more homers. What was a right handed hitter supposed to do in Yankee Stadium, where the dimensions were 301 down the line, 402 to the right of that, 415 to the right of the bullpen gate, 457 in deepest left center, 466 to the left of the center field screen, 461 in center and 407 in deepest right center? He frequently hit balls that would have left other parks. For his career he hit 361 homers but only 148 of those came at Yankee Stadium and 213 on the road. If you double his road total, he would finish with 426 homers.

In 1949, DiMaggio added to the mystique. The Yankees' new manager was Casey Stengel. DiMaggio appeared in only 76 games that season, not playing until June 28 because of a heel injury. The Yankees had a small lead when "Joltin' Joe" returned but the Red Sox, managed by the Yankees' former manager Joe McCarthy, went on a streak and the Yankees had some injuries. DiMaggio had viral pneumonia and lost 10 pounds. Boston came to Yankee Stadium leading by one game with two games to play. But the Yankees took both games to win the pennant. They won the Series easily over the Dodgers, four games to one.

DiMaggio had one more great season in him. In 1950 he hit 32 homers and knocked in 122 runs while slugging .585. The Yankees won their second straight Series, sweeping Philadelphia's Whiz Kids, four games to none. DiMaggio was 35, however, and injuries were taking their toll. He had missed 15 games in 1950 and then missed 38 more in 1951. The injuries, coupled with 12 homers and a .263 average, were enough to tell DiMaggio that the time was near.

On Dec. 11, 1951, the Yankee brass, with DiMaggio standing by, addressed the press from the Yankees' midtown Manhattan offices. "...When baseball is no longer fun, it's no longer a game," DiMaggio said. "And so I've played my last game..." When someone persisted in asking why he quit he answered, "I just don't have it anymore." When asked why Joe quit, his oldest brother Tom – who Joe once said was a better ballplayer than himself, Vince and Dom and could hit the ball further - said, "He quit because he wasn't Joe DiMaggio anymore."

His 13-year run was complete, but his grip on the public was not. A marriage to Marilyn Monroe, his countless appearances at Old Timer's Games and an aloof bearing have given him a regal demeanor nearly 50 years after his retirement. There is much in his bottom line to command such regard. His .579 slugging average is sixth highest all-time. Naturally, that figure is aided by his playing only 13 years and having just 6,821 at-bats, instead of 18 or 20 years and 10,000 or more at bats like Mays, Aaron and Musial.

He played on nine World Series winners and 10 pennant winners with New York. Eleventh place on this list won't be high enough for many people. Listen to many who saw him, and some who didn't, and they speak of his career as if it were utterly flawless. The basis for this conclusion is often misty recollection, or the passed along misty recollection of others, like the fathers and uncles of those too young to see him.

DiMaggio is a heroic symbol of an America that existed half a century ago. Because many believe that America was a better America, and because DiMaggio was a part of that era, it is a loosely formed syllogism in their minds that he must be better than those who have come since. To maintain that DiMaggio was not a great ballplayer would be foolish in the extreme. But it would also be foolish to deny that DiMaggio benefited from nostalgia for an America gone by. As a symbol of that era, his life has long since passed over into mythology.

He aids and abets the myth by remaining scrupulously private. He also aids the myth making by insisting on being announced last and being announced as "the greatest living ballplayer" at Old Timer's games. He was voted "the Greatest Living Ballplayer" in 1969 by the Baseball Writers of America. But there is no logical equivalence between the statements: "Jones was voted greatest" and "Jones is the greatest."

He was a great, great ballplayer. But he was not the greatest ballplayer. Nor is he the greatest living ballplayer.

Best 5-Year Average
1937-1941

R	H	D	T	HR	RBI	AVG	OBP	SLG
121	191	34	11	34	138	.343	.409	.625

Best 10-Year Average
1936-1948 (missed '43, '44, '45)

115	185	32	11	30	128	.327	.391	.583

No 15-year Average (played only 13 years)

Lifetime totals

G	1,736	RBI	1,537
AB	6,821	BB	790
R	1,390	K	369
H	2,214	AVG	.325
D	389	OBP	.398
T	131	SLG	.579
HR	361	SB	30
HR %	5.3	CS	9

12
MICKEY MANTLE
Right Field

"The Commerce Comet"
Born: 10/20/31 Spavinaw, OK, Died: 8/13/95 Dallas, TX
5 feet 11 inches, 198 pounds
Debut: 4/17/51, Played 18 years: 1951-1968 New York (AL)

Those people who missed Mickey Mantle's career should know about four balls that he hit. Then they will understand what the shouting was about.

The first was off Senators' pitcher Chuck Stobbs on April 17, 1953. Batting right-handed, Mantle crushed the ball over the left-center field fence and out of Griffith Stadium. The ball is estimated to have traveled 565 feet. Batting left-handed three years later, he belted one at Yankee Stadium that might have gone further.

This blast was off Pedro Ramos, another Senators' pitcher. A dotted line in the morning Daily News showed the ball's flight. It bounded off the right field facade above the third tier of the Stadium, 387 feet from home and 117 feet high. It hit just 18 inches short of going over the roof.

Seven years later, Kansas City right-hander Bill Fischer was the victim. This blow also tattooed the facade – reports that the ball was still rising are no doubt apocryphal – and missed going out by three feet. No one has hit a ball out of Yankee Stadium and Mantle remains the only one ever to hit the facade.

To get a full appreciation of what The Mick did, try the following exercise when leisure permits. I did. Sit in the "box seats" in the first eight rows of the third deck of Yankee Stadium and then count the dozens of rows still behind you. The players at home plate look more like ants than human beings at that distance. Far above and behind you is the facade. From this vantage point, it is inconceivable that a man could even come close to hitting a ball that far. Dozens of balls have been hit into the first 10 or 15 rows of the upper deck. As great as that is, it is nowhere close to what Mantle did. Yet Mantle did it twice.

After Mantle had turned Bill Fischer's neck, it was Barney Schultz' turn to watch one leave. It was the bottom of the ninth in the third game of the 1964 Series. The score was tied 1-1 and Mantle said to Elston Howard in the on-deck circle, "I'm gonna end this one." Yankees' pitcher Jim Bouton laughed, saying he knew it was going to happen. Mantle turned Schultz' first pitch around, blasting it into the upper deck to give the Yankees a two-games-to-one Series lead. He had made good on his called shot. The blow was also Mantle's 16th World Series homer, moving him ahead of Babe Ruth on that list.

Among Mantle's lasting distinctions are his many moonshots and his power as a switch-hitter. His 536 home runs are more than any switch-hitter ever. Only Eddie Murray, at 504, is even close. Yet another element that distinguishes Mantle from the others is his rare combination of power and speed.

When Mantle, who was born in Oklahoma in 1931, arrived in New York 20 years later, he was a player of near infinite promise. As he hit 27 and then 37 and then 52 homers by 1956, he was already part of base-ball lore, a small-town boy from Spavinaw, a guy who owned one sports coat and whose neck was sore from looking up at the skyscrapers. He had came to the most storied team in sports and succeeded beyond any-one's expectations.

But the course of reality rarely stays the course of fable.

There are holes in Mantle's career, like getting 100 runs batted in only four times in 18 years. Many of the holes owe to non-stop injuries to his legs. By his own admission, he did not nurse leg injuries as much as he nursed drinks into the night while enjoying his stardom. He said he could have played past 36 years old if he had not "wasted" the talents given him. He also said he would have taken better care of himself if he had known he would live longer. No one else in his family, including his father, ever made old age.

He didn't understand why people made such a fuss over his ability, because he knew what they didn't: that his drinking had ended his career, torn apart his family and cut short his life. So while Mantle is the most talked about baseball player since World War II, he also led a life that was the most allegorical. Despite his awesome athletic endowments, his career still has a "what-if" quality. What if he had stayed healthy and not caught his spikes on an outfield drain and torn ligaments in his knee in Game 2 of the 1951 World Series? What if he did not have to endure three knee operations after that one? What if he had more discipline about getting treatment for his injuries?

Even with the subtext of injuries, some of his achievements are spellbinding. Mantle won the Triple Crown in 1956, belting out 52 homers, knocking in 130 runs and hitting .353. His slugging average was .705 and he completely dominated the American League, nay both leagues. And he hit three homers in the World Series, avenging New York's first World Series loss to the Dodgers the year before. In what will forever be remembered as the Don Larsen World Series for his perfect game in game 5, Mantle made a running backhand catch off a Gil Hodges drive into the left-center gap to save Larsen's perfection and hit a homer to give the Yankees a 2-0 win.

The only American league player to rival Mantle's talents was Ted Williams, who had already turned 37; Mantle hadn't reached his 25th birthday by year's end. He rose to prominence at a time when the National League was bringing up the lion's share of black talent and had the most powerful hitters. After Mantle and Williams, the best player in the American League was Al Kaline. The National League had Willie Mays and Eddie Mathews, Hank Aaron and Ernie Banks, Duke Snider and Gil Hodges, Roberto Clemente and Frank Robinson, Orlando Cepada and Willie McCovey.

With Mantle as the most dominant player in the league – and Whitey Ford and Yogi Berra adding to the Yankees' strength up the middle – Mantle's life grew larger and larger. People who didn't follow baseball religiously would turn on their sets in October to find Mantle and the Yankees, as if it were New York's birth right to appear in World Series.

With a healthy Mantle, the Yankees won with a regularity that is frightening. In the fourteen seasons between 1951 and 1964, the Yankees won 12 pennants and seven World Series. To a man, players like Hank Bauer and Gene Woodling and Tony Kubek – and the list goes on and on – swear that Mantle, more than anyone else, is responsible for them cashing World Series checks year in and year out.

His peak years were astounding. In their book *The Hidden Game of Baseball*, Palmer and Thorn rank four of Mantle's years – the 1955, 1956, 1957 and 1961 campaigns – in the top 100 offensive years ever posted. The only players with more top-100 seasons are Ruth with 12; Williams, eight; Gehrig, eight; Hornsby, seven; Cobb, six; and Musial, six. Foxx ties Mantle with four.

As Bill James said, Mantle was the "greatest player of the 50s." The problem is, something else that Bill James said is true. Players' "peak values" are determined in their twenties, but their "career values" are determined in their thirties. Look at Mantle's record and his good seasons are over by 32, after his 1964 season.

He hit his 500th homer in 1967 and that season and the next gave to his last days a final tour kind of quality. He passed Ott and Williams and Foxx in homers. He last hit two homers in a game off Minnesota's Jim Merritt, on August 10, 1968, on Old Timer's day. He retired after the season with 536 home runs. People who mention his 1,710 strike outs (less than 100 per year), rarely add that he walked 1,733 times, leading the league in that category five times, while never leading the league in strikeouts.

Thinking of his moon shots, Billy Martin said "no man in the history of baseball had as much power as Mickey Mantle. No man. You're not talking about ordinary power. Dave Kingman had power. Willie Mays had power. Then, when you're talking about Mickey Mantle, it's an altogether different level. Separates the men from the boys."

His .557 slugging average ties him with Willie Mays for 10th place all-time.

Best 5-year Average
1954-1958

R	H	D	T	HR	RBI	AVG	OBP	SLG
126	168	23	7	38	104	.325	.452	.618

Best 10-year Average
1955-1964

| 108 | 146 | 20 | 4 | 37 | 95 | .314 | .444 | .614 |

Best 15-year Average
1952-1966

| 100 | 141 | 20 | 4 | 32 | 89 | .307 | .416 | .580 |

Lifetime totals

G	2,401	RBI	1,509
AB	8,102	BB	1,733
R	1,677	K	1,710
H	2,415	AVG	.298
D	344	OBP	.423
T	72	SLG	.557
HR	536	SB	153
HR %	6.6	CS	38

13
MIKE SCHMIDT
Third Base

Born: 9/27/49 Dayton, OH
6 feet 2 inches, 203 pounds
Debut: 9/12/72, Played 18 years: 1972-1989 Philadelphia

People who say that most of baseball's best players are the players of bygone years – and I'm one of them – will have to admit that this generation of baseball fans got a long look at a man who is simply the greatest all-around third baseman who ever played. In Baltimore they like to say that Brooks Robinson is the "greatest third baseman of all-time." Correction. Brooks Robinson was the greatest fielding third baseman of all-time. Mike Schmidt is the greatest third baseman of all-time.

Schmidt's preeminence at the position is beyond dispute. His 548 homers are the seventh highest total all-time and the most ever by a third baseman. Before Schmidt, the third base king was Eddie Mathews with 512. Schmidt is also the slugging champ at the position, with a cool .527 average. His home run ratio – one every 15.3 at bats – is ninth place all-time. Schmidt developed a tireless work ethic and took care of his 6-foot-2-inch, 200-pound physique. His teammate Pete Rose once said, "Just to have his body, I'd trade mine and my wife's and throw in some cash."

He won 10 Gold Gloves at third base. What else? In 1980 he led the

Phillies to their first World Series victory ever, hitting .381 with two homers and seven RBIs in a six-game defeat of the Royals. Schmidt took World Series MVP honors that year and won the first of three regular season MVPs, too. He was the greatest slugger of the 1980s, hitting 313 homers for the decade.

The distinctions go on and on. He won eight home run titles.

PLAYERS WITH THE MOST HOME RUN TITLES

Babe Ruth	12	Willie Mays	4
Mike Schmidt	8	Hank Greenberg	4
Ralph Kiner	7	Hank Aaron	4
Mel Ott	6	Mickey Mantle	4
Harmon Killebrew	6	Ted Williams	4
Jimmie Foxx	4		

Naturally, part of the reason he has so many home run titles is that he didn't play in an era when Aaron, Mays, Mantle, Robinson, Mathews, Killebrew, Jackson, Banks and McCovey – all nine with 500-plus homers – were slugging it out with each other. Save for Hank Aaron, who hit 40 in 1973, Schmidt didn't have any of the seven National League members of the 500-homer club, who reached their peaks in the 1950s and 1960s, competing against him during the years between 1972 and 1989.

Nonetheless, his numbers are awfully impressive. He led the league in runs batted in four times and had 100 or more RBIs nine times. He would have been one of 10 players in history to have 10 seasons of 100 or more RBIs, but the strike season in 1981 cost him 60 games and he finished with "only" 91. 1981 looked like Mike Schmidt's all-world season; he slugged his personal best .644. Three times he led the league in on-base percentage and five times more the home run stud led in slugging. What makes Schmidt's slugging percentage remarkable was that he did not hit for average, batting only .267. In fact, Schmidt's slugging record looks about as concentrated as anyone's in baseball history.

Only Aaron and Mays hit more National League homers. He hit 30 or more homers 13 times. Eleven times he hit 35 or more.

Three times he slugged 40 or more. He hit his 500th in 1986, his final MVP season.

Excluding his partial year during the strike season, Schmidt's greatest season was 1980. That year he hit 48 homers, knocked in 121 runs and slugged .624. That year was also the second of six in which he led in home run percentage.

Despite his awesome totals, things didn't always go smoothly for Mike

Schmidt. He was picked by the Phillies in the second round of the 1971 draft. He got his first major league experience in 1973 and his showing was anything but auspicious. He banged out 18 homers but couldn't hit his weight, batting .196 with an amazing 136 strikeouts in 367 at bats. Three years later, in 1976, he had earned his third home run crown, even hitting four homers in a game in an 18-16 win over the Cubs.

And the Philadelphia fans – who own the dubious distinction of once booing Santa Claus – never seemed to be satisfied. Three years after the 1980 World Championship, the Phillies lost to the Orioles in five games. The fans who cheered him just three years ago now shouted "choke, choke" whenever they saw him. As for the sportswriters, Schmidt once said, "Philadelphia is the only city in the world where you can experience the thrill of victory and the agony of reading about it the next day."

Boo Mike Schmidt? Since Boston fans booed Williams, anything may be possible. Booing or not, Mike Schmidt is the greatest third sacker who ever walked and no one on the horizon is even close.

Best 5-year Average
1979-1983

R	H	D	T	HR	RBI	AVG	OBP	SLG
101	137	22	4	40	104	.275	.400	.576

Best 10-year Average
1977-1986

99	142	25	4	36	102	.275	.390	.550

Best 15-year Average
1974-1988

97	142	26	4	35	101	.272	.384	.539

Lifetime Totals

G	2,404	RBI	1,595
AB	8,352	BB	1,507
R	1,506	K	1,883
H	2,234	AVG	.267
D	408	OBP	.384
T	59	SLG	.527
HR	546	SB	174
HR%	6.5	CS	92

14
FRANK ROBINSON
Right Field

Born: 8/31/35 Beaumont, TX
6 feet 1 inch, 195 pounds
Debut: 4/17/56, Played 21 years: 1956-1976
1956-1965, Cincinnati; 1966-1971, Baltimore; 1972, Los Angeles;
1973-1974, California; 1974-1976, Cleveland

Remember the old game of word association? You say a word and learn something about another person by hearing what they say? Try that game with Frank Robinson and see if you don't hear "first black manager" right after you say his name. That was a worthy achievement, no doubt. The answer indicates that people forgot most everything about his career. In fact, Frank Robinson rates a tie as being the most forgotten of my first 13 players. In Stan Musial's case, being forgotten is more understandable, because his career ended nearly 40 years ago. But Frank Robinson's career ended in 1976, so what's the excuse with him?

Play word association with me and I'll think "586" when you say "Frank Robinson." In case you need a primer in baseball history, that's the number of homers he hit and 586 is still fourth on the all-time list, far ahead of any active player. Ken Griffey, Jr.'s, 294 means he just passed *half* of Robinson's total. Now I think Ken Griffey, Jr., is a pretty great player, so you know how great I think Robinson was. He was far greater than some of his contemporaries who routinely get credit for being better. Take Roberto Clemente, for instance.

Whenever I hear the roll call of great players, Clemente is ahead of Robinson. How can this be? Sure Clemente stole the 1971 Series and beat the Birds. But one series does not a career make. Clemente hit 240 homers, 346 less than Robinson. Try explaining away that difference. While you're at it, remember that Robinson slugged .537. Clemente slugged .475. I mention this not to beat up on Clemente, who was a great player. Rather, I do it to show how one player often got the short end of the stick, despite being better. For some reason – or combination of reasons – the fates have conspired to undersell Robinson's career. Why?

Here we go. He played in Cincinnati, which wasn't exactly "Baseball Central" when Robinson came on the scene in 1956. He tied Wally Berger's rookie record with 38 homers that year and led the league with 122 runs to boot. But if you're teaching someone the meaning of the phrase "toil in anonymity," you could use 10 years in Cincinnati between 1956 and 1965 to help explain it. Mays and McCovey and Marichal were grabbing headlines from San Francisco, a guy named Aaron was making waves in Milwaukee, Koufax and Drysdale were scorching batters in L.A., not to mention Gibson in St. Louis, while Robinson averaged 33 homers and 100 RBIs over his 10 years with the Reds.

The one year Cincinnati made waves was 1961. Robinson won the Most Valuable Player Award that year, though his season was hardly better than his great 1959 campaign, which no one noticed. But in 1961 the Reds won the pennant, earning the dubious right to meet the famed 1961 Yankees, who had just set an all-time record with 240 homers. Six Yankees hit more than 20, so it was no wonder they were able to overcome the loss of Mantle, who hit 54 homers, to an abscessed hip. Mantle batted only six times in the Series, but it didn't matter. The Yankees won easily in five games.

Second billing would become the norm for Robinson during the next four years with the Reds. In 1962 he had even a better season – 39 homers, 136 runs batted in and a .342 average. He also led the league in runs and doubles and reached 200 hits. He won the slugging title for the third straight year, an amazing achievement when you consider the competition: Hank Aaron, Ernie Banks, Eddie Mathews and Willie Mays. Robinson slugged .624 in his seventh season, making it his second straight over .600 and seven straight over .500.

What kept Robinson playing at such a high level was determination. His young teammate Pete Rose said he never saw anyone prepare harder than Robinson. That's Pete Rose talking and you know how hard he prepared. Outfield mate Vada Pinson described Robinson as a team leader and a battler. Like Frank, Pinson also graduated McClymonds High in Oakland. He remembers one particular game against the Braves.

"Frank slid into third base hard – like he always does no matter what the score may be – into Eddie Mathews," Pinson said. "Mathews jumped on top of Frank and punched him in the eye. It swelled out to here and nobody thought Frank could possibly play the second game of a double-header that day. But when the game started, there was Frank in the line-up. Not only did he hit a home run to win the game, but he also made a catch and fell into the left field stands – on a ball that Mathews hit, inci-dentally – that saved the game. He got a standing ovation, and I guess that's one of the biggest thrills I've ever felt in baseball."

Following that run, we don't really hear from Robby, the man with the long, whip action swing, until 1965. Some speculate that Robinson, a civil rights advocate who once got in trouble for carrying a gun, may have upset Reds' general manager, Bill DeWitt. DeWitt said of his ten-year star, "We feel he's an old thirty," despite his hitting 33 homers and knocking in 113 that year. So DeWitt traded him, with Dick Simpson, to Baltimore for Milt Pappas and another pitcher named Jack Baldschun. Not since Boston owner Harry Frazee traded Ruth in 1919 did a traded player pay back a bonehead deal with such a monster season.

Robinson settled in Baltimore just fine. New city, same old fire. "Frank was not out to make friends," said Brooks Robinson, "but to knock someone on his tail." In 1966 he hit 49 homers, knocked in 122 and hit .316 to capture the Triple Crown and the Most Valuable Player Award. He also won his fourth slugging crown (.637). Then he hit two homers in the Series as Baltimore pitchers converted the Dodgers into the Hitless Wonders, allowing them a total of two runs in the entire Series. Baltimore swept.

How good was Baltimore pitching? Get ready. They used only four pitchers to cover the 36 innings – Dave McNally, Wally Bunker, Jim Palmer and Moe Drabowsky – and, amazing to tell, the Dodgers didn't score after the third inning of Game One!

Baltimore had its first World Series title. They would win another Series in 1970, not to mention pennants in 1969 and 1971. Milt Pappas had a 17-7 season six years after "The Trade," winning more than 100 games in his 8-year stretch in Cincinnati. But he was a better pitcher in Baltimore and was essentially a .500 pitcher in Cincinnati. Across a four-year spell Jack Baldschun won 9, lost 7 and retired in 1970. All things considered, the Robinson trade is among the worst ever.

During the six years the Orioles had Robinson they were one of the greatest teams ever to take the field. They had it all. The pitching staff was headed by Jim Palmer, who won 20 games eight times in the nine years between 1970 and 1978. Lefty Dave McNally won 100 games between 1968 and 1972. Mike Cuellar won 125 games from 1969 through 1974. The pitching was the best in baseball, comparable to what the Cleveland Indians had in the early fifties (Feller, Wynn, Lemon and Garcia) and what the Braves have put together in the nineties (Maddux, Glavine, Smoltz and Neagle). In 1971 Pat Dobson won 21 and Baltimore had four 20-game winners that season.

Then, look at the Baltimore defense. There may never have been a better left side of the infield than Robinson and Belanger. Yankee announcer and Hall of Fame shortstop Phil Rizzuto would marvel at Belanger, whom he referred to as "the best shortstop I ever saw." Belanger took home eight Golden Glove Awards. And Brooks Robinson won 16 gold Gloves at third, taking home the hardware *every* year between 1960 and 1975. Brooks was simply the best defensive third baseman there ever was. The 1964 MVP would turn the 1970 World Series into his personal showcase, robbing hitter after hitter in the Reds' potent lineup. He also hit two homers and batted .429 in the Series, taking MVP honors as the Birds beat Frank Robinson's old team in five games. Frank chipped in two homers.

The defense also included Paul Blair, who played a shallow center field and still managed to get to everything. Blair won eight Golden Gloves of his own. Toss in four Goldens for Palmer and three more for second baseman Dave Johnson and Baltimore's nine took home 39 Golden Gloves. The hitting was led by Frank Robinson and Boog Powell, but Blair and Brooks also hit.

It was once said that Baltimore belonged to Brooks Robinson but the Orioles were the property of Frank Robinson. He carried the Birds to the Series in 1969, 1970 and 1971. He batted clean-up, ran the bases and played right field. He was also the judge in their clubhouse kangaroo court, putting a mop on his head and handing out small fines when players didn't hustle or made mental errors. But if you need additional reasons for the reputation of Frank Robinson being slightly overlooked, look no further than Brooks' success and popularity. The MVP third-sacker was a legend in Baltimore.

After Frank Robinson's 1966 season, he had problems with nagging injuries. In 1967 he followed up his Triple Crown campaign with 30 homers and 94 RBI, despite missing 33 games. A collision at second base resulted in a concussion and blurred vision. He missed a month. He had the same vision problem the following year, and also suffered from the mumps and a sore arm. In 1969 he stayed healthy, but missed 30 games in 1970 because of a shoulder injury after he ran into a wall.

Most of the playing thrills were over for Robinson after 1971. After the 1971 season, a year in which Robinson hit 28 homers – including his 500th – and knocked in 99 runs, the Orioles inexplicably traded him to the Dodgers. In 1972 Robinson played in only 103 games due to another early season injury.

Then the Dodgers traded him to California for the 1973 season, where he hit 30 homers for the 11th time in his career. He was awarded to Cleveland on waivers the following year and Cleveland made him a player-manager in 1975, the first black manager. How did Robinson feel about it? Proud, to be sure. "It's nice to come into town and be referred to as the manager of the Cleveland Indians," he said in 1975, "instead of the first black manager." He played his 21st and last year for Cleveland in 1976. He later managed the Giants and the Orioles. His best years as a manager were the '87 and '75 seasons, one with the Giants in 1982, the other with the Orioles in 1989. But his overall record was just 680-751 for a percentage of .475. Much of that was due to Cleveland's mediocrity, however. "In Cleveland, pennant fever usually winds up being just a 48-hour virus," Robinson cracked. Robinson held, as he was entitled to, some strong views about the changes in the game from the 1950s to the 1970s. With Baltimore as a minor league manager in 1978 he said about free agency, "The fan is the one who suffers. He cheers a guy to a .350 season, then watches the player sign with another team. When you destroy fan loyalties, then you destroy everything." The tide was changing, and not changing for the best. "Players no longer have to be dedicated," he said, "because performance doesn't always dictate what the salary will be. If a player doesn't have to have a super year to collect a big salary, the motivating factor is missing."

Robinson finished with 2,943 hits and 586 homers. It's not too hard to conceive of him staying around to get both the 3,000th hit and his 600th homer. "People ask me why I didn't stay around to hit 14 more home runs for 600, or 43 more hits for 3,000 and my patent answer is `well, no one wanted to pay me.' But numbers at that time weren't that big of a deal. I played 21 years and if I didn't get those hits or home runs in 21 years, then I was not going to hang around two or three more years just to acquire numbers."

Even without reaching those plateaus, Frank Robinson is one of the most complete players in baseball history. Frank Robinson is the eighth best outfielder – behind only Ruth, Mays, Aaron, Cobb, Musial, DiMaggio and Mantle – and the 14th greatest player of all-time.

Best 5-year Average
1958-1962

R	H	D	T	HR	RBI	AVG	OBP	SLG
107	168	34	5	35	110	.309	.377	.583

Best 10-year Average
1956-1965

R	H	D	T	HR	RBI	AVG	OBP	SLG
104	167	32	5	33	101	.303	.383	.557

Best 15-year Average
1956-1970

R	H	D	T	HR	RBI	AVG	OBP	SLG
101	162	30	4	32	97	.303	.386	.555

Lifetime Totals

G	2,808	RBI	1,812
AB	10,006	BB	1,420
R	1,829	K	1,532
H	2,943	AVG	.294
D	528	OBP	.392
T	72	SLG	.537
HR	586	SB	204
HR %	5.9	CS	77

15
PETE ROSE
Third Base/Second Base/Outfield

"Charlie Hustle"
Born: 4/14/41 Cincinnati, OH
5 feet 11 inches, 200 pounds
Debut: 4/8/63, Played 24 years: 1963-1986
1963-1978, Cincinnati; 1979-1983, Philadelphia;
1984, Montreal; 1984-1986, Cincinnati

It was the spring of 1963 and Pete Rose, who hadn't played a Major League game, was looking to land a job as the Reds' regular second baseman. After watching Rose draw a walk and then sprint to first, Whitey Ford dubbed him "Charlie Hustle." The name stuck and it's no wonder it did. A truer name was never given to any athlete, anywhere. Ten times he played 160 or more games, 15 times 155 or more. No player ever showed up more ready to play, more often, than Pete Rose, the most competitive player I ever saw. Rose played harder than any player of his time, and his time just happened to be 24 years, 1963 through 1986. Pete Rose closes out the first hallowed group, the elite 15 players of all-time.

With all-out desire, with skill surpassed only by will, Pete Rose retired as the all-time leader in three categories: games, 3,562; at bats, 14,053; and hits, 4,256. He was second in doubles with 746, fourth in runs with 2,165 and 11th in walks with 1,566. Sure, Rose liked his statistics and was driven to attain certain statistical markers. But the statistical legacy, awesome though it is, does not tell the whole story.

Those who saw him know that he was driven by excellence and a steady burning desire to come out on top. "Somebody's got to win and somebody's got to lose," Rose once said, "and I believe in letting the other guy lose." He needed to play. "I hate days off 'cause I might get hit by a train," Rose said.

Sure he knew that he was being watched. Hustling to first, spiking the ball into the carpet after a putout at first, sliding head first when he didn't need to, Rose played to the cameras. "I think it's harder to slide head first," he said. "I'd rather have an arm spiked than an ankle – plus you get your picture in the paper!"

You certainly think hustle when you think Rose, but you also think numbers. If you like numbers, go get some chips and kick back in your favorite chair while you peruse these. Like clockwork, every Rose season was a plus: 600-plus at bats, 100-plus runs, a .300-plus average and, often as not, 200-plus hits. We know that Rose is the all-time hit leader with 4,256. He hit .300 or better 15 times in a 17-year stretch between 1965 and 1981. Between his rookie season in 1963 and his last strong year in 1981, when he hit .325 with the Phillies in the strike-shortened season, Rose faced the best arms in baseball history.

The National League was led by Tom Seaver, Juan Marichal, Sandy Koufax, Bob Gibson, Steve Carlton, Ferguson Jenkins, Gaylord Perry, Don Sutton and Phil Neikro. The league ERA in the 1960s – and continuing into the seventies – was the lowest of any decade since the 1910s. Despite the strong-armed excellence of the era, Rose got 200 or more hits 10 times.

Another name for Charlie Hustle might have been "Mr. Consistency." Take a look at what Rose did from 1965 through 1979. In that 15-year span, he averaged 204 hits per season! He is the only other person in the history of the game to do that. Ty Cobb, whose hit total Rose surpassed, averaged 194 hits per year for a 15-year period from 1908 through 1922. Stan Musial was closer, averaging 197 hits for the 15 years from 1943-1958 (he missed 1945).

Besides the 204 hits, Rose's 15-year output included averages of 73 walks, 105 runs and a .316 average. He also hit .300 or better 14 times during that period.

In all, Mr. Consistency led the league in runs four times, hits, seven times; doubles, five times; batting, three times and in on-base percentage once. Not many singles' hitters in the history of the game deserve to be mentioned in Rose's company. Cobb, Speaker, Lajoie, Boggs, Gwynn,

Carew – who else was as consistently pesky an offensive player as Rose?

Rose also played on pennant winners six times and Series winners three times. In seven league championship series he hit .357 or better six times!

In 1981, Rose won his last batting title, hitting .325 at the age of 40. "The only way I won't hit .300," he once bragged, "is if something is physically wrong with me." Or if I get too old, he might have added. When you are the all-time leader in games, at-bats and hits, you've earned the right to brag a little. Aside from that, he is one of the greatest winners ever to play. You can only amass great totals in baseball if you are ready to go to work every day.

Go ahead, make him the butt of jokes about his gambling and his appearances on home shopping channels selling autographed items. Then take the players you root for and see if they will even come close to achieving what Rose did. More than likely they won't. Despite the evidence of Rose's gambling that surfaced later, after his career, he was driven by excellence as a player. His legacy as a player is that of an all-out, consistent, hustling player. Rose the player was driven by winning, not by money.

The Hall of Fame is poorer without him and it is ludicrous that he is not there. He should be put back on the eligible list and voted in.

Best 5-year Average
1966-1970

R	H	D	T	HR	RBI	AVG	OBP	SLG
103	203	36	8	14	66	.303	.377	.472

Best 10-year Average
1966-75

105	203	37	7	10	62	.316	.385	.444

Best 15-year Average
1965-1979

105	204	38	7	8	62	.316	.385	.433

All-time totals

G	3,562	RBI	1,314
AB	14,053	BB	1,566
R	2,165	K	1,143
H	4,256	AVG	.303
D	746	OBP	.377
T	135	SLG	.409
HR	160	SB	198
HR%	1.1	CS	149

16
BARRY BONDS
Left Field

Born: 7/24/64 Riverside, CA
6 feet 1 inch, 185 pounds
Debut: 5/30/86, Played 12 years: 1986-1997
1986-1992, Pittsburgh; 1993-1997, San Francisco

How good is Barry Bonds? If he averages just 25 to 35 homers a year for the next five years, he will finish between 500 and 550 homers. If he averages just 20 stolen bases a year over the same time, he will have 500. So, while people talk about 400 homers and 400 stolen bases for Bonds, 500 and 500 are definitely within reach. Most likely he will also reach 1,700 runs, 1,500 RBI, 500 doubles and 2,500 hits.

Bonds is a three-time MVP and has hit 40 or more homers three times. He and Griffey, Jr., are typically compared as the two best in the game. The difference between them has been stolen bases and on-base percentage, both of which favor Bonds. At this point it must be said that Bonds is better, because he has been playing well for a longer time. But this might change.

Griffey, Jr., is five years and four months younger than Bonds and should surpass Bonds' totals in time. Bonds cannot help that. He can help his own totals.

Seven times he has posted 100-plus runs batted in and six times scored 100 runs. Bonds is a gifted player, a great fielder, hitter and runner. In 1997 he carried the Giants to a Division Title with homer after clutch homer down the stretch. Then San Francisco was swept by Florida.

Post season play has never been his strong suit. Last year he hit .250 making his lifetime playoff average .200 (16 for 80).

For most of his five years in San Francisco, the Giants have been the "pitch-less wonders." In the current lineup Bonds doesn't have any protection and so he's willing to take the walks. He got 145 walks last year, the fifth time in six years he has led the NL in that category. His on-base percentage was a staggering .446; he has led the league in that category four times. Bonds is also a three-time slugging champion, winning that title the same years he won MVPs (1990, 1992, 1993).

It will be exciting to watch Bonds over the next five years, to see just how long he can sustain 35-45 homers per year, to go with the 100 to 125 RBI and the high slugging averages. He has also won four Gold Glove Awards.

It is difficult to project what a player will do. But Bonds has played 12 years and given us a large enough sample from which to draw predictions. The process of making the predictions is called inductive inference and even a conservative prediction will give Bonds the totals I suggested above.

Best 5-year Average
1993-1997

R	H	D	T	HR	RBI	AVG	OBP	SLG
114	153	28	4	40	108	.308	.446	.619

Best 10-year Average
1988-1997

| 107 | 151 | 30 | 4 | 33 | 99 | .297 | .422 | .566 |

12-year Average

| 104 | 146 | 30 | 5 | 31 | 91 | .288 | .408 | .551 |

Lifetime totals

G	1,742	RBI	1,094
AB	6,069	BB	1,227
R	1,244	K	871
H	1,750	AVG	.288
D	359	OBP	.408
T	56	SLG	.551
HR	374	SB	417
HR%	6.2	CS	118

17
ERNIE BANKS
Shortstop

Born: 1/11/31 Dallas, TX
6 feet 1 inch, 180 pounds
Debut: 9/17/53, Played 19 years: 1953-1971, Chicago (NL)

Above all, Ernie Banks will be remembered for three things. One was his temperament; his sunny disposition was summed up in his phrase, "Let's play two." Banks' second distinction is his home run total at shortstop. He finished with 512 homers and is easily first in home runs per season (33) for the nine years he played short. Third, his entire 19 year career was played with one team, the Chicago Cubs. Between 1953 and 1971 the Cubs didn't win a pennant, not even a division title. But as Cleveland manager Jimmy Dykes once said, "Without Ernie Banks, the Cubs would finish in Albuquerque."

Banks won back-to-back MVPs with the "Cubbies" – the National League equivalent of the Boston Red Sox, loved for their perennial ineptitude. The only time one of his teams got so much as a sniff of the post-season, they blew an eight-game lead over the Mets in 1969. The bittersweet moments of playing on losing Cubs' teams still cannot erase the accomplishments of Ernest Banks. He had a slight uppercut in his fluid, long-armed swing, enabling him to power 512 homers, tying him with Eddie Mathews for 12th place on the all-time list, with one more than "Master Melvin" Ott.

Like Ott, Banks benefited greatly from hitting homers in a friendly home park. He hit 290 – or 57 percent – of his 512 homers at Wrigley Field. But closer inspection shows that too much cannot be made of this. What Banks achieved between 1955 and 1960 should not be downplayed. In that six-year period he hit 44, 28, 43, 47, 45 and 41 homers. No short-stop has ever come close to hitting 40 in five of six years. His best year was clearly 1958, when he hit 47 homers, knocked in 129, batted .313 and slugged .614.

In those six years, he won the MVP twice and finished third, fourth and sixth in the voting three other times. For fans of the Cubs – who usually weren't close to coming in first, anyway – what more was there to do than follow Banks' stats and see how he'd come out in the MVP voting? He was clearly the best shortstop of his time and second only to Honus Wagner all-time.

Following that run of 40-homer reasons, Banks hit 29 in 1961 and 37 in 1962. He was 31 years old and had already hit 335 homers. Further, he had knocked in 100 runs and hit 30 homers six times. But he had a colli-sion in 1961 that resulted in a vision problem. That, plus knee injuries, led him to shift to first base in 1962. Over the next nine years, however, he would hit 30 homers only once, in 1968. His strike-out-to-walk ratio hovered between 2-to-1 and 3-to-1. From 1960 through 1971, .353 was his highest on-base percentage, with his mean OBP at .313. That's an on-base percentage you expect from a weak hitting second baseman.

The best evidence for his rapid decline was his slugging average. It had been as high as .614 and usually was between .500 and .590. After 1962, it was usually around .450 and peaked at .469! He had hit 40 homers five times at shortstop but not once at first base.

The only time he came close to winning with Durocher's hapless Cubs was that summer of 1969, when the Cubs pulled a memorable el-foldo. The *quid pro quo* to Dykes' comment about Albuquerque? With Banks, they didn't finish much higher than Albuquerque.

In 1970, Ernie Banks hit his 500th homer, becoming only the ninth member of the 500-homer club. Six others would follow him into the hallowed club. Reaching that plateau ensured his entry into the Hall of Fame and he was elected in 1977.

Best 5-year Average
1955-1959

R	H	D	T	HR	RBI	AVG	OBP	SLG
102	175	27	8	41	115	.299	.361	.585

Best 10-year Average

87	160	26	6	36	104	.282	.341	.538

Best 15-year Average

81	157	25	6	32	98	.277	.331	.508

All-time Totals

G	2,528	RBI	1,636
AB	9,421	BB	763
R	1,305	K	1,236
H	2,583	AVG	.274
D	407	OBP	.333
T	90	SLG	.500
HR	512	SB	50
HR %	5.4	CS	53

18
EDDIE MATHEWS
Third Base

Born: 10/13/31 Texarkana, TX
6 feet 1 inch, 200 pounds
Debut: 4/15/52, Played 17 years: 1952-1968
1952, Boston (NL); 1953-1965, Milwaukee; 1966, Atlanta; 1967,
Houston; 1967-1968, Detroit

Current NBC broadcaster and former light hitting catcher, Bob Uecker had a career year for Milwaukee Braves in 1963, posting an awesome .250 average on four hits in 16 at bats. Before the Braves shipped the lifetime .200 hitter to St. Louis, he said "Between me and my roommate, we've hit 400 major league home runs." His roommate was Eddie Mathews, who then had 399 of those 400.

Only the sixth player ever to hit 500 homers, Eddie Mathews was just 20 when he became a starting third baseman with the Boston Braves in 1952 and was still suiting up for that position when the team moved to Milwaukee in 1953 and Atlanta in 1966. He had a chance to sign with Brooklyn for $10,000 but took Boston's $6,000 offer instead, reasoning that he would get to the major leagues faster with Boston than with Brooklyn, who had a powerhouse team in the early 1950s. Until Mike Schmidt came along in the 1970s, Mathews was the greatest slugger ever to play the hot corner.

Steady Eddie also helped the Braves to a World Championship in 1957 and a pennant in 1958. His two-run homer in the 10th inning won game four of the 1957 Series. The blow turned the Series around: had the Braves lost, they would have been down three games to one. With the bases loaded in game seven, he stabbed a hot grounder with two out in the ninth and tagged third for the force that ended the Series.

But Mathews' career shows that he was a strong hitter for about 15 years. Like Mays, Mantle and Banks, Mathews was born in 1951. Like them, he would also reach 500 homers. Between 1953 and 1955 he slugged .627, .603 and .601. His best year was 1953, when he belted 47 home runs, knocked in 135 runs, hit .302 and slugged .627. Beyond that, he hit 30-plus homers for nine straight years, from 1953 through 1961. The following chart shows those with 30 or more homers the most consecutive seasons:

PLAYERS WITH MOST CONSECUTIVE 30-HOMER SEASONS

Foxx	12	Aaron	7
Gehrig	9	Kiner	7
Mathews	9	Barry Bonds	6
Schmidt	9	McCovey	6
Mantle	8	Mays	6
Ruth	8	Killebrew	6

Hitting 30 or more in consecutive seasons is not the only measure of a great home run hitter. But it shows just how consistent Mathews was.

Mathews' career is also a lesson for those laboring under the mistaken assumption that sluggers are free to strikeout as often as they want. He led the league in walks four times but never in strikeouts. The result was that he had an on-base average of 400-plus six times. Teammate Frank Torre remarked how Mathews put in extra practice to make himself a better third baseman.

He also put up 95-plus runs for 10 straight seasons from 1953 through 1962. Eight times he scored 100 or more runs. Hank Aaron and Mathews formed one of the greatest one-two punches ever, hitting 863 homers as teammates. He slugged .500 or better eight times and hit 40 or more homers four times. But after the age of 30, he never slugged .500 again. Over his last seven seasons, from 1962 through 1968, his mean slugging average was .426.

He started the 1967 season with Houston, hit his 500th homer with them and was traded to Detroit later that year, retiring in 1968 before their World Championship.

He was inducted into the Hall of Fame in 1978, 10 years after his retirement. This begets the obvious question: what took the writers so long?

What does it take to figure out that if a player is just the sixth player to reach 500 homers – and the first ever at his position! – his inclusion in the Hall of Fame must be automatic and immediate? He averaged 33 homers and averaged 95 RBI per year for 15 years – from 1952 through 1966. What were these voters looking at?

He was not as good as Brooks Robinson on defense, but he was a good third baseman. Mathews should have joined Mickey Mantle and Whitey Ford in Cooperstown in 1974. Sam Thompson, Cool Papa Bell and Sunny Jim Bottomley were selected that year – but what in blazes happened to Eddie Mathews? Did his stats get lost in the mail before they arrived at the writers' homes?

Best 5-year Average
1953-1957

R	H	D	T	HR	RBI	AVG	OBP	SLG
105	155	25	5	39	106	.289	.403	.575

Best 10-year Average
1953-1962

| 106 | 156 | 23 | 5 | 37 | 102 | .285 | .394 | .551 |

Best 15-year Average
1952-1966

| 97 | 150 | 23 | 5 | 33 | 95 | .279 | .385 | .522 |

Lifetime Totals

G	2,391
AB	8,537
R	1,509
H	2,315
D	354
T	72
HR	512
HR %	6.0
RBI	1,453
BB	1,444
K	1,487
AVG	.270
OBP	.378
SLG	.509
SB	68

19
HARMON KILLEBREW
Third Base/First Base

"The Killer"
Born: 6/29/36 Payette, ID
5 feet 11 inches, 213 pounds
Debut: 6/23/54, Played 22 years: 1954-1975
1954-1960, Washington; 1961-1974, Minnesota; 1975, Kansas City

And the public address announcer intones: "Playing first base for the all-forgotten team, number 3, Harmon Killebrew." I can hear the announcement now. Forget Rodney Dangerfield. These days Harmon Killebrew gets half the respect Dangerfield gets. "The Killer" was an awesome power hitter who hit a home run every 14.22 at bats, more frequently than anyone in baseball history with the exception of Babe Ruth, Mark McGwire and Ralph Kiner.

The only one of those players who clubbed more than Killebrew was Babe Ruth. Killebrew, on whose back and shoulders you could land small aircraft, hit 573 homers, good enough for fifth place all-time. He was the all-time home run leader for right handed American League batters. People can talk about his size and lack of speed. Killebrew once replied, "there is no correlation between hitting homers and running the mile." In short, 'leave me alone – I hit 'em over the wall and save myself the trouble of running.' In a decade of great power hitters, Killebrew led the

1960s with 393 home runs. He capped off that decade with 49 homers and his only MVP award.

During the 15-year period from 1959 through 1973, Killebrew averaged 36 home runs and 97 RBI.

Born on June 29, 1936, in Payette, Idaho, Killebrew kicked around with Washington from 1954 through 1958 before they decided to give him serious playing time in 1959. After being given the third base job, Killebrew had five two-homer games in 17 days! He belted 42 and tied Rocky Colavito for the league lead. That year he had played only 4 of his 153 games away from third. But the following season he spent most of his time at first base and belted 31 homers. In 1961 the team moved to Minnesota, a change that suited Killebrew just fine.

Playing first base for one year and outfield the following three, Killebrew hit – no misprint – 46, 48, 45 and 49 homers over the next four seasons – an amazing 188 in four seasons – winning the homer title from 1962 through 1964. Then he "cooled" to 25 and 39, before hitting 44 in 1967 to take his fifth homer title and 49 in 1969 to take his sixth. At that point Killer had posted a .500 slugging average 10 times in the last 11 years, including a .606 mark in 1961 and .584 in 1969.

The nickname "Killer" hardly suited this gentle giant. He was reluctant to give offense to other players, so much so that he didn't want writers to mention that he didn't smoke or drink, lest he offend his friends who did. He hit 41 homers for the eighth time in 1970 – a feat matched only by Hank Aaron in his era. He should also have joined the 10-time 100 RBI club, but when he belted 45 in 1963, he got only 96. So he finished with 100 or more RBI nine times.

He hit 28 homers in 1971, including his 500th. He also led the league in RBI for the fourth time and walks for the fourth time. Pitchers apparently gave up pitching to him: seven times he drew more than 100 walks; he finished his career with 1,559 walks. Four times his on-base percentage was above .400

The achievements of guys like Killebrew are downplayed. He quietly went about his business, didn't grab the spotlight with outrageous statements and only once made a World Series. That was 1965, when the Twins, a well-rounded club, won 102 games. Killebrew collided at first with Russ Snyder on August 2 and dislocated his elbow. He missed 49 games but still managed 25 homers.

In his lone series Mudcat Grant bested Don Drysdale in Game One and Jim Kaat bested Sandy Koufax in Game Two to take a 2-0 lead. Over the next three games, however, the Twins scored only two runs, shutout by Claude Osteen and Koufax. Grant won Game Six. Koufax and Kaat, both pitching on two days rest, pitched brilliantly in Game Seven but

Koufax pitched a three-hit shutout in a 2-0 Dodger win. Killebrew hit .286 but the team hit only .195, suffering three shutouts in their four losses.

No parades followed when Killebrew retired 10 years later. A sign of the disrespect was that he wasn't voted into the Hall of Fame in his first year of eligibility, but had to wait until 1984. Who was voting and what were they looking at? Fifth all-time in home runs and a bunch of writers decide that he has to cool his heels in the lobby?

People who love the game should not treat as gospel the verdicts of Hall of Fame voters. When they are required to explain their views and put forth arguments based on evidence and reason, then it will be time to take them seriously. The facts – which are available to anyone's inspection – prove that Killebrew was an awesome home run hitter.

Best 5-year Average
1960-1964

R	H	D	T	HR	RBI	AVG	OBP	SLG
89	140	18	2	44	107	.267	.374	.558

Best 10-year Average
1961-1970

R	H	D	T	HR	RBI	AVG	OBP	SLG
88	135	18	2	40	105	.266	.388	.547

Best 15-year Average
1959-1973

R	H	D	T	HR	RBI	AVG	OBP	SLG
80	120	18	2	36	97	.261	.383	.526

Lifetime totals

G	2,435	RBI	1,584
AB	8,147	BB	1,559
R	1,283	K	1,699
H	2,086	AVG	.256
D	290	OBP	.379
T	24	SLG	.509
HR	573	SB	19
HR%	7.0	CS	18

20
NAPOLEON LAJOIE
Second Base

"Larry"
Born: 9/5/1874 Woonsocket, RI, Died: 2/7/59 Daytona Beach, FL
6 feet 1 inch, 195 pounds
Debut: 8/12/1896, Played 21 years: 1896-1916
1896-1900, Philadelphia (NL); 1901-1902, Philadelphia (AL);
1902-1913, Cleveland; 1915-1916, Philadelphia (AL)

Tommy Leach was a third baseman who played 19 years with three different clubs from 1898 through 1918. Of Napoleon Lajoie he said, "What a
ballplayer that man was. Every play he executed so gracefully that it looked
like the easiest thing in the world." In the Baseball Hall of Fame only one
tablet bears the words "most graceful." It is the inscription for Napoleon
Lajoie. He was known as "Nap," and was an outfielder early on who finished his career as a first baseman. But, in between, he was a second baseman and he will be remembered for his excellence at that position.

He started with the Phillies, for whom he played from 1896 through
1900. But by 1900, his fifth year, he was earning only $2,400, the National
League minimum. When Connie Mack, then in his first year as the A's
manager, offered Nap $4,000, he jumped to the new American League. In
1901, he had a season which can only be described as all-universe.

He led the league in runs with 145 and hits with 232. He led in the power categories, too – 48 doubles, 14 homers and 125 RBIs. He hit .426, still an American League record. His on-base percentage was .463 and his slugging average a hearty .643. He stole 27 bases and led the circuit in putouts (395) and fielding at second base (.960). In addition to leading the league in 10 categories and – winning the Triple Crown – he led the A's to a pennant. The Phillies sued Mack, and eventually the Pennsylvania Supreme Court enjoined Lajoie from playing with the Athletics. American League President Ban Johnson ordered that Lajoie be transferred to Cleveland, outside of Pennsylvania's jurisdiction where he could still play in the American League.

So Lajoie began a 13-year stint in Cleveland in 1902. It is beyond dispute that his consistency at the plate and in the field established him as the best American League player until Cobb got going in 1907.

Lajoie led the league in hits, slugging and batting four times each. While Lajoie would never post another season like his 1901 campaign, he won consecutive batting titles in 1902 (.378), 1903 (.344) and 1904 (.376) and nearly stole one from the Georgia Peach in 1910.

When he got six bunt hits against the St. Louis Browns on the last day of the 1910 season, it seemed he had the title in the bag. Like the rest of the league, St. Louis manager Jack O'Connor detested Cobb and so ordered his third baseman to play on the outfield grass, and all day Lajoie bunted to the left side. Eight players sent Lajoie a congratulatory telegram on winning the batting title – the eight were all Cobb's teammates. A sportswriter Hugh Fullerton retaliated on Cobb's behalf, changing his ruling on a ball Cobb hit that he'd ruled an error earlier in the year, helping to give Cobb a .385 average and the batting title. Seven decades later the controversy got going again. It was discovered that an error had been made in Cobb's favor: a game in which he went two-for-three had been entered twice. So Lajoie had really deserved the batting title after all, .384 to .383.

Both the *Baseball Encyclopedia* and *Total Baseball* still give credit to Cobb. Lajoie never won his fifth batting title.

But the slick infielder called "The American League Wagner" had plenty of other distinctions. By the time of his retirement in 1916 – Connie Mack got him back for his last two seasons – Lajoie had surpassed 3,000 hits, finishing with 3,242. Five double titles had helped him to a total of 652. His lifetime average was .338 and his slugging average was .467, plenty healthy for a second baseman.

It is clear that Hornsby is a greater second sacker than Lajoie. It's not clear that anyone else is.

Best 5-Year Average
1900-1904

R	H	D	T	HR	RBI	AVG	OBP	SLG
101	178	41	11	8	95	.374	.400	.558

Best 10-Year Average
1897-1906

| 90 | 170 | 37 | 11 | 6 | 93 | .362 | .388 | .498 |

Best 15-Year Average
1897-1911

| 81 | 168 | 36 | 9 | 5 | 84 | .351 | .385 | .495 |

Lifetime totals

G	2,480		RBI	1,599
AB	9,589		BB	516
R	1,504		AVG	.338
H	3,242		OBP	.380
D	657		SLG	.467
T	163		SB	380
HR	83			
HR %	0.8			

21
CHARLIE GEHRINGER
Second Base

"The Mechanical Man"
Born: 5/11/03 Fowlerville, MI, Died: Bloomfield Hills, MI
5 feet 11 inches, 180 pounds
Debut: 9/22/24, Played 19 years: 1924-1942, Detroit

He was called "the Mechanical Man." His manager Mickey Cochrane once remarked, "He says 'hello' on opening day and 'good-bye' on closing day and in between hits .350." Would that every manager had nine just like him! Gehringer had an astounding total of seven 200-hit seasons in nine years – from 1929 through 1937. The record confirms one Hall of Famer's recollection of him: "Charlie Gehringer is always in a rut," said Lefty Gomez. "He hits .350 on opening day and stays there all season."

Gehringer the second baseman, appears alphabetically just after Lou Gehrig, the first baseman in *Total Baseball*. Gehringer could not be compared to Gehrig, but how many ballplayers could? He was, however, elected to the Hall of Fame in 1949, after 19 years with the Detroit Tigers, from 1924 through 1942.

Charles Leonard Gehringer was born on a farm in Fowlerville, Michigan, on May 3, 1903. He liked baseball so much as a kid that he and his brother carved out a diamond on the farm so that he could play every day. He played a year at the University of Michigan, distinguishing himself in both baseball and football, but left after his freshman year to play professional baseball, in the Michigan-Ontario League.

His first appearance with the Tigers was auspicious. He was given a try-out by Detroit player-manager Ty Cobb in 1924 and, in the last five games of the season, collected 6 hits in 13 at bats. After a full season with Toronto of the International League, he was called back for the final eight games of the 1925 season. Detroit was his home until he joined the Navy in 1942. He never made more than $35,000 a year playing baseball.

During his 19-year tenure, Gehringer was simply the best fielding second baseman in the American League and a tremendous hitter. In the 14 years between 1927 and 1940 Gehringer hit .300 or better 13 times. His percentage hitting was thus reminiscent of second baseman like Napoleon Lajoie, Eddie Collins and Rogers Hornsby. The comparisons were earned.

He scored 100 or more runs no less than 11 times, leading the league in 1929 (131) and 1934 (134). In two other years he scored 144 runs and in two more he scampered home 133 times! That says nothing of the man's power numbers.

How many second baseman get 100 runs batted in seven times? In seven different full seasons he slugged over .500 and he finished with a .480 slugging average. So while Gehringer was taciturn enough to be called "Sphinx-like" in his personality, always immersed in reading and crossword puzzles in his free time, there was nothing dull about his play.

His fielding was called poetry in motion – and why not? He led the league in fielding percentage seven times and led the league in assists seven times. That alone commanded great respect. But then the hitting. During the 1930s he hit .331, the seventh best average of anyone in that decade. He also totaled 1,003 RBI in the thirties. No other middle-infielder was nearly that high on the list. No wonder Gomez lamented: "Gehringer could hit me in a tunnel at midnight with the lights out."

If anyone doubted what Gehringer could do, the Mechanical Man made believers of them in 1937. All he did that year was score 133 runs, get 209 hits, hit .371, record an on-base percentage of .458 and slug .520 (his fourth straight season above .500) and lead the league in fielding. He was awarded the MVP.

When this marvelously complete player finished his career after just 45 games in 1942 (he had hit .220 in a full season the previous year), he had totals that would make first basemen and outfielders proud. Not only had he hit .320, but he had hit .321 in three World Series, including a .375 mark in the 1935 classic, when the Tigers rebounded from a 1934 Series loss to the Cardinals with a six-game defeat of the Cubs.

Gehringer played in the first All-Star Game in 1933 and five more after that. Upon retiring he said, "Us ballplayers do things backwards. First we play, then we retire and go to work."

Following his retirement and four years as a Navy fitness instructor, Gehringer became wealthy through an auto-accessories business. He then returned to the Tigers in 1951 for a two-year stint as a general manager. He later served as a Tigers vice president.

He died in Bloomfield Hills, Michigan in 1991. He was 89 years old. The legacy is intact. When someone asked Lefty Gomez to defend his opinion that Gehringer was the greatest second baseman in the game, the pitcher remarked: "All if know is that whenever I'm pitching, he's on base."

Best 5-year Average
1934-1938

R	H	D	T	HR	RBI	AVG	OBP	SLG
133	205	43	7	16	111	.346	.434	.520

Best 10-year Average
1929-1938

122	195	42	8	14	102	.334	.411	.506

Best 15-year Average
1926-1940

113	181	37	9	12	92	.317	.404	.490

Lifetime totals

G	2,323	RBI	1,427
AB	8,860	BB	1,186
R	1,774	K	372
H	2,834	AVG	.320
D	574	OBP	.404
T	146	SLG	.480
HR	184	SB	181
HR %	2.1	CS	89

22
GEORGE BRETT
Third Base

Born: 5/15/53 Glen Dale, WV
6 feet, 200 pounds
Debut: 8/2/73, Played 21 years: 1973-1993, Kansas City

Since attention spans are about as long as political sound bites in the
nineties, people may have already forgotten about George Brett, whose
career ended just a short while ago. Too bad, because George Brett was one
of the greatest third basemen ever to play the game. He was a singular hitter – hitting for average, power and getting few strike outs. Said Kansas
City manager Jim Frey, "George Brett could get good wood on an aspirin
tablet."

While he must be ranked behind Mike Schmidt, he is very close to
Eddie Mathews as the third greatest ever to play the position. I think that
Brett should be ranked behind Mathews, because Mathews averaged 33
homers and 95 RBI while slugging .522 in a 15-year run. Brett's best 15-
year run average, from 1976 through 1990, was 19 homers, 84 RBI and a
.522 slugging average. Over his career Mathews is clearly the greater
slugger, hitting 512 homers and slugging .509. Brett hit 317 homers and
slugged .487.

Brett makes up a portion of that gap with his .305 average and his
longevity. Brett got his 3,000th hit in 1992, finishing with 3,154. His

average of .305 was helped along by three batting titles, won 14 years apart in 1977 (.333), 1980 (.390) and 1990 (.329). Brett averaged only 45 strikeouts a season.

Brett was also a winner, a fixture of the division and pennant winning Kansas City teams of the 1970s and 1980s. In their sixth try in the post season they finally broke through in 1985, beating the Cardinals in a controversial seven-game World Series. Brett's post-season exploits were outstanding: in 163 at-bats he hit .344, slugged .638, hit 10 homers and knocked in 23 runs. Brett was one of the greatest clutch hitters of his time.

A unique combination of abilities at the plate, Brett's real hitting talent was in spraying the ball, hitting it where it was pitched. While he could hit singles with the best of them – like Rose and Carew – Brett had something more. Brett had tremendous power, hitting in the gaps and typically getting 60 to 70 extra base hits in a season. In this respect Brett's style was a combination of the power hitting third basemen like Schmidt and Mathews and the percentage hitting third sackers like Rose and Boggs.

A mention of Brett's name usually leads to a discussion of Charlie Lau, the batting coach of the Royals who emphasized hitting "through the ball." "I just helped him concentrate more on seeing the ball and hitting it where it was pitched," says Lau. "He always had all the ability in the world." A fellow member of the 3,000-hit club, Carew could appreciate Brett's batting technique. "There is too much emphasis in the game on hitting home runs," Carew once explained. "George just hits the ball where it is pitched. This might influence others to do the same."

Brett's banner year was the 1980 season, when he hit .390 and had a chance to be the first player in 39 years to hit .400. He was hitting .400 until the final weeks of the season but fell short. To hit .400 he need only have turned five of his 274 outs into hits.

Brett becomes eligible for the Hall of Fame in 1999. Like most other players who have 3,000 hits, he should be a cinch to make it.

Best 5-Year Average
1979-1983

R	H	D	T	HR	RBI	AVG	OBP	SLG
87	161	34	9	20	89	.328	.393	.557

Best 10-Year Average
1977-1986

84	155	34	8	19	85	.317	.389	.534

Best 15-Year Average
1976-1990

83	159	33	7	19	84	.315	.387	.522

Lifetime Totals

G	2,707	RBI	1,595
AB	10,349	BB	1,096
R	1,583	K	908
H	3,154	AVG	.305
D	665	OBP	.373
T	137	SLG	.487
HR	317	SB	201
HR %	3.1	CS	97

23
REGGIE JACKSON
Right Field

"Mr. October"
Born: 5/18/46 Wyncote, PA
6 feet, 195 pounds
Debut: 6/9/67, Played 21 years: 1967-1987
1967, Kansas City; 1968-1975, Oakland; 1976, Baltimore; 1977-
1981, New York (AL); 19892-1986, California (AL); 1987 Oakland

Reggie Jackson is a hot button player. Mention his name – or the nickname "Mr. October" and you will evoke no in-between opinions. Said A's
reliever Darold Knowles, "There isn't enough mustard in the world to
cover that hot dog." He is first in career strikeouts with 2,597. Yet even
his strike outs were button-popping, intimidating feats. He hit 563
homers. He was "Mr. October," owner of a .755 slugging average in fall
classics, the highest in World Series history. Even for his detractors, and
they are many, there is no denying he was one of the greatest big-game
performers baseball has ever seen. "Taters, that's where the money is,"
said Jackson.

    For him, taters were also where the winning was. Winning followed
Jackson like a "just married" sign follows a bumper. Jackson's teams
played in 11 division series, winning six pennants and five World Series.

    Four times he led the league in homers, twice hitting more than 40.

His best year was 1969 when he burst on the American League scene with 47 homers and was two weeks ahead of Maris' pace with 40 in July. He then hit only seven for the rest of the season and finished behind Harmon Killebrew, who clouted 49. Jackson also posted 118 RBIs, a .275 average and a .608 slugging mark that season. He walked 114 times and recorded a personal best .410 on-base percentage.

Over a 15-year period from 1968-1982 he averaged 31 homers and 92 RBI. Jackson also mixed speed with his power, four times stealing more than 20 bases and finishing with 228 steals. His last five years with California and Oakland were decline years, otherwise his slugging average would have stayed above .500.

Despite his statistical legacy, many remember Jackson best for his frequent appearances in the post-season. He missed the World Series in 1972 after suffering a leg injury while sliding home safely in a 1-0 victory over Billy Martin's Tigers in the American League Championship Series. With Jackson out, no one expected the A's to beat Cincinnati. But Gene Tenace mashed four homers and knocked in nine runs and great defense and clutch pitching helped the A's win in seven games.

In 1973 Jackson was league MVP and World Series MVP, hitting a homer in game seven of the Series off the Mets' Jon Matlack. In game six he knocked in two runs off Tom Seaver to pace Oakland's 3-1 win.

In the 1974 Series, Oakland didn't have a hitting star and didn't need one; they won in five games over Los Angeles as the Dodgers could manage only 10 earned runs off Oakland pitching.

"We had a common bond on the A's," said Jackson. "Everybody hated Charlie Finley." While no team had won three Series in a row – Jackson's definition of a dynasty – since the Yankees of the early fifties, Oakland's trifecta was a mere preamble to the Jackson fireworks that followed.

A multi-million dollar free agent at a time when they were few, he was signed by New York in November 1976. Not long after, he announced "I'm the straw that stirs the drink." He later said he was misquoted, to which Thurman Munson replied, "For three fucking pages?" As time went on, however, he lived up to his boast.

The Yankees of 1976 had been swept by Cincinnati and they hit only one homer run while losing. That homer was hit by, of all people, light hitting shortstop Jim Mason, in his only World Series at-bat. They lacked a slugger who could put teams away. Not anymore.

Jackson said if he played in New York they would name a candy bar after him. For a gimmick someone produced the "Reggie Bar." After a tumultuous season adjusting to life with Billy Martin, who said the Yankees could win without him (though they hadn't), Jackson hit four homers off four different pitchers in games six and seven of the World

Series. The man who once said, "Hitting is better than sex," had exploded. The Dodgers' first baseman Steve Garvey later confessed to clapping in his glove after Jackson sent his third sixth game homer crashing into Yankee Stadium's black seats, some 475 feet from home plate. It was the show of shows, with Jackson hitting five homers, knocking in eight runs and wrecking the Dodgers. Even Martin and Munson were patting his back. Mike Torrez, one year before helping the Yankees on another team, won Game Three and Game Six.

Jackson hit .391 with two homers and eight RBI in the 1978 Series. The Yankees returned from being down two games to none, hitting .306 for the series and beating the Dodgers 28-8 over the next four. Munson hit .320 and knocked in seven, and Bucky Dent, the Series MVP, finished his journey through OZ, plating seven more and hitting .417. Third baseman Graig Nettles didn't hit much, but flashed more leather than a dominatrix, turning the Series around in Game Three with a series of plays that cost the Dodgers about five runs.

Jackson would play in the post-season four more times with New York and California – in 1980, '81, '82 and '86 – but never again would he play on the winning side in a World Series, as the Dodgers beat the Yankees four games to two in 1981.

Yankees owner George Steinbrenner admits to one mistake: allowing Jackson, a free agent, to be signed by the Angels in January 1982. At the time Steinbrenner was trying speed, bringing in Dave Collins and Ken Griffey to play in his revamped outfield. The result: it would be 15 seasons (1982-1996) between drinks.

Not until 1996 did the Yankees capture the American League flag, their longest pennant drought in more than 70 years. Jackson returned to the Stadium in April, 1982, and deposited a Guidry slider in the upper deck. Jackson, who Steinbrenner thought was finished, hit 39 homers in 1982.

He hit his 500th homer in 1984 and finished with 15 in his last season for Oakland. He retired after the 1987 season.

While it could be said that Jackson was a "slugger," he was not a great hitter. Not only did he supplant Mantle's total of 1,710 strikeouts, but he went by it in 15 years. He never learned how to strikeout less. If he had made more contact, he would have driven in more runs without hitting homers. He finished with just a .262 average and a .358 on-base percentage. Jackson clearly understood the problem. "When you play this game 10 years and go to bat 7,000 times and get 2,000 hits, you know what this means? That you've gone 0-for-5,000."

One of the most exciting players who ever lived, Jackson was enshrined in the Hall of Fame in 1993.

Best 5-year Average
1969-1973

R	H	D	T	HR	RBI	AVG	OBP	SLG
88	140	28	2	32	91	.271	.366	.518

Best 10-year Average
1969-1978

R	H	D	T	HR	RBI	AVG	OBP	SLG
88	142	28	3	31	95	.273	.362	.514

Best 15-year Average
1968-1982

R	H	D	T	HR	RBI	AVG	OBP	SLG
84	139	25	3	31	92	.272	.362	.515

All-time totals

G	2,820	RBI	1,702
AB	9,864	BB	1,375
R	1,551	K	2,597
H	2,584	AVG	.262
D	463	OBP	.358
T	49	SLG	.490
HR	563	SB	228
HR %	5.7	CS	115

100

24
JOHNNY BENCH
Catcher

Born: 12/7/47 Oklahoma City, OK
6 feet 1 inch, 208 pounds
Debut: 8/28/67, Played 17 years: 1967-1983, Cincinnati

Johnny Bench was simply the best catcher in baseball history. He twice hit 40 homers and knocked in 100 runs six times in an eight-year stretch between 1970 and 1977. But despite being a slugger who hit 20-plus homers for 12 consecutive seasons, Bench's defense also sets him apart from the other greatest catchers - Yogi Berra and Roy Campanella.

Anyone who saw Bench cannot forget his style of one-handed catching and how he threw blue darts to second to nail would-be base stealers. Some runners, like the Yankees' Mickey Rivers in the 1976 World Series, would get thrown out by Bench and then just give up, not even attempting to steal again. "Every time Bench throws," said Orioles VP Harry Dalton, "everybody in baseball drools."

Bench was a trailblazer at the position: the first to wear a protective helmet behind the plate. He also made one-handed catching popular, keeping his throwing hand behind his back to protect it from foul tips. He credits his father, who, "Taught me to throw 254 feet – twice the distance to second base – from a crouch." Ten years in a row – from 1968 through 1977 – Bench won Gold Glove Awards.

Then, too, he was an invaluable part of the best eight-man lineup in decades, comparable to the Dodgers of the early 1950s and two editions of the Yankees – late twenties and the late thirties. It was 1970, the year when a 22-year-old Bench burst on the scene with 48 homers and 148 runs batted in to win his first MVP award that Los Angeles sportswriter Bob Hunter dubbed the Cincinnati collective "The Big Red Machine." Two years later Bench was at `em again, taking MVP honors for hitting 40 homers and plating 140 runs.

Johnny's career contains many "Bench-marks." Consistency was his trademark. He was a 14-time All-Star. The power hitting was unmistakable; not since Berra and Campanella had catchers hit that way. The fielding, too, seemed never to wane.

Then, consider the team itself. The Reds with Bench won six division titles, four pennants and two World Series between 1970 and 1979. Bench did not distinguish himself in the 1970, 1972 and 1975 World Series. But he made the 1976 Series his personal playground. The Reds swept the Yankees and Bench hit two homers, knocked in six and batted .533. After Rivers failed steal attempt, New York did not try another. Yankees' catcher Thurman Munson hit .529. Munson gave his opposite number due praise. "The man deserves all the credit in the world," the Yankees' captain said. A reporter asked Reds' skipper Sparky Anderson what he thought of Munson's 10-hit performance. Anderson praised Munson's effort but added, "Just don't compare him to Johnny Bench." To New York readers the remark came off as callous. In another way it was not. The American League MVP that season, Munson had quite a career. He and Carlton Fisk were the frequent subjects of the argument, "Who is the best catcher in the American League?" But the added qualifier had to be "in the American League." Neither of them were in Bench's class.

And as good as Gary Carter would become in the 1980s, he didn't approach Bench's power numbers either, and even a larger gap exists between them in defense.

The catchers who are closer to Bench come before him. Yogi Berra, Roy Campanella and Bill Dickey all give Bench a run for his money. Because of the "color barrier," Campanella didn't get to the Major Leagues until he was 26 and played only ten years to Bench's 17 and Berra's 19. Campanella came to bat only 4,205 times so his slugging average of .500 had little chance for decline and his totals lag behind. Bench, who slugged .476, had 7,658 at-bats, nearly twice as many as Campanella, and slightly more than Berra, who had 7,555 and slugged .482. Dickey had only 6,300 at-bats and slugged .486. But Dickey wasn't the slugger or run producer that Bench or Berra were. Dickey hit 202 homers and drove in 1,209 runs in 17 years (71 per year), while leading the league in fielding four times. In the same number of years Bench hit 389 homers and drove in 1,376 (23 homers and 81 RBIs per year). Berra had 358 homers in 19 years and 1430 RBIs – 19 homers and 75 RBIs per year. Berra batted .285, significantly better than Bench's .267.

Berra is the only one challenging Bench for king of the hill. But Bench's slight edge in power and production and significant edge in fielding are tie-breakers. So Bench takes first, Berra second and Campanella third. People who just started watching baseball in the sixties or early seventies, and therefore didn't get to see many of the greats of old, can say with assurance that they watched the greatest third baseman of all-time, Mike Schmidt. They also watched the greatest catcher of all-time: Johnny Bench.

Before retiring in 1983, Bench had three sub-par seasons. "I need cortisone for both knees," he said. "I take butazolidin, endizine and muscle relaxer. If I were a race horse, I would be disqualified." Later, he said he contemplated coming out of retirement. But the fancy ended, he said, "When I pulled a muscle vacuuming."

It was fitting that Bench would end his 17-year stint with Cincinnati. It was also fitting that he was elected to the Hall of Fame his first year of eligibility, in 1984. He had broken Yogi Berra's record for career homers by a catcher. Now Bench would cross a generation and get his introduction to Yogi. Yogi sent a telegram that read: "Congratulations on breaking my record. I always thought the record would stand until it was broken."

Best 5-year Average
1970-1974

R	H	D	T	HR	RBI	AVG	OBP	SLG
91	154	26	3	34	113	.267	.350	.499

Best 10-year Average
1969-1978

| 80 | 142 | 27 | 2 | 29 | 102 | .269 | .351 | .493 |

Best 15-year Average
1968-1982

| 70 | 130 | 24 | 1 | 25 | 88 | .269 | .348 | .480 |

Lifetime totals

G	2,158	RBI	1,376
AB	7,658	BB	891
R	1,091	K	1,278
H	2,048	AVG	.267
D	381	OBP	.345
T	24	SLG	.476
HR	389	SB	68
HR %	5.1	CS	43

25
TRIS SPEAKER
Center Field

"The Grey Eagle"
Born: 4/4/1888 Hubbard, TX, Died: 12/8/58 Lake Whitney, TX
5 feet 11-and-a-half inches, 193 pounds
Debut: 9/14/07, Played 22 years: 1907-1928
1907-1915, Boston (AL); 1916-1926, Cleveland;
1927, Washington; 1928, Philadelphia (AL)

A story goes that when Tris Speaker was a young boy in Texas, he fell from a horse and broke his right arm. So he became a left-handed pitcher. Then his left arm was injured in a football accident and surgeons advised amputation. But he refused and learned to throw left-handed.

While still pitching in Texas, he was racked up for 22 hits one day, all for extra bases. "Stay in there kid," said his manager with sarcasm. "They haven't made a single hit yet."

Speaker soon became an outfielder. Over and over again, the center fielders whose names keep coming up in the defensive rating pages of *Total Baseball* are Tris Speaker, Richie Ashburn and Willie Mays. Speaker was a pioneer, the first outfielder to move before the pitch.

The story goes that he acquired the knack as a Red Sox rookie, while fielding fungos hit by Cy Young and trying to figure out which way the ball would go. Said Speaker, "He used to do this for me about 30 minutes a day. He could place the ball just one step out of my reach. So I started watching him to see where he'd hit the ball and thus sharpened my sense of anticipation. In a few days I knew just by the way he swung whether the ball would go to my right or left. Then I began to study the batter during a game; when he started his swing, I knew if he would hit to my left or right and I was on my way."

This anticipation helped Speaker play shallow. Because he could play shallow, he participated in a record four unassisted double plays and he set a record for outfielders with 448 career assists. He led American League outfielders seven times in putouts, five times in double plays, three times in assists, and twice in fielding. Old timers remember him playing virtually in back of second base, robbing hitters of singles on shoestring catches and throwing out base runners on the balls that dropped. Despite playing shallow, he possessed an uncanny ability to retreat on a ball.

Consider all that and then consider he hit .345 and slugged .500. A fleet-footed batsman who hit .356, gave his club 42 doubles, 12 triples and 6 homers on average for a 15-year period, Tris Speaker was a great all-around player who helped the Red Sox win World Championships in 1912 and 1915.

Speaker is too easily overlooked. He played his 22 years between 1907 and 1928 and too often he loses out when compared with Ruth, Cobb and Wagner, who flourished to a greater extent. Yet the "Grey Eagle" had 200 hits four times, 50 doubles five times and drew 1,381 walks while evidence suggests that he struck out about 300 times (we only have records for him from 1913-1928, which doesn't include the first six years of his career). While he slugged well below .500 in the "dead ball" era, starting in 1920, when he was 32, he slugged .562, .538, .606, .610, .510, .578 for the next six years.

His last two years in Boston were Ruth's first. Before that he played on the 1912 Boston team that beat the Giants four games to three. In the seventh game, the Giants went ahead 2-1 in the top of the tenth and Christy Mathewson was pitching. Mathewson had lost game five, pitching well in a 2-1 loss. If the Giants held the lead, they would win the Series.

The Giants center fielder, Fred Snodgrass, dropped a lazy fly hit by pinch hitter Clyde Engle to lead off the bottom of the tenth. Snodgrass then followed that muff with one of the greatest plays of his life, catching a Harry Hooper drive over his shoulder in deepest left-center field. One out. Christy Mathewson walked light hitting second baseman Steve Yerkes. Mathewson got Speaker to pop up, an easy foul off first base. First baseman Fred Merkle could have gotten it, but Mathewson called for catcher Chief Meyers to take it. He never got there and the ball fell in foul territory. "Spoke," as Boston teammate Harry Hooper called Speaker, then yelled to Matty, "you just called for the wrong man. It's gonna cost you this ball game." With a second life, Speaker lined one over first to score Engle and tie the game and put runners on the corners. Larry Gardner, the third baseman, then hit a long fly to right. Yerkes tagged and scored and the Series was over.

The 1915 Series was easier, with Boston defeating the Phillies in five games. By then Speaker was an established star, earning $16,000 a year and a $5,000 bonus for signing a two-year contract. But after nine years with Boston, Speaker was traded to Cleveland for the 1916 season. Owner Joe Lannin had wanted to cut his salary to under $10,000 following the 1915 season. When Speaker refused the deal, he was traded to the Indians for pitcher Sam Jones, second baseman Fred Thomas and $50,000. Adding insult to the Boston fans' loss, Speaker posted his finest year in 1916: he led the league in five categories, including: hits, 211; doubles, 41; average, .386; on-base percentage, .470; and slugging .502. By winning the batting title, he interrupted Cobb's run of titles, which would have been 13 straight. But the Red Sox won without him, beating Brooklyn four games to one.

It was a sign of things to come. With his new team, Speaker enjoyed personal success, hitting above .380 four times. He scored 100 runs four times and got 200 hits three times. But the Indians went nowhere for his first four years while the Red Sox, with a young Babe Ruth, took two World Series in his absence.

That changed in 1920, the year before he was appointed player-manager of the Indians. In 1920 the Indians won the pennant as Speaker posted personal bests with his .388 average and 133 runs scored. To help edge the White Sox in the race, Speaker turned in an astonishing play. With two out and two on in the ninth and Cleveland one run ahead, Shoeless Joe Jackson hit a screaming liner to right center. The Grey Eagle took off and was in flight before Jackson had completed his swing. He made a tremendous leap, crashing into the concrete wall and falling unconscious. But he held on to the ball. Cleveland won the pennant by two games. They then beat Brooklyn five games to two. Speaker was making $40,000, the highest salary in baseball until Ruth signed for $52,000 in 1922.

1920 was Speaker's third World Series victory and his last sniff of the post season. Speaker and Cobb were cleared of suspicions of gambling on games in 1926 and they ended up playing their last seasons together on the Philadelphia A's in 1928.

He was elected to the Hall of Fame in 1937, only the seventh ever to receive that honor, after Cobb, Johnson, Mathewson, Ruth, Wagner and Lajoie.

Even at the time of Speaker's death in 1958, the Boston outfield of Speaker, Duffy Lewis and Harry Hooper was referred to as the greatest of all-time. His 3,514 hits were then second only to Cobb's 4,193. His .345 average is ranked fifth and his 792 doubles rank first. His 227 triples rank sixth and his 1,882 runs are eighth.

Best 5-year Average
1921-1925

AB	R	H	S	D	T	HR	RBI	BB	K	AVG	OBP	SLG
484	100	179	113	46	9	10	86	76	13	.370	.456	.568

Best 10-year Average
1916-1925

AB	R	H	S	D	T	HR	RBI	BB	K	AVG	OBP	SLG
501	98	180	120	43	10	7	80	76	13	.360	.444	.526

Best 15-year Average
1911-1925

AB	R	H	S	D	T	HR	RBI	BB	K	AVG	OBP	SLG
515	101	183	124	42	12	6	79	75	15	.356	.438	.518

Lifetime Totals

G	2,789
AB	10,195
R	1,885
H	3,514
D	792
T	222
HR	117
HR%	1.1
RBI	1,529
BB	1,381
K	220
	(incomplete)
AVG	.345
OBP	.428
SLG	.500
SB	432
CS	129
	(incomplete)

II
The Next 25 Players

26
WILLIE MCCOVEY
First Base

"Stretch"
Born: 1/10/38 Mobile, AL
6 feet 4 inches, 210 pounds
Debut: 7/30/59, Played 22 years: 1959-1980
1959-1973, San Francisco, 1974-1976, San Diego; 1976, Oakland;
1977-1980, San Francisco

When he was inducted into the Baseball Hall of Fame in 1986, Willie McCovey stood tall at the podium. "People ask me how I'd like to be remembered. I tell them I'd like to be remembered as the guy who hit the line drive over Bobby Richardson's head." The remark brought laughter, but it was bittersweet. It reminds anyone who saw the stylish first baseman that a World Championship was the only thing missing from his career. He hit that ball right on the screws. Nothing new, really. He still holds the National League record for the most homers by a left-handed hitter, with 521.

He came to the Giants in 1959, a year after they signed Orlando Cepada. After being called up from Phoenix where he'd been tutored by a pretty fair hitter named Ted Williams, McCovey made his debut on July 30, 1959. In his first game he went 4-for-4, getting two singles and two triples off Robin Roberts. Asked what McCovey likes to hit, Roberts said,

"Everything." In his first seven games he had three homers, nine RBIs and a .467 average. He hit 13 homers and hit .354 in limited time that season, good enough for Rookie of the Year Honors. But one first sacker was a party and two was a crowd for the Giants.

Orlando Cepada and McCovey were both first baseman and both were tried, in the outfield with little success. Cepada was given the first base job and McCovey platooned, occasionally getting innings at first base but mostly platooning in the outfield. He hadn't even played in 350 games by the time his fifth reason rolled around in 1963.

Then he broke loose. Getting 500 at bats for the first time, he led the league with 44 homers in 1963. McCovey would never have gotten the first base job, however, had Cepada not been injured in 1965 and traded to St. Louis the following year. McCovey cashed in. From 1965 through 1970 he hit 30-plus homers ever year, including 45 in 1969, his best year ever. McCovey led the league in four offensive categories that season – the 45 homers (he led the league with 36 the year before), 126 runs batted in, a .458 on-base percentage and a .656 slugging average. He followed that with 39 homers, 126 RBI and led the NL for the third straight year in slugging with a .612 mark. Asked how he would pitch to himself, he replied, "I'd walk me."

Pitchers were agreeing. In 1970 they walked him 137 times, with a record 45 intentional walks. For the second year in a row he had 126 walks. "If you pitch to him he'll ruin baseball," said Reds' manager Sparky Anderson. "He'd hit 80 home runs. There's no comparison between McCovey and anyone else in the league."

But "Stretch" – the name was given to him because of the way he reached out to take all sorts of throws at first – was beginning to show wear and tear by the early seventies. He missed 56 games in 1971 after tearing knee cartilage in spring training. In 1972, the year Mays was traded to the Mets, he missed 81 games after breaking his right arm in a collision with John Jeter in April. He bounced back to hit 29 homers the next year, but he was 35 years old. Following the season he was traded to San Diego for Mike Caldwell. After three declining years with the Padres and Oakland, he returned to San Francisco for what many thought was a last gasp in 1977. He was 39 and little was expected of the 6-foot-4-inch, 210-pound slugger who had his best years behind.

After getting a standing ovation on Opening Day that brought him to tears, McCovey went on to compile a fine season, hitting 28 homers and knocking in 86 runs that earned him Comeback Player of the Year.

In 1978 he hit his 500th home run and ended up two years later with 521, the same number as Ted Williams, his idol and teacher who had helped more than 20 years before. McCovey also holds the career record for grand slams with 18, five behind Lou Gehrig. He never won a World Series but insists to this day that the liner he hit to Richardson, with the bases loaded and two outs in the ninth inning of the 1962 series, was, "The hardest ball I ever hit."

If you missed Stretch at his best, consider that in one game in 1969 the Mets were so fearful of his bat that they played four men in the outfield to stop him. Cleon Jones scraped a ball off the fence near the 396-foot sign to make the strategy pay off.

He finished with only 8,197 at-bats in 22 years - just 372 per year – so his body often failed to do his bidding. But when he was healthy, most everyone was in awe of how he could hit. In 1986 he was elected to the Hall of Fame.

Best 5-Year Average
1966-1970

R	H	D	T	HR	RBI	AVG	OBP	SLG
88	145	25	4	37	109	.295	.421	.587

Best 10-Year Average
1962-1971

83	127	19	3	33	77	.282	.388	.557

Best 15-Year Average
1959-1973

69	110	17	3	28	68	.282	.384	.547

Lifetime totals

G	2,588	RBI	1,555
AB	8,197	BB	1,345
R	1,229	K	1,550
H	2,211	AVG	.270
D	353	OBP	.377
T	46	SLG	.515
HR.	521	SB	26
HR %	6.4		

27
KEN GRIFFEY, JR.
Center Field

"Junior"
Born: 11/21/69 Donora, PA
6 feet 3 inches, 195 pounds
Debut: 4/3/89, Played 9 years: 1989-1997, Seattle

Ken Griffey, Jr., has a chance for a career like Willie Mays, but any judgment to that effect will have to wait another seven or eight years. Teammates of Griffey will say it sometimes looks as if he's not trying that hard, only because the game comes easy to him. He is an incredibly rounded talent. But when one hears people saying Griffey' Jr. is the best player "they ever saw," you have to wonder when it was that they started seeing.

He has done some great things in his nine years in the Major Leagues but you don't start comparing people to Mays, Aaron and Mantle when they haven't put in the time yet. The greatest of the great require about 15 years. Aaron hit 645 homers in a 17-year period from 1957 through 1973. Mays hit 563 homers in his best 15-year stretch from 1954 through 1968. It is impossible to compare the size of those achievements with a 28 year-old who has hit 294 homers in nine years.

Baseball requires a test of time like no other sport. It is a longer, fuller test. People do not ask 15 great seasons of running backs, quarterbacks or shooting guards. But in baseball, to be compared with the great hitters, you need 15 years.

If you don't have 15 years, as in the case of DiMaggio (13 years) or Greenberg (13 years), then you had better be giving us enough of a sample to tell where you were headed for the years you missed.

Griffey has provided a fairly good sample. In nine seasons he has been over 100 RBI five times. Twice he has led in homers. In '97 he paced the league in five categories. He hit 56 homers, knocked in 147 runs, slugged .646, scored 125 runs and posted a homer percentage of 9.2. In the eight years prior, Griffey had only led the league in one category: he hit 40 homers in the strike shortened 1994 season.

So despite the talk of greatness that has surrounded him for years, he has only now begun to dominate the game. Beginning in 1998, he plays his next five years between the ages of 29 and 33. Coming off his monster 1997 season, it looks as if he will peak for a number of years.

He is still behind Frank Thomas, the American League's other great hitter, in several important categories. His average, on-base percentage and slugging average trail the Big Hurt's. Griffey's impatient 76 walks and 126 strikeouts in 1997 is not a combo you'll find on Thomas' resume either. But Griffey looks about ready to make a permanent gear change.

He upped his lifetime slugging average by 13 points last year, all the way to .562. He is the best all-around player in the game and will be by a country mile if he runs off five or eight or ten years like everyone thinks he's capable of. He still needs 366 homers to catch the person he's most likely to draw comparisons to: Willie Mays.

At the moment, he's compared to Barry Bonds, but he may soon be looking at Bonds in the rear-view mirror. Forgetting 1995 – a year he missed 90 games due to a wrist injury – Griffey has posted 45, 40, 49 and 56 homers in the last four years, for a Ruthian average of 47.5 per season.

Griffey must stay healthy, however. His 157 games played and 608 at bats in 1997 are personal bests for a player prone to crashing into walls and missing games. Which brings us to the fielding. He's as good a center fielder as you'll find. He was awarded his fifth consecutive Gold Glove last year.

He's headed for the Hall of Fame. But that's not enough for this kid from Donora, Pennsylvania, the same town Stan Musial came from. Griffey has a chance to be in the top 10 or five of all the players who ever played.

We'll just have to wait and see if he finishes what he's started.

Best 5-Year Average
1993-1997

R	H	D	T	HR	RBI	AVG	OBP	SLG
102	147	26	2	41	106	.303	.393	.622

Career Average
1989-1997

R	H	D	T	HR	RBI	AVG	OBP	SLG
91	154	29	3	33	97	.302	.381	.562

Lifetime totals

G	1,214	RBI	872
AB	4,593	BB	580
R	820	K	755
H	1,389	AVG	.302
D	261	OBP	.381
T	24	SLG	.562
HR	294	SB	123
HR%	6.4	CS	48

28
RICKEY HENDERSON
Left Field

"Man of Steal"
Born: 12/25/58
5 feet 10 inches, 195 pounds
Debut: 6/24/79, Played 19 years: 1979-1997
1979-1985, Oakland; 1985-1989, New York (AL);
1989-1993, Oakland; 1993, Toronto; 1994-1995, Oakland;
1996-1997, San Diego; 1997, Anahiem

Ricky Henderson started the 1998 season with 1,231 stolen bases, nearly 300 ahead of anyone who ever played. He has used a .286 average and 1,772 walks to feed his thievery, which in turn feeds his run scoring. He began the year with 1,913 runs – 100 per season for 19 years. Reggie Jackson once called him, "a walking triple." On the day he broke Lou Brock's record of 938 steals, victimized Milwaukee pitcher Doc Medich said, "He's like a little kid in a train station; you turn your back on him and he's gone."

Just try telling any of this to Yankee fans. Rarely has a ballplayer been maligned so often for so little as Rickey Henderson was maligned in New York. Many Yankee fans, not wanting to be confused with the facts, think that Henderson was shiftless, a malingerer who "jaked it." By contrast, Henderson once said, "If I haven't gotten my uniform dirty, I haven't done anything in a baseball game." So two views exist on Henderson, the player. Let's see which is perception and which is reality.

For starters, let's look at the record of Henderson's time in New York to see just how badly he was performing. Between 1985 and 1989, in 596 games and 2,302 at-bats with the Yankees – essentially the equivalent of four healthy years at 149 games per year – he put up the following numbers:

Totals	Per-year Average	Totals	Per-year Average
513 runs	128	.288 batting average	.288
80 homers	20	.394 on-base pct.	____
326 stolen bases	82	.455 slugging pct.	____
663 hits	166		

Even with those numbers, 90 percent of Yankee fans thought he was "dogging it." There were contract problems in 1989 and the hue and cry was such that Henderson was traded to Oakland on June 21. The Yankees finished 74-87 that year and Oakland finished 99-63, taking game, set and match, finishing off San Francisco in a four-game sweep. Henderson hit two homers, stole eight bases, scored eight runs and took the MVP of the five-game League Championship Series against Toronto. He then hit .474 in the Series.

In 1990 Henderson won the MVP, hitting 28 homers, knocking in 61, walking 97 times and batting .325. His on-base average was .441 and he slugged .577 – while batting leadoff! The Yankees, now free of their trouble-making malingerer and bolstered by the trade spoils of Eric Plunk, Greg Cadaret and Luis Polonia, finished dead last with a 67-95 record. You had to go back to the time of flannel uniforms to find their previous last-place finish: 1966.

The ripples in the pond continued. In 1991 the Yankees finished fifth, 20 games under .500 at 71 and 91. They finished 10 games under .500 the next year and didn't play .500 ball until 1993. In the four full seasons they had Henderson, they played .602 (1985), .556 (1986), .549 (1987) and .528 (1988). You be the judge about Henderson's impact.

Henderson has been the best leadoff hitter in history. Henderson's average of 101 runs per year has been achieved despite three years – 1979, 1987 and 1994 – where he failed to play 100 games. In fact, Henderson, due mostly to leg injuries, has averaged only 129 games per season in his 19-year career. Nonetheless the run productivity is incomparable. *Total Baseball* divides statistical achievements into eras. In the era covering the last 20 years, Henderson leads all players with .78 runs per game. The last two players to average that many runs per game were Joe DiMaggio (.80) and Ted Williams (.78).

Rickey Henderson started his career the same year as Tim Raines.

Both are speedsters, good hitters with power and great base stealers. As good as Raines has been, Henderson is better. Henderson has led the league in runs five times and has scored 100 or more runs 12 times.

Three times he led the league in walks. Even when he doesn't hit he changes games. In 1996 he hit .241 but had a .412 on-base-percentage because he drew 125 walks! If he scores 87 runs in 1998, he'll have 2,000 runs in 20 years.

Then, consider his stolen bases. He overtook Lou Brock's career total of 938 in 1989. Eleven times Henderson has led the league in pilfery and his 1,231 stolen bases puts him nearly 300 ahead of Brock. The "Man of Steal" has stolen 100 bases three times and shattered Brock's previous record of 118 by swiping 130 in 1982. He has been caught only 288 times in his career, so his success rate is 81 percent. Even in 1997, at the age of 38, he was successful on 85 percent of his attempts. Henderson led the American League in steals every year between 1980 and 1991, except 1987. That year he missed 67 games with a damaged hamstring.

All this tells us it is irrelevant whether or not people like him or suspect him of not giving his all. If he is not giving his all, then it behooves every major league manager to find eight more just like him who are not giving their all.

Numbers measure performance. With his combination of awesome power and speed, he is one of the most gifted players of the last 25 years. Since Mays retired in 1973 and Aaron in 1976, how many more talented players than Henderson have played the game?

Power, speed and a *Total Baseball* rating of 31st lifetime among all defensive players – Henderson is a complete player.

The Baseball Writers of America who vote will know all about his steals. If they also take five minutes to look at his runs scored and on-base percentage, they cannot escape the conclusion that he is a first ballot Hall of Famer. Of course, if Rickey failed to give them the right quote when they were on deadline, there could be a different result.

Best 5-year Average
1989-1993

R	H	D	T	HR	RBI	AVG	OBP	SLG
106	137	23	2	17	56	.287	.409	.435

Best 10-year Average
1984-1993

| 111 | 144 | 25 | 3 | 18 | 57 | .290 | .407 | .459 |

Best 15-year Average
1980-1994

| 107 | 141 | 23 | 4 | 14 | 52 | .290 | .407 | .441 |

Lifetime totals

G	2,460	RBI	921
AB	8,931	BB	1,772
R	1,913	K	1,276
H	2,550	AVG	.286
S	1,813	OBP	.404
D	426	SLG	.431
T	59	SB	1,231
HR	252	CS	293
HR%	2.8		

29
HANK GREENBERG
First Base

"Hammerin' Hank"
Born: 1/1/11 New York, NY, Died: 9/4/86 Beverly Hills, CA
6 feet 3-and-a-half inches, 210 pounds
Debut: 9/14/30, Played 13 years: 1930-1947
(missed 1931-32, then 1942-44)
1930-1946, Detroit; 1947, Pittsburgh

Hank Greenberg signed with Detroit in 1929 for $9,000 a year, ignoring the advice of Yankee scout Paul Krichell. "I was a slugging first baseman," Greenberg explained later, "and the Yankees had the best in Lou Gehrig. So I chose Detroit."

Before a "Hammerin' Hank" Aaron, came Hammerin' Hank Greenberg. While the world saw some of Greenberg, it didn't see nearly enough. In the early 1930s he spent many prime years in the minors and then was drafted into the Army on May 7, 1941, the first baseball star to go into military service. He was discharged on December 5, 1941 under a rule allowing those over the age of 28 to cut short their terms. But when the Japanese attacked Pearl Harbor, he was recalled by the Army Air Corps. He missed all but 19 games in 1941 and then all of 1942, 1943 and 1944. He returned to play 78 games in 1945. But the damage was done.

By the time he retired at the age of 36, he had played just 13 seasons and had gotten 500 at-bats in just seven of them. But even during his brief major league tenure, which included barely more than 5,000 at-bats, Greenberg gave enough evidence of what might have been.

Harry Benjamin Greenberg was born in New York City in 1911 and grew up on the Lower East Side and then in the Catona Park neighborhood of the Bronx. By his own admission he was gawky and ungainly but worked hard at improving his fielding and hitting. He enrolled at NYU in 1929 but dropped out to sign a baseball contract with Detroit.

With the Tigers, Greenberg played more than 1,100 games at first base, but played another 200 or more in the outfield, mostly in left field. A teammate of Charlie Gehringer, Greenberg had some of his best years during four pennant winning seasons. He first broke through in 1934. That year the 6-foot-3-and-a-half inch, 210-pound first baseman recorded an incredible 63 doubles, 201 hits and knocked in 139 runs. He hit .339 and slugged .600 – a slugging plateau that became typical for Greenberg.

In fact, Greenberg slugged .600 or better for the following six years as Detroit captured three pennants and a World Series. After the pennant in 1934 and the World Series win over the Cubs in 1935, the Tigers repeatedly finished behind the Yankees' dynasty team from 1936 through 1939. They broke through in 1940, winning the pennant but losing the Series to the Cincinnati Reds in seven games.

But even as the Yankees of Gehrig, DiMaggio, Dickey, Lazzeri, Gomez and Ruffing grabbed the spotlight, Greenberg put up some ungodly numbers. It began in the World Championship season of 1935. That year Greenberg led the circuit with 36 homers and 170 runs batted in and was selected MVP. After missing all but 12 games of the 1936 season with injuries, Greenberg absolutely terrorized American League pitching in 1937. He had 200 hits – 103 of them for extra bases! – and knocked in 183 runs, the third highest RBI total in baseball history. The following year he staged an all-out assault on Ruth's home run record of 60 set in 1927. Greenberg finished with 58, having to battle young Bob Feller and fanning twice on the last day of the season. His RBI "slipped" to 146 in 1938, but he led the league with 144 runs, 119 walks and posted a personal best .683 slugging average.

He led the Tigers to their third pennant in seven years in 1940, Greenberg's last MVP season. While the Tigers gave up a three-two Series lead and suffered a disappointing Series loss to the Reds, Greenberg posted great individual marks. He hit 41 homers, knocked in 150 runs and slugged .670. During the season he moved from first base to left field so the Tigers could move their young power hitter Rudy York into the lineup.

While Greenberg missed most of the 1945 season due to military service, he led Detroit to another league flag and even hit the pennant clinching homer, a grand slam against the St. Louis Browns on Sept. 30, 1945. Detroit then beat the Cubs in the Series, as they had 10 years before. Greenberg hit two homers and knocked in seven runs in the classic.

Greenberg led the league with 44 homers and 127 RBIs in 1946 but decided to retire. Hearing of Greenberg's retirement plans, John Galgreath, the Pirates' owner, signed him to a $65,000 contract, plus options, making Hammerin' Hank the highest paid player in baseball. When Greenberg sold back those options after the 1947 season, he had what was believed to be the first $100,000 contract. In a part-time role in 1947, Greenberg hit 25 homers and helped the Pirates' young slugger Ralph Kiner to his second of seven consecutive home run titles by urging him to be more selective at the plate.

Greenberg's bottom line, though impressive, shouts out, "What if." Though he entered the major leagues at 19 years old, he played only nine full seasons. So his 331 home runs and 1,276 runs batted in were far short of what he could have piled up in 15 or 17 full seasons. It is Greenberg's percentage numbers, not his totals, which must be studied.

His .92 RBI per game is matched only by Lou Gehrig in this century. He hit a homer every 15.68 at-bats, which is the 11th best home run percentage all-time. Three times he had 150 or more runs batted in and four times 40 or more home runs. Every time he had more than 500 at-bats he slugged 600 plus, including .668, .683 and .670 in a 5-year period between 1937 and 1940.

In appreciating what Greenberg did, the discerning fan must take his average season and use inductive inference to predict what he would have done in a normal 15 to 20-year career. Give Greenberg 15 full years instead of nine and, with his full-season averages, he would have hit 525 homers and knocked in about 1,980 runs.

Despite his truncated totals, he was elected to the Baseball Hall of Fame in 1956, the first Jewish player to be so honored. It is unbelievable, however, that he failed to get the necessary number of votes several years before that. In 1986, Greenberg died at the age of 75 in Beverly Hills, California.

Best 5-year Average
1935-40 (not counting '36)

R	H	D	T	HR	RBI	AVG	OBP	SLG
129	186	42	10	42	98	.327	.426	.655

Best 10-year Average
1933-1947 (not counting '36, '41-45)

103	159	37	7	33	83	.314	.410	.607

Lifetime totals

G	1394	RBI	1276
AB	5193	BB	852
R	1051	K	844
H	1628	AVG	.313
D	379	OBP	.412
T	71	SLG	.605
HR	331	SB	58
HR%	6.4	CS	26

30
CAL RIPKEN
Shortstop/Third Base

Born: 8/24/60 Havre De Grace, MD
6 feet 4 inches, 215 pounds
Debut: 8/10/81, Played 17 years: 1981-1997, Baltimore

And the beat goes on. It's over 2,475 consecutive games played and counting. Since he started at shortstop in the second game of a double-header on May 29, 1982, in the middle of former President Ronald Reagan's first term in office, Cal Ripken's name has been in the starting lineup. Not two weeks later, on July 1, 1982, he took over shortstop, replacing an eight-time Gold Glove man, Mark Belanger. Midway through the 1996 season, on July 15, he was moved from shortstop – where he played 2,216 consecutive games – to third.

Despite the streak, he has taken criticism of late from those who think that he and the team could benefit if he took an occasional rest. If you argue Ripken's too tired or injured to play well, one test would be his post-season work, where you would think he'd be exhausted. In 110 post-season at bats, Ripken has 37 hits for a .336 average. In 1997, at 37 years old, Ripken gave his team 166 hits, 30 doubles, 17 homers, 84 RBI and a .270 average. That's better production than more than half of the starting third basemen in both leagues.

A 6-foot-4-inch, 215-pound shortstop who, despite his size, led the league in fielding four times, Ripken is set to post several more land-mark numbers. Before long he'll have 10,000 at-bats, 2,500 straight games, 1,500 runs, 3,000 hits, 400 homers and 1,500 RBI. That combination of numbers is singular at shortstop. Like another shortstop, Ernie Banks, Ripken won two MVPs, in 1983 and 1991. In 14 of his 16 full-time seasons, he has knocked in between 81 and 114 runs. Four times he has gotten 100 RBI, including the 102 he got in 1996. His batting average, and per-year runs, hits and extra-base hits, are declining now. But name a great player's numbers that didn't decline after 35 years old?

When Ripken broke Gehrig's record he already knew of Gehrig's 493 homers and .340 average and said in a humble vein, "The only thing I have in common with Gehrig is the streak." He is the most durable player in baseball history, breaking the record at shortstop, not first base as Gehrig did. His streak of 10 straight years of 20 or more homers, which was stopped in 1992, is the most ever by a shortstop (Banks did it eight years in a row). Ripken didn't weigh his team down in the field, either. His four fielding titles and two Gold Gloves have come since 1990, after he was 30 years old. He started seven straight All-Star games, led the league in double plays and putouts four times and assists six times. His 534 assists in 1983 set an American League record. He was able to contribute in the field because he was a smart position defender with sure hands.

What can be wrong with a player who wants to play as much and win as much as Ripken? Take the story of how he badly injured his hand sliding on artificial turf against Seattle in 1983. He couldn't grip the bat but handled the pain and got five hits, two of them homers, tying an Oriole club record for total bases in a game.

Streak or no streak, one can only hope he continues to the year 2000 and beyond. The night of Sept. 6, 1995, when he broke Gehrig's record with 2,131 straight games, is the best shot in the arm baseball has had in years.

Best 5-year Average
1982-1986

R	H	D	T	HR	RBI	AVG	OBP	SLG
106	184	37	4	27	94	.291	.354	.487

Best 10-year Average
1982-1991

97	175	34	3	26	94	.280	.352	.469

Best 15-Year Average
1982-1996

91	170	32	3	24	91	.279	.347	.457

Lifetime totals

G	2,543	RBI	1,453
AB	9,832	BB	1,016
R	1,445	K	1,086
H	2,715	AVG	.276
D	517	OBP	.344
T	43	SLG	.450
HR	370	SB	36
HR %	3.8	CS	34

31
MEL OTT
Right Field

"Master Melvin"
Born: 3/2/09 Gretna, LA, Died: 11/21/58 New Orleans, LA
5 feet 9 inches, 170 pounds
Debut: 4/27/26, Played 22 years: 1926-1947, New York (NL)

Mel Ott hit 511 home runs very quietly. How he hit them, where he hit them or how many he ever collected in one year will never change the bottom line of 511. When he died suddenly after a car accident on Nov. 21, 1958, only Ruth and Foxx had more homers that he did. Mel Ott and Ernie Banks, who hit 512 homers, benefited more from playing in their home parks than all of the other 13 members of the 500-home run club. That being said, 500 home runs is still a stellar achievement. If anyone thinks it isn't, then why have only 15 men done it?

Mel Ott, with that timing maneuver of lifting his right leg, started cranking homers in the Polo Grounds for the Giants at a time when the Yankees, playing across the Harlem river, were the toast of the town. In 1929, at the age of 20, Ott hit 42 homers and knocked in 151 runs. He was the youngest ever to hit 40 homers and never reached that homer or RBI total again. But Ott managed between 18 and 38 homers per season – most of the time in the high 20s or low 30s – for the next 16 years. In the years when Foxx and Gehrig were leading the American League, Ott was leading the National

League, copping the homer title six times between 1932 and 1942.

Ott was amused that his career got started as a result of a penny post card. He received the card in the summer of 1925, when he was 16 years old. He was playing ball with a semi-pro team called the Paterson Grays. The card read: "Report to John McGraw, Polo Grounds, New York." It was signed: John McGraw.

Ott thought somebody was pulling a joke on him and paid no attention to it. Several weeks later Harry Williams, a close friend of McGraw's, tracked the tardy Ott down and chased him to New York. Ott was a catcher but McGraw thought his heavy legs would knot up from the grind of catching and made him an outfielder. McGraw didn't want anyone tampering with Ott's high leg kick and so did not allow Ott to go to the minors. He would stay with New York from 1926 through 1947.

Whoever thought of the phrase "slow and steady wins the race" could have been describing Ott. He did not hit homers in bunches of 40 like Gehrig or in 50s like Foxx, but he was a steady producer.

For Ott's ability to pull pitches over the close Polo Grounds fence, a sportswriter gave him the name "Master Melvin" early on.

The name stuck. While the center field fence was impossibly far, ranging from 485 at the start of Ott's career to 505 feet in 1930 and 484 when he retired, the right field fence was a constant tease. It was 258 feet away all the time he played there. It quickly jutted out to 440 feet in right center, but Ott took aim at the close quarters down the line. He hit 323 homers (63 percent) at home and 188 (37 percent) on the road.

Ott was also particularly adept at drawing walks. He had 100 or more free passes 10 times, leading the league six times in walks. This gave him an exceptional career on-base percentage of .414, and helped him to nine seasons of 100 or more runs.

Ott's temperament matched his steady production at the plate. He was quiet, obliging and a gentleman. These characteristics put him in stark contrast to his manager, John McGraw, whose mercurial temper and dictatorial ways earned him the name "Little Napoleon." The story goes that Leo Durocher had Ott in mind when he said, "Nice guys finish last."

The phrase doesn't really apply to Ott. His teams won as often as Durocher's did. In 22 years, Ott played on three pennant winners and a World Series champion. In 26 years of managing, Durocher did the same, not winning a Series until his New York Giants won in 1954 – Durocher's 16th attempt at a World Championship. And you can't compare the two as hitters. In 17 seasons, Durocher, a shortstop, hit 24 homers and batted .247. Between 1925 and 1929 he was on the Yankees with Ruth, who called Durocher, "The All-American Out."

In 1933, the Giants matched up with the Washington Senators, led by future Hall of Famers Joe Cronin and Goose Goslin. But the 26-year-old Ott got the Giants cruising with a two-run homer in Game One. Giant ace Carl Hubbell got the win. Hubbell also won Game Four to give the Giants a commanding 3-1 lead. In Game Five Ott's homer in the top of the tenth broke a 3-3 tie and Dolf Luque shut down the Senators in the bottom of the inning. The Giants were champions. Ott was the hitting star for the Giants, batting .389 with two homers and four RBIs. Giant aces Schumacher and Hubbell turned in the pitching performances.

Ott returned to the fall classic in the 1936 and 1937 seasons, but those years were the beginning of the Yankees' post-Ruth dynasty. From 1936 through 1939 they won four consecutive World Series. The Giants lost the two Series, four games to two and four games to one. Lefty Gomez won a combined four games for the Yankees.

In 1942 the Giants followed the practice of the day of turning players into player-managers. In Ott's first year at the helm he also managed to lead the league in homers with 30! While Ott managed without distinction through 1948, he remained one of the batting stars through the War-depleted forties. In fact, the 18 homers hit in 1943 were good enough for second in the league. He hit all 18 at home. His playing career ended in 1947, two years after he hit his 500th home run. In 1948, Ott was relieved of his field duties and moved into the front office and the flamboyant Durocher took over the managing. Ott was elected to the Hall of Fame in 1951, just four years after he retired.

He was working as broadcaster in Detroit before his death in 1958. Just 49 years old, Ott died on Nov. 21 from injuries suffered in an auto crash a week before. Ott was in St. Louis and had just pulled away from a highway restaurant on U.S. Highway 90 when his car collided with another.

Ott's career certainly merits a second look. He had 100 RBI 9 times in a 10-year period between 1929 and 1938. He walked 1,708 times while striking out only 896 times, a ratio of about two to one. He was the youngest ever to hit 40 homers, hitting 42 at the age of 20 in 1929. He led the 1930s in games with 1,473. His 308 homers in the 1930s were third behind Foxx (415) and Gehrig (347). His 1,135 RBI in the decade were also third behind Foxx (1,403) and Gehrig (1,358).

He is still in the top 10 ten all-time in runs, RBI and walks. Ott hit .304 for his career and slugged .533 and certainly left his mark on the history of the game.

Best 5-year Average
1928-1932

R	H	D	T	HR	RBI	AVG	OBP	SLG
110	165	30	5	30	117	.322	.423	.580

Best 10-year Average
1929-1938

| 115 | 173 | 30 | 5 | 30 | 121 | .315 | .417 | .566 |

Best 15-year Average
1928-1942

| 107 | 164 | 28 | 4 | 30 | 108 | .310 | .415 | .548 |

All-time totals

G	2,730	RBI	1,860
AB	9,456	BB	1,708
R	1,859	K	896
H	2,876	AVG	304
D	488	OBP	414
T	72	SLG	533
HR	511	SB	89
HR%	5.4		

32
ROBERTO CLEMENTE
Right Field

Born: 8/18/34 Carolina, PR, Died: 12/31/72 San Juan, PR
5 feet 11 inches, 175 pounds
Debut: 4/17/55, Played 18 years: 1955-1972, Pittsburgh

When I think of Clemente the man, I think of an altruistic person who died young doing a great deed. The reason he was on the overloaded DC-7 plane that was flying food to Nicaragua was that he learned soldiers in Nicaragua were stealing supplies and selling them. "If I go to Nicaragua, the stealing will stop," he said. "They would not steal from Roberto Clemente." He was warned that the plane's cargo might be too heavy but he insisted on going. As the plane was banking to turn back to Puerto Rico after the engines sputtered, 60-pound bags of sugar which were not carefully tethered, shifted, causing the plane to go down. He was not the kind of man to attach his name to charities, sign a check and walk away.

When I think of Roberto Clemente the ballplayer, the name calls up several images. The first set of images are framed by the 1971 World Series, when Clemente collected 12 hits, homered twice, made plays in the outfield and ran with reckless abandon to lead the Pirates back from two games to none to beat the Orioles in seven. The other images, disconnected with any particular games, are of him making a catch and whirling to fire a strike to cut down a runner at second or third.

While these images call up a gifted, all-around athlete and perhaps the greatest fielding right fielder ever to play, the record shows that Clemente's game lacks an element that other great players of his time – Mays, Aaron, Mantle and Robinson included – had in abundance. The element is power. One cannot peruse the numbers in a record book without having Clemente's home run total and slugging average jump out. He hit 240 homers and slugged .475. Mays hit 660 homers and slugged .557; Aaron, 755 and .555; Mantle, 536 and .555; and Robinson 586 and .537. The power gap between Clemente and the others is just far too great. This is not to say that Clemente was not a great player.

He won four batting titles, leading the circuit in 1961, '64, '65 and '67. He had 200 hits four times and batted .317 for his career. He won the MVP in 1966, his best year in home runs and RBI with 29 and 119. He also hit .317 and slugged .536, the latter figure 61 points above his lifetime average. He had 846 extra base hits and his last hit was his 3,000th. Add all this to 12 Gold Gloves and a gun of a throwing arm from right field and he's a great player. No question.

Clemente was frequently angry at not getting the recognition that Mays and Aaron got in the National League. But the record shows that he didn't deserve the same recognition. His best 15-year run, from 1958-1972, shows averages of 15 homers, 78 RBI, a .325 average, a .370 on-base percentage and a slugging average of .491. Compare these averages with Mays', Aaron's, Mantle's and Frank Robinson's – the best of those who began playing in the 1950s.

15-Year Averages
Averages

	HR	RBI	AVG	OBP	SLG
Clemente 1958-1972	15	78	.325	.370	.491
Aaron 1957-1971	38	113	.313	.383	.577
Mantle 1952-1966	32	89	.307	.416	.580
Mays 1954-1968	38	104	.311	.387	.586
Robinson 1956-1970	32	97	.303	.386	.555

The numbers reflect that Mays, Aaron, Mantle and Robinson are substantially better in the slugging and run-producing categories.

Further, Clemente's walks to strikeout ratio is horrendous. The reason his on-base percentage is poor is that he walked only 35 times per year while striking out 68 times.

In 1971, the year everyone thinks was representative of his career, he hit 13 homers, knocked in 73 runs and hit .341. Good numbers, yes. But earthshaking totals for all time? No. He had a great seven games in October and so people who don't think about statistical ideas like "sample size" think those numbers tell the story of his career. They do not. They did showcase what he was capable of doing.

Having made an argument that Clemente was in no way the equal of Aaron, Mays, Mantle or Robinson, I hasten to add that he was still a great player. To hit .317 and collect 3,000 hits during the era when pitching was the best in baseball history is truly a great accomplishment.

The Roberto Clemente Award given each year is the one that should be remembered, not just MVP, Cy Young and batting champions. Clemente was a hero, a word too often used. The normal five-year waiting period for the Hall of Fame was waived in his case. He was voted elected in just 11 weeks, selected on 93 percent of the ballots.

Best 5-Year Average
1966-1970

R	H	D	T	HR	RBI	AVG	OBP	SLG
87	175	23	11	21	87	.332	.386	.534

Best 10-Year Average
1961-1970

89	184	26	10	18	83	.331	.379	.509

Best 15-Year Average
1958-1972

84	166	25	9	15	78	.325	.370	.491

Lifetime totals

G	2,433	RBI	1,305
AB	9,454	BB	621
R	1,416	K	1,230
H	3,000	AVG	.317
D	440	OBP	.362
T	166	SLG	.475
HR	240	SB	83
HR %	2.5	CS	46

33
AL KALINE
Right Field

Born: 12/19/34 Baltimore, MD
6 feet 2 inches, 180 pounds
Debut: 6/25/53, Played 22 years: 1953-1974, Detroit

Al Kaline delivered very early on his promise. In 1955, at the age of 20, he hit .340 and won a batting title, becoming the youngest player in major league history to do so. He was second in the MVP voting to Yogi Berra. Within a few years, Ted Williams was saying: "There's a hitter. In my book he's the greatest right-handed hitter in the league. There's no telling how far the kid could go." What was intended as a compliment became a burden.

The only problem was that he would never win another batting title, nor a home run or RBI title. But Kaline played consistently well and after his 22-year career ended in 1974, it could be said he was one of the greatest players the Detroit Tigers ever produced.

A pitcher who played from 1956 through 1963, Jim Brosnan had Kaline in mind when he said, "Fans want the player to be not what he inherently is but what they think he ought to be." He never hit 30 homers, never hit .340 again and only went above 100 RBI three times. He won the Gold Glove Award every year from 1957 to 1967, except 1960. It never seemed enough.

At 11 years old, Kaline flung a softball 173 feet and six inches to set a new elementary school record. When the judges did not believe it, he had to throw the ball again. Then he became a pitcher, as the best kids on sandlots often do. Kaline signed with the Tigers on the day he graduated high school for a $30,000 bonus-salary arrangement and got into the lineup a week later.

Shortly after, he threw out runners at second, third and home in successive innings. At Yankee Stadium, with the Tigers ahead by one run and the Yankees threatening with two outs and two on in the last of the ninth, Mantle hit a ball so far that the Yankees' broadcaster shouted, "The Yankees win 5-4." But Kaline raced to the old auxiliary scoreboard near the 407-foot marker. He leaped supported his body with his bare right hand, and made a backhanded catch to end the game.

"I was there because I was a fielder," Kaline said after his first few years. "That's what kept me in the league. The question was: did I have enough bat?" In the 1955 season, Kaline's .340 was better than Mantle by .34 points and Mays by .21 points. He followed up that campaign with 27 homers, 128 RBIs and a .314 average, the same year Mantle won the Triple Crown with 52 homers, 130 RBIs and a .353 average. Kaline would go on to play in 16 All-Star Games. So what exactly was the problem?

The problem was his winning a batting title at the age of 20 and the expectations that created. Kaline got his share of boos. After the 6-foot-1-inch, 150-pound kid won the title, the pitchers, in Kaline's words several years later, "Have been cuter with me ever since."

Speaking in 1964, he felt resentment at the expectations heaped on his shoulders. "The worst thing that happened to me in the big leagues was the start I had," he said. "This put pressure on me. Everybody said, `This guy's another Cobb, another Joe DiMaggio.' How much pressure can you take? What they didn't know is that I'm not that good a hitter. They kept saying I do everything with ease. But it isn't that way. I have to work as hard if not harder than anyone in the league. I'm in spring training a week early every year. I've worked with a heavy bat in the winter, swinging it against a big bag. I've squeezed rubber balls all winter long to strengthen my hands. I've lifted weights, done push-ups, but my hitting is all a matter of timing. I don't have the kind of strength that Mantle or Mays have, where they can be fooled on a pitch and still get a good piece of the ball...I'll tell you something else. I'm not in the same class as players like Mays, or Musial or Henry Aaron, either. Their records over the last five seasons are much better than mine."

It was refreshingly honest of Kaline to admit that he wasn't as great as others of his day. The consequence was that Kaline – who was receiving a $62,000 salary that ranked high in the league in the early sixties and plenty of outside income – was not having any fun with the game. He went into depressions because he could not give fans what they hoped he would. He ended up playing only 131 games in 1967 after slamming his hand into a bat rack and breaking it. In 1968 the A's Lew Krausse hit him with a pitch and broke his arm. Kaline returned as a first baseman six weeks later. The Tigers won 103 games and lost 59, beating out Baltimore by 12 games in the standings. By World Series time Kaline was ready to play the outfield.

The Cardinals took a three-games-to-one lead behind the pitching of Gibson, who allowed Detroit a combined 10 hits in 18 innings, while striking out 27. Kaline singled in the tying and go-ahead runs in game five. In game six he singled twice in a 10-run third inning. He led the Tigers with two homers, 8 RBIs and a .379 average. Only Mickey Lolich's three victories, the last in St. Louis on two days rest, kept Kaline from grabbing the Series MVP.

It was Kaline's 15th season and his first and last World Series. Kaline would play through the 1974 season, getting 3,007 hits and finishing with 399 homers. Bill James makes an excellent point about Kaline's career in his Historical Abstract. Both Kaline and Clemente were born in 1934, both were excellent right fielders, both had career highs of 29 homers. Many people start with the assumption that Clemente was better, a conclusion supported by his batting average, .317, which was much higher than Kaline's .297. But let's go further.

Kaline has a huge edge in homers (399-240), walks (1,277-621) and on-base percentage (.379-362). Kaline also slugged higher (.480-.475), scored more (1,622-1,416) and drove in more (1,583-1,305). Clemente may have been the more spectacular player, but was he more steady? He had the 1971 World Series, when he made his case for being an all-around player. But seven games are only seven games and Kaline, in a more quiet fashion, had a 1968 Series which was itself quite good. Of the greats who began in the fifties, Mays, Aaron, Mantle and Robinson all get the nod over Kaline. And one might add Banks, Mathews, McCovey, Killebrew and Clemente. Like Kaline's, their careers were broad but, unlike his, their peaks were higher. Kaline was good enough, long enough, to make a list of the greatest ever.

Best 5-Year Average
1959-1963

R	H	D	T	HR	RBI	AVG	OBP	SLG
89	160	26	4	23	88	.309	.381	.511

Best 10-Year Average
1955-1964

| 91 | 169 | 28 | 6 | 23 | 91 | .310 | .381 | .507 |

Best 15-Year Average
1955-1969

| 85 | 153 | 26 | 4 | 22 | 85 | .304 | .383 | .502 |

All-time Totals

G	2,834	RBI	1,583
AB	10,116	BB	1,277
R	1,622	K	1,020
H	3,007	AVG	.297
D	498	OBP	.379
T	75	SLG	.480
HR	399	SB	137
HR %	3.9	CS	65

34
YOGI BERRA
Catcher

Born: 5/12/25 St. Louis, MO
5 feet 8 inches, 194 pounds
Debut: 9/22/46, Played 19 years: 1946-1963, 1965 New York (AL)

"I really didn't say everything I said," Yogi said, when asked about all the malaprops. People smirk when they hear the name and the funny lines attributed to him. Keep laughing. But the last laugh was his and he was often laughing on the way to the bank. Yogi Berra cashed 10 World Series checks, more than any player in baseball history. As Casey Stengel said, "He was a peculiar man with amazing ability." He was the best catcher of his time – slightly better than Campanella because of his longevity – and the best catcher on the best team in baseball history.

Berra is ranked second to Bench for the same reason that Aaron is just behind Mays, and Robinson is just behind Schmidt. The differences between these pairs of players is so slight that people need to be reminded just how close they were. Yogi Berra joined the Yankees in 1946 and became their full-time catcher in 1948. In the 19 years he played for the Yankees, New York won 14 pennants and 10 World Series. That means he played on more winners than all the Yankee greats – Ruth, Gehrig, DiMaggio, Ford and Mantle. In fact, he played on more winners than anybody in baseball history.

Between 1949 and 1961 he gave the team, on average, 25 homers and 93 runs batted in while hitting for a mean average of .277. Those are good numbers for an outfielder. For a catcher they are not only good but unmatched in the history of baseball, with the exception of Johnny Bench's numbers. While part of Berra's legacy is to be celebrated for his goofy sayings and ungainly physique, this amusing image has tended to obscure just how good he was.

He was a notorious clutch hitter. He was a bad ball hitter who could turn high fast balls around and deposit them over the 344-foot sign in Yankee Stadium. Berra played healthy enough, long enough, to knock in 100 runs five times and more than 90 runs four other times. On a team that boasted Mantle and Ford and consistent strength up the middle, it was Berra who walked off with MVP awards in 1951, 1954 and 1955. When he retired, he managed and won pennants in each league, with the Yankees and the Mets.

His cumulative World Series time is equal to a good half season. He is first in World Series games with 75, first in at-bats, 259; first in hits, 71; first in doubles, 10; third in home runs, 12; second in runs, 41; second in RBIs, 39; third in walks, 32.

Berra not only played on the greatest "long dynasty" in history – the Yankees from 1947 through 1964 – but he played on the greatest short one, too: the `49-`53 Yankees that won five straight Series. During that five-year run, he hit 132 homers (26 per year), drove in 509 runs (102 per year), and batted .295. DiMaggio was gone after 1951 and Mantle didn't join them until that year. So Berra was their most important offensive player during that time.

The story of Berra's entry into baseball bears repeating. Branch Rickey, the Cardinals' GM in 1942, offered Berra $250 to sign with St. Louis, $250 less than he was offering Berra's friend Joe Garagiola. Berra turned down the money. Berra signed with the Yankees for the $500 bonus the next year. Soon after, the Yankees refused $50,000 from the Giants' GM Mel Ott, who had seen Berra play in the International League. Post script: Garagiola played for four teams in nine seasons and never had a regular job with any of them. Berra became a 15-time All-Star and was elected to the Hall of Fame in 1972 at about the same time Garagiola was a broadcaster and telling funny stories about Berra.

The Dodgers took advantage of Berra's early defensive liabilities, running wild on him in the 1947 World Series. Berra had to be replaced and share receiving duties with Sherm Lollar and Aaron Robinson. Then he was tutored by Bill Dickey. Ten years later, he would set a record, handling 950 chances without an error between July, 1957 and May, 1959.

Berra had his last good year in 1961, at the age of 36. That championship squad, which won 109 and lost 53, seems to have an equal claim with "Murderer's Row" of 1927 to being the greatest team ever. Berra, who played 87 of his 119 games that season in the outfield, was one of six Bronx Bombers to hit 20 homers as the team combined for 240.

In his second stint as a Yankee manager (he managed them to the pennant in 1964), Berra was fired by George Steinbrenner after the Yankees started out 6 and 10 early in 1985. Rickey Henderson, who went on to score 145 runs that season, was injured when Berra was fired. The team's only living great who played on all five of the '49-'53 championship teams, Berra vowed never to return to the Stadium while Steinbrenner was owner. He has kept his word, not attending a single Old Timer's game since. The Yankees are poorer for his absence.

On a team that has fielded one great catcher after another – starting with Bill Dickey in 1929 to Elston Howard in 1955 right through Thurman Munson in 1979 – Berra is the best of the lot.

Best 5-Year Average
1950-1954

R	H	D	T	HR	RBI	AVG	OBP	SLG
95	165	23	4	27	108	.299	.362	.502

Best 10-Year Average
1949-1958

84	148	22	3	26	102	.287	.351	.492

Best 15-Year Average
1947-1961

75	136	20	3	23	91	.286	.347	.485

Lifetime totals

G	2,120	RBI	1,430
AB	7,555	BB	704
R	1,175	K	414
H	2,150	AVG	.285
D	321	OBP	.350
T	49	SLG	.482
HR	358	SB	30
HR %	4.7	CS	26

35
ROY CAMPANELLA
Catcher

Born: 11/19/21 Philadelphia, PA, Died: 6/26/93 Woodland Hills, CA
5 feet 8 inches, 200 pounds
Debut: 4/20/48, Played 10 years: 1948-1957, Brooklyn

Roy Campanella was just 36 years old in 1958 when his car skidded on an icy road in Glen Cove, New York and slammed into a telephone pole. That accident, which left him a quadriplegic, meant that he only played 10 years in the major leagues. Because of the color line, he did not start his career until the age of 26. So if we are to assess Campanella's greatness, we must look at what he did achieve and use that as a barometer to infer what he would have achieved had he not started his career late and ended it early.

In his 10 years in the major leagues, Campanella averaged 24 homers and 86 RBIs. He hit .276 and slugged .500. Before his career-ending injury, he had consecutive poor seasons, hitting .219 and .242. He hit only 33 total homers in those two years – 1956 and 1957 – and his slugging average dropped to .394 and .384. In fact, Campanella was 33 when he had his last good season in 1955. He won his third MVP award that year, hitting 32 homers, knocking in 107 and hitting .318, while slugging .583.

I suggest that we can get a conservative estimate of what his totals might have been if we simply add to his existing totals the totals of five years: his first three years with the Dodgers and his last two. He hit 95 homers and knocked in 351 runs in those five seasons, which would bring his numbers to 337 homers and 1,207 RBI for a 15-year career.

The conservative estimate has the virtue of using numbers that reflect lower totals as he entered the league (where he would still be adjusting to major league play and/or playing less games and getting less at-bats) and reflecting a decline in performance as he got older. I see no reason for adding totals based on his best five years (1951-1955). His best five years were his fourth through eighth seasons. Even using this conservative estimate, Campanella is no worse than the third greatest catcher in baseball history and is very close to Bench and Berra.

Campanella's peak years are every bit as good as were Berra's or Bench's. In five of his first seven full seasons he slugged .498, .551, .590, .611 and .583. In his best year (his sixth in 1953) he hit 41 homers, drove in 142 to lead the league, hit .312, and slugged .611, the highest slugging mark for a catcher in baseball history. Since he was the catcher and steady run producer it can be argued he was the most valuable part of one of the greatest teams in baseball history.

Between 1949 and 1956, the Dodgers won five pennants and a World Series. For three of those years – '41, '53 and '55 – Campanella was voted MVP.

The Dodgers' record for those years were:

1949: 95-57	1953: 105-49
1950: 89-65	1954: 92-62
1951: 97-60	1955: 98-55
1952: 96-57	1956: 93-61

That's a cumulative record of 765-466 and an average season of 96 wins and 58 losses (.621). Those teams were anchored by a catcher with a rocket arm and a powerful bat.

Ebbets Field probably helped the right-handed hitter's totals. Of those 211 homers we know about, he hit 120 of them (57 percent) at home and 91 (43 percent) on the road. The year he started it was 343 feet in left field, 351 in left center, 393 in deep left center, 384 in center, 376 just right of the center field grandstand, 403 in deepest right center and 297 down the right field line. Campanella hit well at home and on the road.

As valuable as his hitting was, an equally important influence may have been his leadership on those teams. When the Dodgers were leaving the dugout for the ninth inning of the seventh game of the 1955 World Series, in quest of their first World Championship, several players were suddenly advising Johnny Podres how to pitch to the Yankees. "Let him alone," Campy yelled. "He's done fine for eight innings." Podres completed the 2-0 shutout.

Dodger fans often wondered what would have happened in the 1951 playoffs had Campanella been catching. Could he have coaxed Don Newcombe through that ninth inning? Campanella missed the last two games of that best-of-three playoff with a pulled hamstring muscle. "I begged Charlie Dressen to let me play," Campy said, not long before his death in June, 1993, "begged him; but he wouldn't let me play." Monte Irvin added, "If Campanella hadn't injured himself in Philadelphia, he might have settled Branca down after one high strike to Bobby Thompson." Campanella always said he got started as catcher because other players in high school didn't want to play the position and it was the surest way for him to make the team. "From the start, catching appealed to me as a way of being in the thick of the game continuously," he said after his career.

Born in Philadelphia in November, 1921, Campanella was the son of an Italian father and a black mother. After playing some high school ball, at 15 he joined the Bacharach Giants, a semi-pro black team. At 16 he was the first-string catcher for the Baltimore Elite Giants, one of the top clubs in the Negro Leagues. A three-time All-Star with the Elite Giants, he eventually made $3,000 a month as a full-fledged star. There he would end up catching as many as four games in a single day. "You didn't get hurt in the Negro Leagues," the workhorse explained. "You played no matter what happened to you because if you didn't play, you didn't get paid." He polished his talent by playing winter ball in Venezuela. He was in demand there: he could manage teams and speak Spanish.

Brooklyn GM Branch Rickey, who had already signed Jackie Robinson to a minor league contract, offered Campanella $185 a month to play for the Nashua New Hampshire team of the New England League. He took a cut in pay by leaving the Negro Leagues, but he thought he'd get to the majors sooner. Walter Alston was his manager and Don Newcombe was his roommate. By 1947 Campy was playing for Montreal, where Robinson had played the year before.

In 1948 Campanella had made the Dodgers and was earning $5,000 a year. Rickey then sent Campy to St. Paul of the American Association, not because he wasn't good enough for the Brooklyn club but because Rickey wanted him to break the color barrier there. Campy thus had another $1,500 tacked onto his salary.

At Leo Durocher's urging, Campanella was called back to the Dodgers after 35 games and stayed with the team.

Like most catchers, Campanella found it difficult to stay healthy for entire seasons. Only twice did he play more than 140 games and his per-season average was 122. Nerve damage resulted from injuries to his left hand and his hitting was declining as a result of it.

He knew that he could not play baseball forever and decided to find a business that would provide security for his wife and five children. He opened a liquor store in Harlem. It was while driving from the store to his home in Glen Cove, Long Island on Jan. 28, 1958, that he suffered the injury that fractured two of his vertebrae. An operation saved his life, but could not restore movement to his body below the shoulders. He underwent rehabilitation at the Rusk Institute of New York University-Bellevue Medical Center. When Dr. Howard Rusk told him how hard he would have to work and how discouraged he would get and asked Campanella if he was ready for it, Campanella responded, "When do we start?"

Further setbacks ensued. His first marriage deteriorated, his home had to be sold to pay debts but Campanella's determination shone through it all. As much fame as he had achieved as Brooklyn's backstop during the glory years, he won more praise and respect for his fighting spirit.

The largest crowd in baseball history did not attend the Brooklyn-New York seventh game of the fall classic. On May, 8, 1959, 93,103 paying fans, filled Los Angeles Coliseum for an exhibition game between the Dodgers and the Yankees. With the stadium lights dimmed, matches were lit in honor of Campanella, who received $75,000 from the gate receipts.

Ten years later Campanella became the second black player – Jackie Robinson was first – to be elected to the Baseball Hall of Fame. "This completes my baseball career," Campanella said. "All my disappointments are behind me. There is nothing more I could ask for in baseball."

The television movie "Lucky to be Alive," was released in 1974. Based on Campanella's life, it followed a book of that title.

Best 5-Year Average
1949-1953

R	H	D	T	HR	RBI	AVG	OBP	SLG
80	142	22	2	30	104	.299	.378	.542

10-Year Average
1948-1957

| 63 | 116 | 18 | 2 | 24 | 86 | .276 | .362 | .500 |

Lifetime Totals

G	1,215	RBI	856
AB	4,205	BB	533
R	627	K	501
H	1,161	AVG	.276
D	178	OBP	.352
T	18	SLG	.500
HR	242	SB	25
HR %	5.8		

36
TONY GWYNN
Right Field

Born: 5/9/60 Los Angeles, CA
5 feet 11 inches, 200 pounds
Debut: 7/19/82, Played 16 years: 1982-1997, San Diego

Tony Gwynn has won eight batting titles since 1984. Six of those times he hit above .350 and in 1993, a year he didn't win, he hit .358. As he gets older, he gets better.

He has raised his career average every year since 1993, when he was 33 years old. In `93 he hit .358; in `94, .394 – the highest since Williams' .406 – and slugged .568, his personal best. In 1995 he hit .368, in `96, .353. So you figure he would tail off a little at the age of 37. Not even close. He hit .372 and slugged .547 and knocked in a personal best 119 runs. He also reached peaks in doubles with 49 and homers with 17. Like Wade Boggs, Gwynn has met with Ted Williams and read his book *The Science of Hitting*. While he could never slug with Ted Williams, his life-time .340 mark is approaching Williams' .344.

He is a remarkable hitter, one of the very best average hitters of all-time. That being said, it is fatuous to maintain, as a *Sports Illustrated* cover story in the summer of 1997 did, that he is, "The best hitter since Ted Williams." They must have been in need of a story. If we put the word "average" between the words "best" and "hitter," then I have no problem with SI's headline.

But the optimal kind of hitting is not average hitting alone, but hitting for average and power. For 16 years, not counting three years he slugged above .500, Gwynn has not been a power hitter. Several hitters since Ted Williams combine average and power, and deserve to be put above Gwynn. Stan Musial is one. Stan "The Man" hit .331, but also hit 475 homers and slugged .559. Hitting homers and winning seven batting titles made Musial a lethal hitter. I would also put Gwynn behind Mays and Aaron as hitters, since both hit above .300 and crashed the long ball. Mays slugged .557 and Aaron slugged .555. In general, power hitting plus average hitting is preferable to just average hitting. In doing this little exercise I'm also making points for Gwynn supporters. Besides Musial, Mays and Aaron, how many others since Ted Williams have combined average and power and are better than Gwynn? Over the last five years he has averaged .368 and slugged .509. Those numbers are reminiscent of Cobb's, who hit .367 and slugged .512 for his career. He has become a better slugger, run producer and average hitter over his last five seasons. His on-base percentage is also rising, over .400 in each of his last five years.

1984 was the only time that the San Diego Padres made it to the World Series. To get there they had to beat the Cubs. "There's no tomorrow if we don't win tomorrow," said Gwynn, after being down two games to none. San Diego rallied to take three straight, with Gwynn hitting .368 in the Series. Detroit then ambushed San Diego in the World Series, four games to one.

But Gwynn's calling card will always be his batting titles. His eight titles rank second all-time as the following chart shows.

MOST BATTING TITLES

Ty Cobb.................12	Rogers Hornsby....7	Ted Williams.........6
Tony Gwynn 8	Stan Musial...........7	Wade Boggs..........5
Honus Wagner 8	Rod Carew 7	Dan Brouthers 5

Besides more batting titles, the next marker for Gwynn will be 3,000 hits.

Best 5-Year Average
1993-1997

R	H	D	T	HR	RBI	AVG	OBP	SLG
79	183	37	2	10	76	.368	.416	.508

Best 10-Year Average
1988-1997

R	H	D	T	HR	RBI	AVG	OBP	SLG
77	179	32	5	7	69	.342	.393	.462

Best 15-Year run
1983-1997

R	H	D	T	HR	RBI	AVG	OBP	SLG
80	182	30	5	7	64	.341	.393	.457

All time totals

G	2,095	RBI	973
AB	8,187	BB	707
R	1,237	K	390
H	2,780	AVG	.340
D	460	OBP	.392
T	84	SLG	.455
HR	107	SB	308
HR %	1.3	CS	121

37
WADE BOGGS
Third Base

Born: 6/15/58 Omaha, NE
6 feet 2 inches, 197 pounds
Debut: 4/10/82, Played 16 years: 1982-1997
1982-1992, Boston; 1993-1997, New York

Wade Boggs owns a career batting average of .331, the highest of all-time for a third baseman. His .422 on-base percentage is also highest among all active players. This means that for the 15-year period beginning in 1983, when Boggs became a full-time third baseman with the Boston Red Sox, he has been nothing less than the toughest out in all of base-ball.

"I played a lot of guys in my career and if you need a guy to get a sin-gle, and hit the ball hard, Wade Boggs is the best I've ever seen," says Rick Cerone, a catcher for 18 years. "He hit .366 (in 1988), led the league in hitting and only pulled about 10 pitches the entire year!" Says Braves third baseman Chipper Jones, "There's a saying among baseball players that there's a lot of money to be made from up the middle to the oppo-site side of the field. He's certainly a guy that's made a living from sec-ond base over."

Nonetheless, Boggs received only 353 at bats in 1997. In Wade Boggs' five years in New York, he batted .302, .342, .324, .311 and .292 and in the 1997 Divisional Playoffs still played behind, who's that again? Charlie Hayes, whose salient career markers are changing teams eight times in 10 years and a .265 average. The Yankees lost in five games to the Indians as Charlie Hayes had 15 at-bats to Wade Boggs' seven.

In a playoff Series played as tightly as that one was, with hitting quite scarce, you look for veterans to give a team the edge. Before the Series began, some people thought that Raines and Boggs might be the veterans to tilt the field in New York's favor.

The most frequent rationale given for sitting Boggs and playing Hayes were the latter's "range" at third base and his "pop." If range means he has a half step over Boggs to his left and right, let's weigh that against Boggs making four errors in 104 games to Hayes' 13 errors in 100 games. Further, Boggs has a .961 career fielding percentage to Hayes' .952. Boggs has two Gold Gloves; Hayes, none. Hayes never reminded anyone of Brooks Robinson or Graig Nettles at third.

Now to the issue of "pop." The statistic that measures pop is slugging average and both players slugged .397 in 1997. Hayes' career slugging average is .403 Boggs? .447. Not even close.

Several New York beat reporters, who made cracks about Boggs' age and ego when he was traded to Tampa didn't make a peep about Boggs getting just seven at bats in the Division Series while the Yankees mustered little offense against Cleveland's pitching.

After game one, in which Boggs had a hit to begin the winning rally, Hayes started the rest of the games. Typically level and sober in his decision making, Joe Torre looked like a man deciding on emotion – some suspect a dislike of Boggs – and then justifying that emotion with reasons. One caller to a talk radio station, citing Boggs' .350 batting average since the All-Star break, was moved to utter frustration: "I can't believe this (the matter of who plays third base) is still being evaluated on a game-by-game basis."

Neither could anyone else. Hayes' view of the situation? "The manager will play the best player," meaning him, Charlie Hayes.

One of the most unreported truths of the Series was how a journeyman third baseman, whose career has been mediocre at best, got one less at bat than Wade Boggs, Chad Curtis and Mike Stanley combined. Bob Costas, regarded by some as the Zeus of broadcast journalism, remained silent on the subject. And Bob Uecker, whose broadcasting skill is rapidly approaching his playing skill, said nothing. To make the case more perplexing, Curtis and Boggs were the Yankees' most valuable players after the All-Star break, while Hayes' average fell from above .290 to its season-ending .258.

In five years with the Yankees, Boggs averaged .313 – good enough for only seven at bats in a five-game playoff, when a second consecutive

World Championship was clearly there for the taking.

Boggs is now journeying to play on the field with the Tampa Bay Devil Rays. He needs 200 hits to make 3,000. When asked in 1997 about getting 3,000 hits while in a platoon situation, Boggs thundered, "I will get 3,000 hits, here or somewhere else." After being traded to Tampa Bay, he said, "the countdown is on."

Aside from being a great percentage hitter, consider the staggering matter of Boggs' on-base record. Boggs had four consecutive years with an on-base percentage above .450. How did he do it? In 1986 Boggs was the first since Stan Musial in 1953 to get 200 hits and 100 walks in the same season. In the midst of seven consecutive 100-run seasons, Boggs performed the following amazing, but little known, feat:

PLAYERS WITH 200 HITS AND 100 WALKS IN THE SAME SEASON
The Records of 10 Great Percentage Hitters

Lou Gehrig	7 times	Joe Jackson	0 times
Wade Boggs	4 times	Rod Carew	0 times
Babe Ruth	3 times	Rogers Hornsby	0 times
Ty Cobb	3 times	Tony Gwynn	0 times
Stan Musia	12 times	Eddie Collins	0 times
Napoleon Lajoie	2 times	Ed Delehanty	0 times
Pete Rose	0 times	Willie Keeler	0 times
Honus Wagner	0 times		

One player in history, Lou Gehrig, has more 200-hit / 100-walk seasons than Wade Boggs. Boggs always had a tremendous batting eye, which he demonstrated by working a walk against Atlanta's Steve Avery to knock in the deciding run in Game Four of the 1996 Series. Speaking of Boggs' batting eye, George Brett once cracked, "There'll be a woman president before Boggs gets called out on strikes!"

Besides winning five batting titles, Boggs had seven consecutive 200-hit seasons.

MOST 200-HIT SEASONS

Pete Rose	10 times	Steve Garvey	6 times
Ty Cobb	9 times	Stan Musial	6 times
Lou Gehrig	8 times	Sam Rice	6 times
Willie Keeler	8 times	Al Simmons	6 times
Paul Waner	8 times	George Sisler	6 times
Wade Boggs	7 times	Bill Terry	6 times
Charlie Gehringer	7 times	Kirby Puckett	5 times
Rogers Hornsby	7 times	Tony Gwynn	5 times

Boggs also won the on-base title six times and posted 40 doubles in seven consecutive years. His best year was 1987, when he hit .363, had a .467 OBP and slugged .588. Between 1982 and 1989 his worst average was .325.

How has he done it? His former teammate Mike Stanton remembers facing Boggs as a reliever in Texas. "I got him out one time, actually struck him out looking. The next time he hit it off the Green Monster at Fenway. It wasn't the same pitch but I was going the same direction with it. He's the type of guy that you really have to mix it up with. He's a smart hitter and usually knows his pitchers. That's one thing people don't understand." Official scorer Bill Shannon has seen enough of the thinking man's hitter. "When he first came from Boston," Shannon recalls, "he was hitting fly balls to left center that were doubles in Fenway but were getting caught here. He made the adjustment right away. Another things about Boggs is that pitchers knew him as a hitter who took the first strike. So he would set up pitchers – take the first one in one at-bat and swing away at the first one the next time."

"I don't know what my end-of-career numbers are going to be, because I don't know how long I'm going to play," says Boggs. "So I don't know if I'm going to get 3,000 hits, or 3,300 or 3,500. It's a little premature." Then he adds, "I'm not going to retire until I get 3,000." Getting 3,000 hits will probably take Boggs until the 1999 season. Five seasons after he retires he should end up in the Hall of Fame.

Best 5-year Average
1985-89

R	H	D	T	HR	RBI	AVG	OBP	SLG
117	211	45	5	10	70	.353	.452	.493

Best 10-year Average
1982-1991

| 102 | 195 | 40 | 4 | 8 | 64 | .341 | .434 | .468 |

Best 15-year Average
1982-1996

| 91 | 180 | 35 | 4 | 7 | 60 | .333 | .425 | .449 |

Lifetime Totals

G	2,227	RBI	933
AB	8,453	BB	1,328
R	1,422	K	668
H	2,800	AVG	.331
D	541	OBP	.422
T	56	SLG	.447
HR	109	SB	20
HR %	1.4	CS	33

38
ROD CAREW
First Base/Second Base

Born: 10/1/45 Gatun, Canal Zone
6 feet, 182 pounds
Debut: 4/11/67, Played 19 years 1967-1985
1967-1978, Minnesota; 1979-1985, California

Chicago White Sox' infielder Alan Bannister marveled at Rod Carew's hitting. "He is the only guy I know who can go 4-for-3," said Bannister. More than 10 years after his retirement, Carew is a standard bearer, a hitting machine who turned major league pitching into line drive batting practice for 19 years. Carew was as mechanically invariable a hitter as they come. He had a slump-defying stroke, waving the bat like a wand and using a short stroke to serve the ball over the shortstop, on a line to center or just about anywhere he wanted.

Gaylord Perry, the Hall of Fame junk man who loaded up the ball and smirked while hitters swung too hard, said he couldn't get Carew out. "Carew is the only player in baseball who consistently hits my grease," Perry said. "He sees the ball so well; I guess he can pick out the dry side."

Along with Tony Gwynn and Wade Boggs, Rod Carew is at the top of the list of the greatest percentage hitters of the last 50 years. A seven-time batting champion, Carew won four of his titles hitting .350 or better. In 1973, he hit .350 for Minnesota, then .364 in 1974 and .359 in 1975. He failed to

146

win the title in 1976, hitting "only" .331. He then hit an astounding .388 in 1977, still the third best average since Williams' .406 in 1941.

That was Carew's peak year: he led the league in runs (128), hits (239), triples (16), and on-base percentage (.452). His .570 slugging average, while not a league leading total, was his personal best. In all, he won seven batting titles in the 10-year period from 1969 through 1978. "When I'm hitting," he said, "the ball comes up to the plate like a basketball. You can see the stitches and the writing on the ball. When you're not hitting, you don't see anything." Adept at bunting, Carew would place handkerchiefs down third base and practice bunting on top of them. He stole 353 bases and tied Pete Reiser's major league record by stealing home seven times in 1969. While he did not have the lengthy run of 200-hit seasons that Pete Rose had, he is comparable to Gwynn and Boggs in his ability to find holes and spray line drives all over the diamond.

How many hitters have more batting titles than Rod Carew? Only three: Cobb, Wagner and Gwynn. Carew's seven titles tie Hornsby and Musial. He even influenced umpires with his style. "If he has two strikes on him and fouls off five pitches and then takes the sixth down the middle, I'm calling it a ball," said umpire Ron Luciano.

Carew twice led the league in triples and could hit the long ball, too. But when he won the batting title in 1972, he was the first to do so without hitting a homer since Zack Wheat did it in 1918. In the 1970s Carew hit .343 for the decade, 23 points ahead of decade runner-up Bill Madlock.

When he collected his 3,000th hit in 1985, he was the first infielder to achieve the honor since Eddie Collins. After the season he decided to call it quits and was elected to the Hall of Fame in 1991, his first year of eligibility.

Carew would surely have traded that honor to avoid a personal tragedy. His daughter Michelle died in 1996 after a long fight with leukemia. Rod Carew is starting to slip through the cracks. But what he accomplished should not be forgotten.

Best 5-Year Average
1973-77

R	H	D	T	HR	RBI	AVG	OBP	SLG
100	210	30	10	10	77	.358	.424	.490

Best 10-Year Average
1969-78

| 84 | 181 | 26 | 8 | 7 | 64 | .344 | .406 | .460 |

Best 15-Year Average
1969-1983

| 79 | 170 | 25 | 7 | 5 | 57 | .338 | .405 | .444 |

Lifetime totals

G	2,469	RBI	1,015
AB	9,315	BB	1,018
R	1,424	K	1,028
H	3,053	AVG	.328
D	445	OBP	.395
T	112	SLG	.429
HR	92	SB	353
HR %	1.0	CS	187

39
EDDIE COLLINS
Second Base

"Cocky"
Born: 5/2/1887 Millerton, NY, Died: 3/25/51 Boston, MA
5 feet 9 inches, 175 pounds
Debut: 9/17/06, Played 25 years: 1906-1930
1906-1914, Philadelphia (AL); 1915-1926, Chicago (AL);
1927-1930, Philadelphia (AL)

In the 25 years that Eddie Collins played for the Athletics and White Sox between 1906 and 1930, he was one of the greatest average hitters the game has ever seen. He finished with 3,315 hits and, despite the lengthy career, his average remained incredibly high at .333. While Collins' name would not be with those of Hornsby and Lajoie in a discussion of the greatest second baseman of all-time, only three players in the history of the game had more hits – Cobb, Speaker and Wagner - when he died on March 25, 1951.

Look next to the name "Eddie Collins" for most any year he played and he consistently got between 175 and 200 hits, stole 50 to 80 bases, and scored 90 to 125 runs, making him one of the most valuable offensive players of his age. He had a hard time winning batting titles because his best years with the A's and the White Sox coincided with the best of Cobb, who won 12 batting crowns in 13 years. Collins was also an excellent second baseman, leading the league in fielding eight times.

Collins played on six pennant winners and four World Series winners with Philadelphia and Chicago and ended his active career as a player-manager with the pale hose from 1924 through 1926.

Born in Millerton, New York, in 1887, Collins made the Columbia University varsity as a freshman, starred on the team and was elected captain for the senior team. But he didn't play his senior year for the Lions because he had already joined the Athletics in the summer of 1906. He tried to disguise his professional status to the college by playing under the name of "Eddie Sullivan." The school found out and he was declared ineligible for his senior year.

But the 20-year-old stayed at college until he got his degree. College grads in pro ball were as rare as triple plays, so Collins automatically got the label "smart player." Not that he needed college to get the label. Collins could build a run with a hit or walk and a steal. Once aboard, he was expert at stealing the other team's signs.

The Athletics tried him at several positions in 1907 but it was at second base where he raised eyebrows. His manager Connie Mack said, "He'll be the greatest in the game in a couple of seasons." Mack was clairvoyant: in 1909 Collins batted .346. Now Collins was a part of Philadelphia's famed $100,000 infield. The figure didn't represent the total of their salaries but the price Mack said he would refuse if he was offered. The infield included Stuffy McInnis at first, Jack Barry at short and Frank "Home Run" Baker at third.

Collins remained with the Athletics through the 1914 season, when Mack dismantled the team that had won fall classics in 1910, 1911, 1913 and had lost to the "Miracle Braves" in the 1914 Series. Mack was fed up with what the Federal League competition had done to his payroll and auctioned off his stars one-by-one. Collins hit .429 in the 1910 Series when the A's beat the Cubs in five. He hit .286 when the A's repeated against the Giants in 1911 and then .421 the following series. He is still tied with Lou Brock for the most stolen bases in World Series history – 14. The White Sox had to ante up $100,000 to buy Collins in 1914, then the highest price ever paid for a player. In 1917 he was back in the Series with the White Sox, hitting .409 as they beat the Giants in six games. The Sox were already loaded with "Black Sox," the players who would conspire with gamblers to throw the 1919 Series.

Before that infamous Series, the 1917 Series featured "Zim's Boner," the culmination of some very bad fielding by the Giants. The Sox were ahead three games to two and were hitting in the fourth inning of a scoreless game at the Polo Grounds. Collins was on third when Happy Felsch hit a grounder to Rube Benton, the Giants' pitcher. Rube wheeled and threw to third baseman Heinie Zimmerman, hanging Collins up between third and home. A rundown ensued between the catcher, Bill Rariden, and Zimmerman. But neither Benton nor Walter Holke, the first baseman, backed up the catcher in protecting the plate. Seeing an opening, Collins dashed home with Zimmerman behind him. The only one near the plate was umpire Bill Klem. No contest, Collins scored.

After the inning, Chicago had a 3-0 lead and held on for a 4-2 victory to win the Series. When Zimmerman was asked about the play later, he snapped, "Who the hell was I gonna throw the ball to – the umpire?" The White Sox have not won a World Series since.

Some say that Collins never hit it off with the White Sox, a team more comprised of individualists and cliques than Collins was accustomed to confronting. Collins hit just .226 in the 1919 World Series but was never implicated in the fix. He never forgave those of his mates who sold out and threw the Series. In turn, they had disliked him even before the thrown Series.

Buck Weaver thought Collins was soft. Collins was by far the highest paid player on the team and Weaver said Collins never got with the program and sharpened his spikes like the rest of them. He was also accused of bailing out at second base to avoid getting into collisions.

One thing is sure: In 1924, Collins, unlike eight of his former teammates, was still in baseball. That year he hit .349 and finished second in the MVP voting to Walter Johnson. In 1925 and 1926 Collins was player-manager for the White Sox and was replaced by Ray Schalk in November, 1926. A month later he was signed again by the Athletics, playing very sparingly in 1927 and 1928 and then assisting Connie Mack as a coach during the 1929 and 1930 championship seasons.

Later Collins became general manager and vice president of the Red Sox. Members of the Baseball Writers Association of America, in their fourth vote in 1939, elected Collins to the Hall of Fame. That June he took part in the centennial celebration at Cooperstown, N.Y.

As an executive with the Red Sox, Collins distinguished himself as he had as a player with the Athletics and White Sox. As general manager, Collins led the Red Sox to their first pennant in 28 years in 1946. Years before, at owner Tom Yawkey's insistence, he went on a scouting trip to the Pacific Coast. He was on the trip to look over a shortstop named Eddie Mayo. But he ignored Mayo and selected a second baseman instead. He also purchased a young outfielder who caught his fancy. That's how the Red Sox got Bobby Doerr and Ted Williams. If a more productive scouting trip has occurred in baseball history, no one has heard of it yet.

He continued to work as an executive with the Boston Red Sox until his death at the age of 63 in 1951. His legacy is that of a winner, a player who not only hit .333 and gathered 3,315 hits, but also a player who had a walk-to-strikeout ratio of about 5 to 1. His final on-base percentage was .424 and he ended with 744 steals, 5th best all-time. He could beat you in many ways.

Lifetime Totals

G. 2,826
AB. . . . 9,949
R. 1,821
H 3,315
D 438
T 187
HR. 47
HR % 47
RBI. . . 1,300
BB . . . 1,499
K 286
      (incomplete)
AVG 333
OBP 424
SLG 429
SB 744
CS 173
      (incomplete)

Best 5-Year Average
1909-1913

R	H	D	T	HR	RBI	AVG	OBP	SLG
108	188	23	12	2	69	.345	.421	.446

Best 10-Year Average
1909-1918

101	172	20	12	2	66	.329	.421	.424

Best 15-Year Average
1909-1923

98	177	21	11	2	67	.334	.420	.428

40
PAUL WANER
Right Field

"Big Poison"
Born: 4/16/03 Harrah, OK, Died: 8/29/65 Sarasota, FL
5 feet 8-and-a-half inches, 153 pounds
Debut: 4/13/56, Played 20 years: 1926-1945
1926-1940, Pittsburgh; 1941, Brooklyn; 1941-1942, Boston (NL);
1943-1944, Brooklyn; 1944-1945, New York (AL)

If you are looking for famous brother combinations in the history of baseball, look no further than Lloyd and Paul Waner. The former was known as "little poison" and the latter as "big poison." Since both of them were just under 5-feet-9 inches, the nicknames don't owe to exceptional size. Rather, the monikers tell us who was older and who had the biggest sting.

Paul Waner was 23 when he became a regular right fielder with the Pirates in 1926. Not long before, a scout for the New York Giants took a look at him and reported back to Giants' manager John McGraw, "That little punk don't even know how to put on a uniform." Then McGraw got a chance to see Waner with his own eyes. "That little punk don't know how to put on a uniform," McGraw repeated, "but he's removed three of my pitchers with line drives this week. I'm glad you didn't scout Christy Mathewson."

Younger brother Lloyd joined the Pirates the following season at the age of 21. The duo batted out 200 hits in the same season three times. Those years, 1927 through 1929, were dominated by the Yankees and the Athletics, high voltage powerhouses with players like Ruth, Gehrig, Foxx and Simmons. The batting skills of the Waners, though considerable, would have been better suited to the station-to-station game being played 10 years earlier, before Ruth changed it.

With the Waners leading the way, the Pirates of the late twenties showed that you could still win games with base hits. Under manager Donnie Bush, the Pirates, with the Waners and third baseman Pie Traynor, who hit .342 with 106 runs batted in, won 94 games and lost 60, earning the right to play the Yankees in the 1927 World Series. When the Yankees came into Pittsburgh for batting practice, the Waners sat in the stands and watched as Gehrig and Ruth hit booming shots into the seats. "Boy they're big," said Paul to his younger brother. When Ruth saw them he said, "Why they're just little kids; if I was that little I'd be afraid of getting hurt." Four games later the Pirates were swept, another pit stop for a Yankees' juggernaut that won 110 and lost 44.

It's only rumor that the lingering effects of the shell shock kept the Pittsburgh Pirates from seeing more World Series action until 1960, 33 years later. That year Pittsburgh beat New York four games to three.

Paul kept on hitting until the end of his career in 1945. The 155-pounder won his first batting title in 1927, hitting .380. He also led the league in hits, 237; triples, 18 and runs batted in, 131. He won batting crowns again in 1934 and 1936, hitting .362 and .373 in those seasons.

Paul left the Pirates after the 1940 season, playing with Brooklyn and then the Boston Braves in 1941. He went back to Brooklyn in 1942 but was traded to the Yankees during the season. He played just one game in 1945 without getting an at-bat. He was 42 and it was time to retire. His brother Lloyd retired that year, too, finishing his career with the Pirates.

Paul moved to Sarasota, Florida, where he operated a batting-practice range and indulged hobbies like golf, hunting and fishing. Despite playing 20 years, Waner was able to face the end. "An old ballplayer is just like an old piece of furniture," Waner once surmised. "Everyone's wondering just how much wear is left. When a young fellow comes along, somebody has to move over, and now it's me; I have no regrets." When he retired, he was second among all National Leaguers in hits with 3,152, trailing only Honus Wagner.

He helped organize the first National Baseball Players' golf tournament in 1934. He had won the championship in 1938, battling Babe Ruth in the final round before winning.

He was elected to the Baseball Hall of Fame in 1952 and didn't downplay the honor. "I have realized my life's ambition," he said. "Thank God I have lived to see the day."

His legacy in the game was still the line drive. Eight times in 11 years he reached 200 hits. He batted .300 14 times. Waner died on August 29, 1965, 20 years after his retirement. Only Stan Musial had been added to the list of National Leaguers ahead of him in hits. His 605 doubles are still 10th best all-time, as are his 191 triples. His lifetime average was .333. He and Lloyd, who was elected in 1967, are the only brother tandem in the Baseball Hall of Fame.

Best 5-year Average
1926-1930

R	H	D	T	HR	RBI	AVG	OBP	SLG
121	211	40	18	9	95	.359	.427	.537

Best 10-year Average
1926-1935

| 112 | 204 | 40 | 16 | 9 | 86 | .345 | .412 | .512 |

Best 15-year Average
1926-1940

| 100 | 191 | 37 | 12 | 7 | 78 | .340 | .404 | .490 |

All-time total

G	2,549	RBI	1,309
AB	9,459	BB	1,091
R	1,527	K	376
H	3,152	AVG	.333
D	605	OBP	.404
T	191	SLG	.473
HR	113	SB	104
HR %	1.2		

41
JOE MORGAN
Second Base

Born: 9/14/43 Bonham, TX
5 feet 7 inches, 160 pounds
Debut: 9/21/63, Played 22 years: 1963-1984
1963-1979, Cincinnati; 1980, Houston; 1981-1982, San Francisco;
1983, Philadelphia; 1984, Oakland

He could field, hit, hit for power, get on base with a walk, steal a base. By a country mile, Joe Morgan was the best second baseman of his time. Morgan's achievements are a litmus test for second basemen like Roberto Alomar, Chuck Knoblauch and others who have come after him. No one in quite a long time has been as multifaceted as Morgan was at second.

Starting with Houston in 1963, Morgan played 22 years. Eight times he scored 100 or more runs. He was the only second baseman to win back-to-back MVPs awards, accomplishing the feat in 1975 and 1976. He won five straight Gold Gloves between 1973 and 1977. When you look at Morgan's numbers, it's plain that 1972, his first year in Cincinnati after Houston, was his coming-out party. That was already his 10th year, so it took some time for him to define the kind of player he would become. The signs were there: he led the league in runs (122), on-base percentage (.419) and walks (115). He hit (.292), and hit for some power (16 homers, 73 RBIs). He also stole 58 bases.

He would score 100 runs in each of the next five seasons, leading the league in on-base percentage three more times and he even showed the league that a middle infielder could lead in slugging, which he did in 1976 (.576). His two MVP awards came in the years when the Big Red Machine won consecutive World Series.

Look at Morgan's career and you find that being let out of the Astrodome was like being let out of a cage. He reached personal bests in home runs, RBIs, walks, average, on-base average and slugging percentage his first year in Riverfront and the numbers got better thereafter. He was no slouch in Houston however. He was runner-up Rookie of the Year to Jim Lefebvre in 1965. From Nellie Fox, who played his last two seasons in Houston in 1964 and 1965, Morgan learned to keep his back arm up and Fox thought that Morgan's "chicken flap" motion with the left arm would help him.

Some will remember Morgan as the man who got the game-winning single in Game Seven of the 1975 Series. Morgan experienced the ebb and flow of fortune first hand in that Series, one of the best ever. In the eleventh inning of Game Six at Fenway, Morgan batted with a runner on first and hit a vicious liner toward the right field stands. Dwight "Dewey" Evans raced back and backhanded a ball that was headed for the seats. He spun and threw to first to compete a double play. In the bottom of the twelfth came Fisk's famous body English homer. Morgan's humpback single in the ninth inning of Game Seven won it for Cincinnati, 4-3.

Little Joe made five other post season appearances. The first was in 1972, when the Reds came from behind in the bottom of the ninth, scoring two against Pittsburgh to take the League Championship series three games to two. Morgan hit two homers in that series but hit just .125 in the World Series, as the A's, without Reggie Jackson, beat the favored Reds in seven games. In the 1973 league series the Reds lost in five games, with Morgan hitting just .100 (2 for 20). He then hit .273, .000, .000, .154 and .067 in the next five league series in 1975, '76, '79, '80 (with Houston) and `83 (with Philadelphia). It is surprising to find Morgan with only 13 hits in 96 at bats, for a .135 average in seven NLCS.

In the World Series he fared somewhat better. Aside from the .125 performance against Oakland, he hit .259 against Boston in 1975, .333 against New York in 1976 and .263 with two homers against Baltimore in 1983. His World Series average was .235 and his overall post-season average was .182.

Cincinnati was the most powerful team of the 1970s, but they ended up winning fewer World Championships than Oakland in that decade and the same number as New York. Mediocre pitching was the reason they didn't win more. They had the best eight-man lineup in baseball year in and year out but never the best pitching in baseball.

Morgan was a free agent after the 1979 season and was picked up by Houston, where he had his poorest season in more than a decade. He followed with one mediocre season and one very good in San Francisco before being traded to Philadelphia in December, 1982. After hitting 16 homers and stealing 18 bases with the pennant winning Philly club, he was a free agent, and picked up by Oakland in December, 1983.

1984 was his last season. The record was impressive. Besides hitting 268 homers, Morgan had 1,650 runs, 1,865 walks (third all-time) and 689 steals (ninth all-time). His lifetime on-base average was an impressive .395. The Hall of Fame came calling in 1990.

Morgan was a full-blown talent at second; he could win a game by setting up a run with a steal, a category in which he led the league three times. He could hit the long ball and could make the plays in the field.

In the 15 years since he has retired, no second baseman is up to the standards he set.

Best 5-year Average
1973-1977

R	H	D	T	HR	RBI	AVG	OBP	SLG
111	156	29	4	23	86	.303	.433	.508

Best 10-year Average
1969-1078

| 103 | 147 | 27 | 5 | 17 | 73 | .280 | .404 | .447 |

Best 15-year Average
1969-1983

| 90 | 133 | 24 | 4 | 15 | 64 | .272 | .397 | .432 |

Lifetime totals

G 2,649	RBI...... 1,133
AB 9,277	BB 1,985
R 1,650	K 1,015
H 2,517	AVG ...... .271
D......... 449	OBP ...... .395
T.......... 96	SLG ...... .427
HR....... 268	SB........ 689
HR % 2.9	CS........ 162

42
LOU BROCK
Left Field

Born: 6/18/39 El Dorado, AK
5 feet 11-and-a-half inches, 170 pounds
Debut: 9/10/61, Played 19 years: 1961-1979
1961-1964, Chicago (NL); 1964-1979, St. Louis

Babe Ruth for cash, Frank Robinson for Milt Pappas and Lou Brock for Ernie Broglio. Those are three of the worst deals in baseball history. The Chicago Cubs could have played out the 1960s and early seventies with Lou Brock, Billy Williams, Ernie Banks, Ron Santo and Ferguson Jenkins. But they traded the prospect Brock, who had shown very little power, speed or anything else besides an ability to strike out, in the four seasons he played with the Cubs until the trade in June, 1964.

Brock became a different player after the trade. He stole bases, hit for power and hit for average. In the 16 years he spent in St. Louis, he hit .300 eight times, led the league in steals eight times and averaged better than 90 runs per year. The Cardinals played three World Series in five years, beating the Yankees in 1964 and the Red Sox in 1967 before losing to the Tigers in 1968.

By the time it was over in 1979, Brock had stolen 938 stolen bases, 47 more than Ty Cobb, who had held the career record for more than 50 years. Today the annual NL stolen base leader receives the Lou Brock

Award. Only Rickey Henderson has surpassed Brock as a base stealer.

Brock was a different kind of leadoff man. For 11 straight years (1964-1974) he recorded more than 600 at bats. Four times during that stretch, he posted 200 hits and four other times gathered more than 190. He stole between 43 and 118 bases in those years and could even hit the occasional long ball. The only thing he couldn't do was draw a walk. In nine years he struck out more than 100 times during that run of years and ended up with more career strikeouts than Mickey Mantle. The result is a .344 on-base percentage and 1,730 strikeouts – both embarrassments for a lead-off man.

Brock's power was no surprise to people who saw him early on. While still with the Cubs, Brock hit a ball into the center field stands in the Polo Grounds (the fence was 483 feet from home), a feat that only Joe Adcock had accomplished. People watching the 1968 Series against Detroit will also recall a homer that Brock hit in the upper deck in center field at Tiger Stadium, where the fence is 440 feet away.

But the dividends for St. Louis went beyond distance. The Phillies led by six-and-a-half with 10 games to play in 1964, when Gene Mauch decided to pitch only Jim Bunning and Chris Short. The Phillies lost 10 in a row to hand the pennant to the Cardinals. During that stretch Brock hit .461 to help St. Louis win its first flag since 1946. That St. Louis team beat the Yankees in seven games with Brock hitting .300 and getting nine hits but not stealing a base and scoring only two runs. Ken Boyer hit two homers and drove in six runs and Bob Gibson was a work horse, going 2-1 and striking out 31 Yankees in the 27 innings he pitched.

Three years later, the Cardinals had to go seven to beat the Red Sox. Gibson was essentially untouchable, allowing the Sox only three runs and striking out 26 in the 27 innings he pitched. Roger Maris, who knocked in seven runs, was the hitting star, along with Brock. Brock showed the Red Sox the entire package, getting 12 hits, stealing seven bases, scoring eight runs and batting .414. Carl Yastrzemski finished his dream season, a Triple Crown year in which he got clutch hit after clutch hit, with three World Series homers.

In the 1968 World Series Brock stole seven more bases – he still holds the series record with 14 – and got 13 hits. Six of those hits were for extra bases. But the Cardinals squandered a three-games-to-one lead – and a 3-0 lead in Game Five – losing Game Five in Detroit and Game Six in St. Louis. With Mickey Lolich pitching on two days rest, the Tigers bested Bob Gibson in Game Seven. Lolich got his third victory of the series to take MVP honors.

Brock could not have imagined that his post-season play was over at the age of 29 and that he would play the last 11 years of his career without a division title or a pennant. His .391 World Series average is fourth all-time and his .655 slugging average is sixth. But many personal goals still lay ahead for Brock.

Before 1974, Brock's stolen base totals were usually between 50 and 70 per season. Maury Wills was winning the stolen base title six years running, between 1960 and 1965, helping the Dodgers to two World Championships. Brock stole 74 in 1966, the beginning of eight titles in nine years. But now he was in his 30s and he didn't figure to approach that mark again.

Wills' 104 in 1962 had broken Cobb's record of 96 set in 1915. Brock shattered that mark, stealing 118 in 1974, while being caught only 33 times, a .781 percentage. He accomplished the feat at 35 years of age.

Next came Cobb's 19th century record of 891 stolen bases (Sliding Billy Hamilton stole 912 between 1888 and 1901). Brock, now 38, broke Cobb's career mark in 1977, finishing the season with 900 thefts. He finished his career in 1979, with 938 steals. Brock achieved another milestone in his final season, recording his 3,000th hit. It was also Rickey Henderson's first year.

All that remained for the fleet left fielder was to be elected to the Baseball Hall of Fame, an honor that came to him in 1985.

Brock again came to prominence when Henderson broke his record in 1982, stealing 130. Brock supporters might hold on to his success rate of .781 during the 1974 season, slightly better than Henderson's .755 percentage on 130 steals in 172 attempts. Henderson broke the total of 938 in 1991 and now has 1,231.

Best 5-Year Average
1964-1968

R	H	D	T	HR	RBI	AVG	OBP	SLG
103	191	31	11	14	54	.293	.331	.443

Best 10-Year Average
1964-1973

| 105 | 194 | 31 | 10 | 11 | 54 | .299 | .348 | .444 |

Best 15-Year Average
1962-1976

| 97 | 180 | 29 | 9 | 9 | 52 | .296 | .345 | .418 |

All-time totals

G	2,616	RBI	900
AB	10,332	BB	761
R	1,610	K	1,730
H	3,023	AVG	.293
D	486	OBP	.344
T	141	SLG	.410
HR	149	SB	938
HR %	1.4	CS	307

43
PAUL MOLITOR
Designated Hitter/Third Base/Second Base

Born: 8/22/56 St. Paul, MN
6 feet, 185 pounds
Debut: 4/7/78, Played 20 years: 1978-1987
1978-1992, Milwaukee; 1993-1995, Toronto; 1996-1997, Minnesota

Paul Molitor's career represents a reversal of the norm. Most ballplayers are healthy in their early years and have to battle injuries later on. Molitor missed nearly 500 games in his first 10 seasons and then got healthy. He played his 20th season in 1997. In 12 of those seasons he hit above .300 and in four of them he had 200 hits.

After his 30th birthday, he hit for the following averages: 31: .353; 32: .312; 33: 315; 34: .285; 35: .325; 36: .320; 37: .332; 38: .341; 39: .270; 40: .341; 41: .305. During 1996, when he hit .341 at 40 years old, he got his 3,000th hit. He has 495 stolen bases and 576 doubles. It is a cinch that Molitor, whose "aging" totals truly amaze, will be elected to the Hall of Fame.

Some people don't understand the challenge to be consistent. When they think of statistics, they think only of the highest highs. But it's a mistake to think that way. Molitor has achieved excellence over time. After hitting .300 just three times before his 30th birthday, he has done it eight times since! His best year was 1987, when he hit .353 and slugged .566, scoring 114 runs.

Molitor has also played on two pennant winners. On the 1982 Brewers, a powerhouse club that belted 216 homers and scored 891 runs, Molitor led the team to a three-games-to-two advantage against the Cardinals. He set a World Series record with five hits in a 10-0 route in Game One. He paced the Milwaukee attack with 11 hits, but Milwaukee couldn't hold a 3-1 sixth inning lead in Game Seven and the Cardinals triumphed 6-3. Molitor, who had batted .316 and hit two homers in the League Champion Series, hit .355 in the World Series.

He waited 11 years to get back to the fall classic. In 1993, the Blue Jays beat the Phillies in six games and Molitor hit .500 to win the Series MVP. He scored 10 runs, while going 12 for 24, including two doubles, two triples, two homers and eight RBIs. His .418 World Series average is first all-time and his .636 slugging average is seventh.

Molitor could always hit right out of bed. The young Molitor had a bigger swing. Now he has a picture swing, a short, quick swipe that's conducive to a high average. The seven-time All-Star also has been successful on 79 percent of his steal attempts.

Something about Molitor's staggering continuity and no-nonsense consistency makes the real baseball enthusiasts want to check the box scores each morning and root for him every year. This writer thought he was a shoo-in for the Hall of Fame after the 1993 Series.

He absolutely sealed his entry into the Hall when he got his 3,000th hit three years later and is still going strong with 3,178 hits, more than 900 of which are for extra bases.

Best 5-Year Average
1990-1994

R	H	D	T	HR	RBI	AVG	OBP	SLG
99	179	32	7	15	79	.322	.392	.488

Best 10-Year Average
1985-1994

96	174	32	6	14	69	.317	.386	.472

Best 15-Year Average
1982-1996

91	165	30	6	13	66	.310	.378	.461

Lifetime Totals

G	2,557	RBI	1,238
Ab.	10,333	BB	1,049
R	1,707	K	1,203
H	3,178	AVG	.308
D	576	OBP	.371
T	109	SLG	.451
HR.	230	SB	495
HR %.	2.2	CS	129

44
EDDIE MURRAY
First Base/Designated Hitter

"Steady Eddie"
Born: 2/24/56 Los Angeles, CA
6 feet 2 inches, 200 pounds
Debut: 4/7/77, Played 21 years: 1977-1997
1977-1988, Baltimore; 1989-1991, Los Angeles;
1992-1993 New York (NL);
1994-1996, Cleveland; 1996, Baltimore; 1997, Anaheim

It is fitting that Eddie Murray should follow Paul Molitor in the pecking order of greats. Murray was a model of consistency. During Eddie Murrray's two years in New York (1992-1993), all one heard about was how he didn't talk to reporters in the clubhouse. On talk radio I heard so much of this psychobabble about Murray, the "cancer in the clubhouse," that I was sure the half-dozen hosts making comments had completely lost sight of what was important.

He was 36 and 37 years old during his New York tenure, yet I never heard from these radio "experts" that he played 310 of a possible 324 games those two years. Neither did I hear that he led the team in RBI both seasons!

Murray was born in early 1956 and had been knocking in 75 runs or more for 20 consecutive years, 1977-1996. In every one of those seasons he had gotten between 78 and 124 RBI, totaling 1,899 RBI – 95 per year for two decades! Six times he got 100-plus RBI and six other times 90-plus. The consistency extends beyond the RBI totals. After he was traded to Cleveland in December, 1993, John Franco said on the radio, "He had `100 RBI – why did he have to go?"

A self-taught switch hitter, Murray played 160 or more games six times and 150 or more 16 times. Playing for Baltimore in 1996, he became only the 15th member of 500-home run club and ended his career with 504. Seven times he hit above .300 and three times had a 400-plus on-base percentage. He got his 3,000th hit on June 30, 1995 and now has 3,253, 10th place on the all-time list. When he got his 500th homer, he became only the third player – Mays and Aaron are the others – to have 500 homers and 3,000 hits.

The part of his career that Murray might like forgotten is his World Series play. He hit .294 in 14 LCS games but his Series play in 1979, 1983 and 1995 was poor. He hit .154 in the seven-game loss to the Pirates' "We Are Family" bunch in the 1979 Series. In 1983 he played on the winning team as Baltimore dumped Philadelphia in five games and Murray hit two homers. In 1995 he hit only .105 in 19 at-bats against Atlanta, a Series in which the Indians' bats were quieted to .179 by Braves' pitching. His lifetime Series average was .169, though he did hit four homers in 65 at-bats.

Less known than his on-the-field achievements are some things he did off the diamond. His involvement in medical, educational and religious foundations earned him the Roberto Clemente Humanitarian Award in both 1984 and 1985.

For those who can get past their personal gripes with him, he will be recalled for consistent production. Cal Ripken said he learned how to approach the game by watching Eddie Murray, who for 12 years in Baltimore went about his business without a hitch. His 504 homers are second to Mantle among all switch-hitters who ever played. His 1,914 RBIs put him in seventh place all-time.

Best 5-Year Average
1981-1985

R	H	D	T	HR	RBI	AVG	OBP	SLG
93	163	29	2	29	106	.304	.393	.530

Best 15-Year Average
1977-1986

88	168	30	2	28	102	.298	.377	.505

Best 15-Year Average
1977-1991

85	167	28	2	27	98		.292	.371	.488

Lifetime totals

G	3,017	RBI	1,914
AB	11,329	BB	1,331
R	1,627	K	1,514
H	3,253	AVG	.287
D	560	OBP	.362
T	35	SLG	.476
HR	504	SB	109
HR %	4.4	CS	43

45
ROBIN YOUNT
Shortstop/Center Field

"Rockin' Robin"
Born: 9/16/55 Danville, IL
6 feet, 170 pounds
Debut: 4/5/74, Played 20 years: 1974-1993, Milwaukee

A man wins a slugging title, a Gold Glove and an MVP at shortstop, then moves to center field and wins an MVP there. He later reaches 1,600 runs, 1,400 RBI, 271 stolen bases and 3,000 hits, nearly one thousand of which are for extra bases. Sounds good enough to me.

Why, then, on the day Don Sutton is selected for the Hall of Fame, does the conversation on a major sports radio station drift from whether or not Sutton belongs (the verdict was that he didn't), to whether or not Yount belongs. Sutton won 324 games, which ties Nolan Ryan for 12th place all-time (and for seventh among those pitching exclusively in this century). He obviously belongs in the Hall of Fame. Ditto for Yount.

No question Robin Yount belongs in the Hall of Fame. An MVP at two of the most demanding fielding positions on the diamond, his 3,142 hits rank him 15th among all those who ever played. Don't forget he played nearly half his games as a middle-infielder, where less is expected of a player in the way of offense, and throw in that he hit 251 homers and drove in 100 runs three times.

As recounted in *Total Baseball*, Yount was a high school All-American in Woodland Hills, California, and was the third pick overall in the 1973 draft (behind David Clyde and John Stearns and ahead of Dave Winfield). He went to spring training with the Brewers in 1974 and became their starting shortstop at age 18. In the spring of 1978, he left the Brewers to become a pro golfer, then returned a few months later to stay. He was still with the Brewers in 1993, the year he retired.

Over his career, Rockin' Robin had two stellar seasons and about four other awfully good ones. In 1982 he was all-everything on the pennant winning Milwaukee team. He got 210 hits, 46 doubles, 12 triples and 29 homers, batted .331, slugged .578 and had an on-base average of .384. He led the league in three categories, including slugging. He topped it off by getting 12 hits, knocking in six and hitting .414 to lead the Brewers in the Series. With Paul Moiltor, who played second, third and later DH in Milwaukee from 1978 though 1992, the Brewers had a formidable one-two punch for a decade-and-a-half.

His other MVP year was 1989, when he hit .318, pounded 21 homers and knocked in 103 runs. He also slugged .511. Yount was 34 then, and it was his last good year.

On Sept. 9, 1992, at County Stadium, he became the 17th player to get 3,000 hits. He and Honus Wagner are the only shortstops to get 3,000-plus hits.

He should be in the Hall of Fame any time now. The suggestion that he shouldn't be is absolutely absurd and owes to a complete ignorance of his statistics and their historical ranking.

Best 5-Yr Average
1980-1984

R	H	D	T	HR	RBI	AVG	OBP	SLG
102	171	36	9	19	82	.303	.358	.498

Best 10-Year Average
1980-1989

96	173	34	8	17	82	.305	.366	.485

Best 15-Year Average
1978-1992

89	164	31	7	15	78	.292	.353	.477

Lifetime totals

G	2,856	RBI	1,406
AB	11,008	BB	966
R	1,632	K	1,350
H	3,142	AVG	.285
D	583	OBP	.346
T	126	SLG	.430
HR	251	SB	271
HR %	2.3	CS	105

46
WILLIE STARGELL
Left Field/First Base

"Pops"
Born: 3/6/40 Earlsboro, OK
6 feet 2 1/2 inches, 225 pounds
Debut: 9/16/62, Played 21 years: 1962-1982, Pittsburgh

Willie Stargell played nearly 60 percent of his major league games in the outfield, mostly in left field. He is more remembered, however, as the burly first baseman "Pops" – likely far beyond the 225 pounds listed in the media guide – who led the Pittsburgh Pirates to the 1979 World Championship. As the slugger and avuncular leader of that "We Are Family" club, he won both the World Series and NLCS MVP awards.

He was also awarded co-MVP for the regular season with Keith Hernandez, a honor that was not deserved. Hernandez hit .344 to Stargell's .282, knocked in 105 runs to Stargell's 82 and Hernandez led the league in runs (116), doubles (48), average (.344) and on-base percentage, (.421). He also won the Gold Glove at first base. But somehow ignoring all that, the baseball writers declared them equal.

Despite that gift, Stargell had a very good career. He slugged .500, 13 times (twice over .600) and finished with a .529 slugging percentage, a very good one and especially good for a player whose 1,936 strikeouts are second only to Reggie Jackson's 2,597.

His best season was in 1973. He had 43 doubles, 44 homers, 119 RBIs and a .646 slugging average, leading the league in those four categories. Six times he hit 30 or more homers and twice he hit 40-plus. His two-to-one ratio of strike outs to walks explains his mediocre on-base percentage.

Stargell fought injuries his entire career and was able to get more than 500 at-bats only five times in 21 years. Over his last eight seasons, from 1975 through 1982, he never reached 500 at-bats. He injured his left thigh muscle twice and broke a rib. In 1976, he worried terribly over his wife Delores, who developed a blood clot in her brain in May. His concern over her health plus his own injuries caused him to miss 45 games that year. In 1980 he injured his left knee and found out it was arthritic, a condition he probably had played with for several years.

One of those years might have been 1979. Stargell had played on the 1971 Pirates, a team that beat the Orioles in the Series. The 1971 Series was Clemente's show and Stargell hit only .208 with no homers and one RBI. 1979 was magical in Pittsburgh, but "Pops" had played only 126 regular season games and logged only 424 at-bats. But then he turned it on.

The Pirates swept the Reds and in the three games he hit two homers and knocked in six, hitting .455. The Orioles went up three games to one in the Series and had Flanagan, Palmer and McGregor to close out the job. But they were outscored 15-2 over the last three games. Stargell hit three homers and knocked in eight in the Series, including a two-run homer against McGregor in the sixth inning of Game Seven to put Pittsburgh ahead for good. Kent Tekulve saved three games for Pittsburgh and Stargell's 12 hits – including a record seven for extra bases – took Series MVP honors.

The victory was a culmination of a year in which "Pops" gave out gold stars for hustle and smart plays. Big salaried players put out a little more to get a "Stargell Star," and the contagious family atmosphere had the country singing "We are Family" and rallying behind the Pirates.

Stargell's total of 475 homers was attained without any home park benefit. Neither Forbes Field nor Three Rivers Stadium offered him any advantages for hitting the long ball. Many Stargell blasts were of the tape measure variety. Stargell hit seven of the 16 balls blasted out of Forbes Field (Ruth did it first, on May 25, 1935). He also is the only player to ever hit a ball out of Dodger Stadium. He did that twice.

His infectious personality tended to rub off on people, too. "When they start the game," Stargell would say, "they don't yell 'work ball.' They say, "play ball.'" Joe Morgan once told him, "Some people are only super stars statistically, but you are a .400 hitter as a person." He was also the master of the quip. When his teammate Dave Parker called Stargell his idol, Stargell said, "That's pretty good, considering that Dave's previous idol was himself."

He was inducted into the Hall of Fame in 1988, his first year of eligibility.

Best 5-Year Average
1969-1973

R	H	D	T	HR	RBI	AVG	OBP	SLG
89	147	30	3	37	107	.292	.375	.583

Best 10-Year Average
1969-1978

75	130	27	3	29	92	.290	.374	.556

Best 15-Year Average
1965-1979

71	130	25	3	29	90	.285	.364	.540

Lifetime Totals

G	2,360	RBI	1,540
AB	7,927	BB	937
R	1,195	K	1,936
H	2,232	AVG	.282
D	423	OBP	.363
T	55	SLG	.529
HR	475	SB	17
HR %	6.0	CS	16

47
DUKE SNIDER
Center Field

"The Duke" "The Silver Fox"
Born: 9/19/26 Los Angeles, CA
6 feet, 190 pounds
Debut: 4/17/47, Played 18 years: 1947-1964
1947-1957, Brooklyn; 1958-1962, Los Angeles (NL);
1963, New York (NL); 1964, San Francisco

The Duke of Flatbush achieved a mark between 1953 and 1957 than only Babe Ruth and Ralph Kiner accomplished before him: Snider hit 40 or more homers five years in succession (Ruth did it seven consecutive years, from 1926-1932). Snider was constantly compared to two other New York center fielders in the 1950s. The threesome, Mantle, Mays and Snider, were baseball's gift to New York City, three center fielders who between them would hit 1,603 homeruns.

He was a good outfielder with a strong arm, leading Ralph Kiner to say, "I'd say Duke covers more ground, wastes less motion, and is more consistent than anyone since Joe DiMaggio." "Willie, Mickey and the Duke," (the name of Terry Cashman's popular song) named the trio that played together in New York. Snider was not as good as Mays or Mantle but for a four-year period he was probably better than either of then.

In 1954, the threesome averaged 36 homers, 114 RBI and a .327 average. In '55 they averaged 43 homers, 121 RBI and a .313 average. By 1956 the average read: 40 homers, 105 RBI and a .314 average. In 1957 the tally was 36 homers, 94 RBI and a .324 average. During the four-year period, Snider led them with 165 homers and 449 RBI. Mantle led in average with .330. Snider also ended up leading everyone in homers and RBI for the decade of the 1950s.

Reams of paper have been spent on the "Golden Years" of New York baseball, from 1947 through 1958. In 11 of those 12 seasons, at least one New York team played in the World Series. In seven of those years, two New York teams played against each other in the Series! The Dodgers hit their high note from 1952 through 1956, winning four pennants and their first World Championship.

When the Dodgers were at their best, Snider was at his best. There's no denying it. Between 1952 and 1956 the Dodgers won 484 and lost 284, an average of 97 wins a year and a winning percentage of .630. Snider won two slugging titles, a homer title, an RBI title and he led the league in runs over those five seasons. During his best five years, he averaged 41 homers, 117 walks, 116 runs, 117 RBIs and a .311 average, while slugging .618. His best year was 1955, when he clubbed 42 homers, knocked in 136 runs and hit .309, with a slugging average of .628. He would go on to slug .500 or better 10 times.

Snider was probably the Dodgers' best World Series performer, too. He played in each of their six Series appearances between 1949 and 1959 and was at his peak in 1952 through 1956. In those four fall classics he hit 11 homers, batted .324 (33 for 102) and collected 24 RBI. He hit four homers in both the 1953 and 1955 Series; his 11 World Series homers are still fourth best all-time.

But when the Dodgers went west for the 1958 season, Snider's power numbers went south. He had hit 40 homers his last year in Brooklyn but only 15 his first year in Los Angeles. In Los Angeles Memorial Coliseum, he never learned to hit to left field, where the "Bamboo Curtain," a 42-foot high mesh screen, stretched from the foul line on out, 140 feet toward center. The fence was only 250 feet from home.

A left-handed pull hitter like Snider had to contend with a center field fence at 425. The right field fence was 301 down the line but cut dramatically back to 440 in right center. In this stadium where track events were held, a total of 193 homers were hit in the first year: 8 to right, 2 to center and, it's true, 183 to left.

Snider had thrived at Ebbets Field, where center field was 384 feet in 1948 (moved to 395 in 1954); deepest right-center fluctuated from 403 to 405 and right field was 297. During his run of 40-homer seasons Snider hit 90 (43 percent) on the road and 117 (57 percent) at home.

It wasn't just fence distances that hurt him in Los Angeles; his productivity dwindled due to back trouble. Over Snider's last seven seasons in Los Angeles, New York and San Francisco, his highest at-bat total was 354. He dealt with knee problems and a broken elbow, too.

He hit his 400th homer with the New York Mets in 1963. "It's another record for Duke!" shouted the Mets' colorful broadcaster Lindsey Nelson. "He's the first person ever to hit his 400th homer on color television." The Duke retired after the next season. He finished with 407 homers, a .295 average and a .540 slugging average.

The "Silver Fox" made it to the Hall of Fame in 1980 – his election, inexplicably, delayed a full decade after he was first eligible. He offered a perspective on his own time and the new time in baseball. "My high salary for one season was $46,000 and a Cadillac. If I were to get paid a million, I would come in at six in the morning, sweep the stands, wash the uniforms, clean out the offices, manage the team and play the game."

The major difference between Mays, Mantle and Snider was that Mays and Mantle had 15-year runs of excellence. Snider's numbers were already declining between his 10th and 15th seasons.

Best 5-year Average
1953-1957

R	H	D	T	HR	RBI	AVG	OBP	SLG
116	172	34	6	41	117	.311	.407	.618

Best 10-year Average
1950-1959

97	161	27	6	33	103	.308	.390	.569

Best 15-year Average
1949-1963

81	135	23	5	27	86	.300	.384	.550

Lifetime totals

G	2,143	RBI	1,333
AB	7,161	BB	971
R	1,259	K	1,237
H	2,116	AVG	.295
D	358	OBP	.381
T	85	SLG	.540
HR	407	SB	99
HR%	5.7		

48
CARL YASTRZEMSKI
Left Field/First Base

"Yaz"
Born: 8/22/39 Southampton, NY
5 feet 11 inches, 182 pounds
Debut: 4/11/61, Played 23 years: 1961-1983, Boston

These are the numbers for Dave Winfield and Carl Yastrzemski:

	AB	HR	RBI	AVG	OBP	SLG
Winfield	11,003	465	1,833	.283	.355	.475
Yastrzemski	11,988	452	1,844	.285	.382	.462

Given "Yaz'" advantage of having nearly 1,000 more at-bats, Winfield was a better home run hitter. His slugging average is higher. Despite those advantages, Yaz led his league in 23 offensive categories during his career; Winfield, only one. Yaz led the AL in on-base percentage (OBP) five times, slugging average three times, batting average three times, runs three times, doubles three times, walks twice, hits twice and homers and RBI once each.

In a word, his peaks were higher than Winfield's. While playing in an era when the National League was winning the All Star games and had most of the best players, and while Mays, Aaron and Robinson were the game's best, American Leaguer Yaz was still one of the best players of his era, as shown by the number of times he led the league in various categories.

Continuing the Winfield-Yaz comparison, Yaz hit 40 or more homers three times, while Winfield never even hit 35 in a single year. Yaz had 100 walks in a season six times; Winfield, not once. Given two players like Winfield and Yastrzemski, whose totals are about even, the tie-breaker is Yaz' peak years.

The son of a Bridgehampton, Long Island potato farmer, Yaz played on a semi-pro team, the Lake Ronkonkoma Cardinals. He batted third and played short, his father, Carl Sr., played third and batted cleanup. They last played together in 1958, with junior hitting .375 and pop batting .410.

Offers from 14 teams rolled in while Yaz enrolled at Notre Dame. Carl senior coaxed the bidding up to an offer of $125,000 from Cincinnati, but his son took slightly less from the Red Sox in 1959 so that he could play closer to home. When Ted Williams first saw Yaz with bat cocked high, he said what Lefty O'Doul had once said to him: "Don't you ever let them change your batting stance."

Williams retired in 1960 and Yaz had to deal with all the pressure of being "the next Williams." He played first base in 1961 and took over in left field the following year. He won the first of three batting titles in 1963, hitting .321. Twenty years later he would still be with the Sox.

His best season was 1967, his Triple Crown year when he lead the league in seven categories: runs, 112; hits, 189; home runs, 44 (tie with Killebrew); RBI, 121; average, .326; on-base percentage, 421 and slugging average, .622. That was the first and last time he slugged .600. 1967 was an utterly complete year for Yaz, a year in which he drove in important run after important run down the stretch. He hit .523 over the last two weeks of the season, including 10 hits in his last 13 at bats.

It was the season of "The Impossible Dream," and Boston clinched the pennant on Oct. 1, beating Minnesota 5-3 as Jim Lonborg bested Dean Chance. Yaz went 4-for-4 in the game. Detroit could have tied for the lead with a sweep of California, but split a doubleheader. The top four teams combined for a 6-12 record over the last week and Boston won with 92 wins and a .568 percentage, the lowest in league history. Yaz didn't accept the Triple Crown trophy because his name was misspelled on it. Collector extraordinaire Barry Halper now owns the trophy.

Yaz waved a magic wand in the Series, too, hitting .400 against the Cardinals with three homers. Boston fell behind three games to one and rallied to even the Series. But they still had to get by Bob Gibson in Game Seven. Playing in Boston, Gibson hit a homer and bested Longborg 7-2, notching his third victory while striking out 10 Sox.

Yaz would have two more sniffs of post-season play. In 1975 the Red Sox won 95 games and played the Reds in the Series. Yaz hit .310 in the

Series, but he hit no homers and had just four RBI. Bill Lee, staked to a 3-0 lead in Game Seven, could not hold it and the Sox lost 4-3. It was one of the greatest World Series ever played, but Yaz, eight years removed from 1967, was no longer the Sox' best player.

In 1978, the Yankees and Red Sox each finished the first 162 games with 99-63 records. Both teams could play the "what-if" game. Boston had squandered a 14-and-a-half game lead in mid-July. New York overtook them in September and led until the last day of the season when they lost and Boston won. The two would play one game to determine the Eastern Division championship.

On Oct. 2, in a game that mirrored the ebb and flow of the entire season, Yaz hit a homer and the Red Sox jumped out to a 2-0 lead. But Bucky Dent's three-run homer, barely reaching the screen above the Green Monster as Yaz kneeled in agony below, gave New York a 3-2 lead. They held on to win 5-4, as Yaz popped up off Rich Gossage to end the game. Yaz had contributed something, just as he had always done in Boston. But for his 23 years it was not enough.

One of the gaping holes in Yaz' record is his slugging .500 only five times in his 23-year career and only once in the last 14 years, from the ages of 32 through 44! This lack of slugging shows in his homer totals, too. He didn't hit 23 homers in a season after he turned 31, a drought that lasted the last 13 years of his career.

But Yaz played long enough and well enough to reach some important milestones. He got his 3,000th hit versus New York on a grounder past Willie Randolph on Sept. 12, 1979, becoming the first AL player to reach 3,000 hits and 400 homers.

He retired after the 1983 season and went into the Hall of Fame with Johnny Bench in 1989.

Best 5-year Average
1966-1970

R	H	D	T	HR	RBI	AVG	OBP	SLG
101	171	30	2	33	98	.297	.405	.526

Best 10-year Average
1961-1970

92	170	34	4	24	87	.297	.390	.495

Best 15-year Average
1963-1977

87	159	29	3	22	85	.291	.394	.477

Lifetime totals

G	3,308	RBI	1,844
AB	11,988	BB	1,845
R	1,816	K	1,393
H	3,416	AVG	.285
D	646	OBP	.382
T	59	SLG	.462
HR	452	SB	168
HR %	3.8%	CS	116

49
DAVE WINFIELD
Right Field

Born: 10/3/51 St. Paul, MN
6 feet 6 inches, 220 pounds
Dubut: 6/19/73, Played 22 years: 1973-1995 (missed 1989)
1973-1980, San Diego; 1981-1990, New York; 1990-1991, California;
1992, Toronto; 1993-1994, Minnesota; 1995 Cleveland

Was Dave Winfield a great player, or did he just play a long time and put up great numbers? In 22 years, from 1973 through 1995 (he missed all of 1989 with a herniated disk), he led the league in only one category - driving in runs in 1979. That was one of only three years that the 6-foot-6-inch, 220-pound right fielder hit 30 homers. He was a very good player, but rarely did his performances dominate the league.

Three important things can be said on Winfield's behalf. First and foremost, there is no doubt Winfield's greatest attribute was his ability to knock in runs. In the 15 years he played between 1977 and 1992, he batted in 1,478 runs. That rounds off to 99 per year. He had 100-plus RBI eight times and 90-plus three more times. At his best, he hit full arms extended, sizzling liners, like the one he hit in the "Pine Tar Game" in July, 1983. George Brett watched that homer never get more than 15 feet off the ground and sail over the 430-foot marker in left-center field. "It's the hardest ball I've ever seen hit," said Brett.

The second salient Winfield attribute is his all-around play. He was a very good fielder, winning seven Gold Gloves, though nothing about his total chances or chances per game in the outfield supports the conclusion that he was a great fielder. He stole bases (223) and was rarely thrown out despite his very aggressive ways on the paths.

Third, Winfield showed great resiliency and determination by putting up impressive totals between the ages of 38 and 41. Recall that he missed all of 1989 with a back operation and had he not returned at 38 years old to start the 1990 season, he would have had only 2,421 hits, 357 homers and 1,438 RBI – good totals, but not Hall of Fame markers. However he earned respect from this corner with four great comeback seasons.

He joined the Angels in 1990, leaving a sour relationship with the Yankee owner behind. Steinbrenner bristled when he found he owed $7 million more in cost-of-living expenses than the $23 million he signed Winfield for in 1981. He hired a convicted felon, Howard Spira, to deliver damaging information about Winfield. It blew up in Steinbrenner's face: he was banished from baseball by Commissioner Fay Vincent. "I felt better since I left," Winfield said after departing New York. "I don't have a grey hair anymore."

Over the next four seasons – with California, Toronto and Minnesota – he hit 96 homers and knocked in 348 runs. He got his 3,000th hit in 1993 and finished with 3,110. He got his 400th homer in 1991 and finished with 465. Now he's a shoo-in for the Hall.

There is a downside. After Yankee owner George Steinbrenner expressed regret over trading Reggie Jackson (whom he wouldn't pay $1 million for the 1982 season after shelling out $23 million over 10 years for Winfield the season before), he said he had gotten rid of "Mr. October" and kept "Mr. May." Of all the idiotic things that Steinbrenner has said and done, he was on the mark this time. Winfield was big enough and talented enough to carry a team on his shoulders. But he rarely did.

In 101 post-season at-bats, he had 21 hits, two homers, nine RBI, and an average of .208. That's the performance of a platooned middle-infielder, not a franchise player. He was 2-for-13 in the 1981 League Championship Series and then played the World Series from hell, getting one hit (a meaningless single in a losing effort in Game Five) in 22 at-bats. Standing on first, he called time and asked the umpires to take the ball out of play – a truly bizarre occurrence.

The Yankees took a two-games-to-none lead in the Series against the Dodgers. Reggie Jackson was back from an injury for game three. Obviously you can't sit Reggie Jackson in the World Series. Given the choice between sitting Jerry Mumphrey – his regular and best defensive center fielder and a switch-hitting .300 hitter – or Winfield, who was already 0-for-8, manager Bob Lemon with some coaxing from Steinbrenner, sat Mumphrey. The decision cost him. Against Valenzuela's screwball, curving away from right-handed hitters, Winfield was useless. Then in Game Four Lemon played Bobby Brown in center field. An inconsistent player, Brown botched a fly ball that opened the flood gates and erased a Yankee lead. The Yankees lost that game and the Series.

In some people's mind, Winfield's 1-for-22 performance in the 1981 Series was erased by his performance in the 1992 Series between Toronto and Atlanta. In the top of the twelfth inning of Game Seven in Atlanta, Winfield hit a two-hop double off Charlie Leibrandt past third. The ball rolled into the left field corner, scored two, and Toronto held on for a 4-3 win to take the Series. Winfield, going 5-for-22, hit .227 in the Series.

His career was about accumulating impressive numbers, but it cannot be said that he was ever the best player in the game. In 22 years he slugged .500 or better only five times and hit .300 or better only four times. He hit nearly twice as many homers as Roberto Clemente but his slugging average (.475) is the same and this hardly qualifies him as a great slugger. Clemente hit .317 to Winfield's .283. Winfield's on-base percentage of .355 is low. In only two of 22 years did he walk more than strike out.

His most impressive number, as I've pointed out, is the 15-year RBI average. It shows consistency in run production. Winfield was a 12-time All-Star who will make, and deserves to make, the Hall of Fame.

Best 5-Year Average
1979-1983

R	H	D	T	HR	RBI	AVG	OBP	SLG
84	154	25	7	27	99	.288	.362	.512

Best 10-Year Average
1979-1988

90	163	29	5	26	102	.291	.364	.499

Best 15-Year Average
1977-1992 (missed all of '89)

89	162	28	5	25	99	.290	.361	.493

Lifetime totals

G	2,973	RBI	1,833
AB	11,003	BB	1,216
R	1,669	K	1,686
H	3,110	AVG	.283
D	540	OBP	.355
T	88	SLG	.475
HR	465	SB	223
HR %	4.2	CS	96

50
FRANK THOMAS
First Base

"The Big Hurt"
Born: 5/27/68 Columbus, GA
6 feet 5 inches, 240 pounds
Debut: 8/2/90, Played 8 years: 1990-97, Chicago (AL)

That old fun quiz question – "name the guys at each of the nine positions who have won back-to-back MVPs" – is showing its age. It used to be that the question showed real symmetry: just one player had won back-to-back MVPS at each position. Jimmie Foxx was the only first baseman, which smart readers already knew. He's not alone anymore. "The Beast" (or "Double-XX" if you prefer the less imaginative moniker) now has company. In 1993 and 1994 Frank Thomas earned back-to-back MVPs, too.

We're talking Frank Thomas as in the 6-foot-5-inch, 240-pound "Big Hurt," not the Frank Thomas who had a fine 16-year career, hit 286 homers (including 34 with the win-challenged 1962 Mets) and retired in 1966. After consecutive home run totals of 41, 38, 40 and 40 between 1993 and 1996, this Frank Thomas had an "off-year" last season. He hit 35 homers, knocked in 125 and hit .347, giving him his first batting title. He also had an on-base average of .456 and slugged .611. The 1997 *Baseball Almanac* called him "the best all-around offensive player in baseball."

Let's interpret "all-around" for a moment. If we mean by "all-around" that he is able to hit for power and for average, then there's no doubt about it. The Hurt's lifetime average is .330. But that's just the appetizer. He has drawn between 109 and 138 walks each of the last seven years. Thus, his on-base percentage now stands at .455 and his slugging average at .600. Both figures are tops among active players!

If and when Thomas continues to fulfill his promise over the next five to 10 seasons, he may be qualified to enter baseball's top 10 of all-time.

What can't he do? Well the big guy can't steal bases – just 19 in his eight-year career – and probably won't win any Gold Gloves at first. But don't expect the White Sox to trade him for those reasons. If this man was playing for the Cubs, the darlings of the Windy City despite not winning anything since 1908, the town would be commissioning statues. Can you imagine Frank Thomas hitting in Wrigley? The baseballs would be covered in ivy stains.

Let's just nibble on the numbers for a bit. Thomas has seven consecutive 100-RBI years (ranging from 101-134), seven consecutive 100-run years (between 102 and 110) and four OBP titles. Thomas peaked with a .729 slugging average in 1994. Note the most recent five-year average (from 1993-1997): 39 homers, 120 RBI, .334 average, .459 OBP and a .631 slugging average.

Thomas has 257 homers and 854 RBI now. Give him eight more seasons and stand back. He will have between 500 and 550 homers, between 1,700 and 1,800 RBI and an average between .325 and .335. His slugging average will probably be between .575 and .615. The only thing that can stop the Big Hurt is an unforeseen hurt. Barring injuries, he is on a first-ballot Hall of Fame run. No question about it.

While Ken Griffey, Jr. got his first MVP, Thomas keeps getting league-leading numbers. Thomas has had 12 league-leading statistics so far – runs (once), doubles (once), walks (four times), average (once), OBP (four times), slugging (once). By contrast, in nine years, Griffey, Jr., has had six league leading totals.

Here is a comparison of their careers:

Griffey, Jr.'s nine-year average:

	R	HR	RBI	AVG	OBP	SLG
(1989-1997)	91	33	97	.302	.381	.562

Thomas' eight-year average:

	R	HR	RBI	AVG	OBP	SLG
(1990-1997)	98	32	107	.330	.455	.600

On offense, Thomas wins hands down over Griffey, Jr. What Thomas hasn't done is have that monster home run season. He has hit 40 three times and his best chance for a 50-homer season was the 1994 strike season when he had 38 homers in 113 games. Griffey, Jr. hit 49 and 56 in 1996 and 1997. But Griffey's longer, uppercut swinging has its own cost-benefit dividends: he strikes out much more than Thomas, walks much less and slugs lower. Thomas is adept at hitting to all fields and, like Ted Williams, is a slugger who is content to take the base-on-balls.

In the field and on the bases, Griffey comes out way ahead.

It's almost like comparing Willie Mays to Jimmie Foxx. Foxx' offensive numbers will impress you more. But then Mays runs the table on the other skills. I said almost. Foxx versus Mays on offense is – once factors like the era they played are included – very close. Thus far, Griffey, Jr. versus Thomas is not very close. Anyone who says that Griffey, Jr. has been better than Thomas as an offensive player so far is either (a) a Seattle fan, (b) a member of the Griffey, Jr. fan club, (c) a person who doesn't respect numbers, or (d) someone just not right in the head.

One of the really fun and interesting things will be watching Thomas tear his way into the next millennium with a bat.

Best 5-Year Average
1993-1997

R	H	D	T	HR	RBI	AVG	OBP	SLG
107	167	32	0	39	120	.334	.459	.631

8-Year Average

| 98 | 158 | 31 | 1 | 32 | 107 | .330 | .455 | .600 |

Lifetime totals

G	1,076	RBI	854
AB	3,821	BB	879
R	785	K	582
H	1,261	AVG	.330
D	246	OBP	.455
T	8	SLG	.600
HR	257	SB	18
HR%	6.7	CS	15

III
The Next 25 Players

51
DAN BROUTHERS
First Base

"Big Dan"
Born: 5/8/1858 Sylvan Lake, NY, Died: 8/2/32 E. Orange, NJ
6 feet 2 inches, 207 pounds
Debut: 6/23/1879, Played 19 years: 1897-1904 (missed 1897-1903)
1879-1880, Troy (NL); 1881-1885, Buffalo (NL); 1886-1888,
Detroit (NL); 1889, Boston (NL); 1890, Boston (Players League);
1891, Boston (American Association); 1892-1893, Brooklyn (NL);
1894-1895, Baltimore (NL); 1895, Louisville (NL);
1896 Philadelphia (NL); 1904, New York (NL)

We go from Frank Thomas, to Dan Brouthers, a slugger akin to Thomas
100 years before. "Big Dan" Brouthers was the greatest slugger of his
day. Born in Sylvan Lake, New York, in 1858, Brouthers played his first
year with the Troy Haymakers in 1879. His .342 lifetime average is still
the highest of anyone who played first base. In addition, his .518 slugging average is the highest of anyone who played before 1900.

By 1881, the first baseman was an established player with the Buffalo
Bisons of the National League. For the next six years, Brouthers led the
league in slugging average, never falling below .541 and going as high as
.581. He also won his first of five batting titles and first of five on-base
percentage titles. From 1881 through 1896, he ran up 16 consecutive

averages of .300 or better. With a keen eye and tremendous power, Brouthers was the game's best slugger in the late 1880s and his percentage and power hitting continued in the early 1890s.

The Bisons were short on money and sent Brouthers and three other members of Buffalo's "Big Four" – Hardy "Old True Blue" Richardson, Jack Rowe and James "Deacon" White to the Detroit Wolverines for $7,500 in September 1885. Detroit earned its first flag with the foursome in 1887. When that team folded in 1888, Brouthers was awarded to the Boston Beeneaters. There he won his third batting title (.373) in 1889. Then he hopped to the Boston Reds, a Players League Team. When that team disbanded, he joined another of the same name. His new squad won the American Association Pennant in 1891, a year when Brouthers copped his fourth batting title (.350). His fifth crown (.335) came with the Brooklyn Superbas in 1892 and he went with Wee Willie Keeler to the Baltimore Orioles in 1894.

Then 36, Brouthers had his last great year, hitting .347, slugging .560 and enjoying his personal best with 128 RBI. Baltimore, with Willie Keeler in right field and John McGraw at third, won its first ever pennant that season. But in a Temple Cup best-of-seven tournament, the New York Giants swept Baltimore, finishing them off on Oct. 8 with a 16-3 win.

Brouthers went to Louisville and Philadelphia before retiring in 1896 at the age of 38. At 46 he came out of retirement to play with the Giants. He worked as a press box attendant at the Polo Grounds until his death in 1932 at the age of 74.

Brouthers' final numbers show that he took advantage of what was available. While homers were scarce in his era, Brouthers hit for average, amassing 460 doubles and 205 triples. His .519 slugging average was the best of his time, and his .423 on-base percentage spoke of his ability to draw walks as well as hit.

He was elected to the Hall of Fame in 1945.

Best 5-Year Average
1882-86

R	H	D	T	HR	RBI	AVG	OBP	SLG
93	149	32	14 8	74		.360	.408	.562

Best 10-Year Average
1881-90

| 102 | 149 | 31 | 13 8 | | 80 | .342 | .414 | .532 |

Best 15-Year Average
1881-95

| 98 | 145 | 29 | 13 7 | | 82 | .344 | .418 | .526 |

Lifetime totals

G	1,673	HR %	1.6
AB	6,711	RBI	1,296
R	1,523	BB	840
H	2,296	K	238
D	460	AVG	.342
T	205	OBP	.423
HR	106	SLG	.519

52
AL SIMMONS
Left Field

"Bucketfoot Al"
Born: 5/22/02 Milwaukee, WI, Died: 5/26/56 Milwaukee, WI
5 feet 11 inches, 190 pounds
Debut: 4/15/24, Played 20 years: 1924-1944 (missed 1942)
1924-1932, Philadelphia (AL); 1933-1935, Chicago (AL); 1936,
Detroit; 1937-1938, Washington; 1939, Boston; 1939, Cincinnati;
1940-1941, Philadelphia (AL); 1943, Boston; 1944, Philadelphia (AL)

"I hate all pitchers," Al Simmons once said. "Hits are my bread and butter. They're trying to take the bread and butter out of my mouth. I hate
them." They must have hated him, too. The Yankees' right-hander
Charlie "Red" Ruffing once remarked that, "With men on bases, Foxx can
be a pain, but Simmons is a plague." The record shows that Ruffing was
right. Beginning in 1924, Simmons knocked in 100 runs for the first 11
years of his career. He averaged 125 RBI for those 11 seasons. He is thus
one of nine players in baseball history to have batted in 100 runs 10 or
more times.

His real name was Aliases Harry Syzmanski. "When I was a kid in
Milwaukee," said Simmons, "I dreamed of playing in the big leagues. And
like every other kid in the country I wanted to play for John McGraw. So
I wrote Roger Bresnahan at Toledo, a Giant farm team, and all I asked for

was expenses, which amounted to about $150. When Bresnahan refused, I signed on with the (American Association) Milwaukee Brewers."

The story goes that while playing with the Brewers, where he hit .398, he saw a sign advertising Simmons Hardware and decided to adopt the name. Purchased by Philadelphia for $50,000 in 1924, Simmons was known by spectators for stepping away from the pitch and putting his leading left foot "in the bucket." His foot never stepped toward the pitcher. Instead, the foot ended up pointing toward third. He soon became jeered as "Bucketfoot Al." His manager Connie Mack quieted the criticism. "If he can hit .398 for Milwaukee, I don't care if he stands on his head."

He was the first player in American League history to get 100 RBI in each of his first two seasons. In his second year he barely missed Sisler's hit record of 257, getting 252. He hit over .300 the first 11 years of his career, winning batting titles in 1930 and 1931 when he hit .381 and .390. Six times he got more than 200 hits.

Simmons was at his best during the A's three consecutive Series appearances between 1929 and 1931, hitting .365, .381 and .390 in consecutive seasons while batting in 450 runs over the three years. Simmons could also hit for power, slugging over .500 10 times in his career, including three seasons over .600 and another over .700. He hit 307 career homers. The fans may have never gotten used to his unorthodox bailing-out batting stance, but Mack kept praising him. "If only I could have nine players like Simmons," he said.

Simmons was 31 when he was traded to the White Sox in 1933 but he still managed 100 RBI in three of the next four seasons. His slugging did decline, however. In only two of his last 11 seasons did he slug over .500. While he played until he was 42, he was passed around between several clubs after his 1935 season in Chicago. He played with Detroit in 1936, Washington in 1937 and 1938, the Braves and Cincinnati in 1939, back to the Athletics for the next two years, on to the Red Sox in 1943 and back with the A's for his last season in 1944.

While he never led the league in homers – his best was 36 in 1930 – the clutch homers were the ones he savored. One homer started the greatest rally in World Series history. In 1929 the Cubs were trailing the A's two games to one but had an 8-0 lead in the seventh inning of Game Four. Simmons lead off the inning with a home run off Charley Root, famous for surrendering Babe Ruth's "called shot" in the 1932 Series. Five of the next six batters singled. Art Nehf relieved Root, but Hack Wilson lost a fly ball in the sun for a three-run homer. The score was now 8-7. After a walk, Nehf was replaced by Sheriff Blake, who allowed two singles. The game was tied when Pat Malone took the mound. He hit a batter and allowed a two-run double to Jimmy Dykes. He struck out the next two batters but it was too late: the A's had 10 runs and won 10-8.

The dispirited Cubs still managed to take a 2-0 lead into the ninth inning of Game Five. Then a single and a two-run homer by Mule Hass tied it. With two outs, Simmons doubled, Foxx received an intentional pass and Bing Miller doubled to end the Series. The A's hit six homers in the series – two by Foxx, two by Haas and two by Simmons.

Simmons also homered twice in the 1930 and 1931 Series. In 19 fall classic games, he hit .329 and slugged .658. He was known as a good outfielder with a strong, accurate arm.

In 1934 the "Duke of Milwaukee" was further immortalized by Carl Hubbell in the All-Star Game. Hubbell started the game badly, giving up a single to Gehringer and a walk to Heinie Manush. He then struck out Ruth, Gehrig and Foxx to close out the first and then Al Simmons and Joe Cronin to start the second. Simmons was one of five Hall of Famers – with more than 2,000 homers between them – to take a seat against King Carl.

It wasn't the strikeout but everything else that the voters remembered when they put him in the Hall of Fame in 1953.

Best 5-Year Average
1927-1931

R	H	D	T	HR	RBI	AVG	OBP	SLG
107	189	38	12	24	113	.375	.417	.641

Best 10-Year Average
1925-1934

108	201	38	11	23	128	.359	.402	.589

Best 15-Year Average
1925-1939

95	179	33	9	20	113	.339	.384	.549

Lifetime totals

G	2,215	RBI	1,827
AB	8,759	BB	615
R	1,507	K	737
H	2,927	AVG	.334
D	539	OBP	.380
T	149	SLG	.535
HR	307	SB	88
HR %	3.5	CS	64

53
MARK McGWIRE
First Base

Born: 10/1/63 Pomona, CA
6 feet 5 inches, 225 pounds
Debut: 8/22/86, Played 12 years: 1986-1997
1986-1997 Oakland; 1997, St. Louis

Mark McGwire's most amazing feat is his frequency of home runs. Babe Ruth hit a homer every 11.76 at-bats. McGwire is just behind him at one per 11.94 at-bats. Ruth hit 714 homers in 8,399 at-bats, compared to McGwire's 387 in 4,622 trips to the plate. What's his secret? Catcher Mike Stanley thinks it's no secret at all. "He has arms like those columns over there," said Stanley, pointing to the cement pillars in the Yankees' clubhouse.

While Mark McGwire is already 34 years old, several factors make it difficult to predict how he will end up. Give him 500 at-bats and watch him go. He hit 39 homers with only 317 at-bats in 1995! When he hit 58 homers in 1997, it was only the fourth time in his career he got 500 at-bats. Repeated injuries have kept this tower of power on the bench.

In four seasons, between 1993 and 1996, he missed 340 games. Give him back 300 of those games at four at-bats per game and give him his present rate on a homer every 11.94 at-bats and you can tack another 100 homers onto his present total. In 1997, McGwire played 156 games, tying his attendance record of 1990. For the second consecutive year he hit more than 50 homers. While he hit 58 homers in 1997 and 52 in 1996, his 1996 season was far superior:

	HR	RBI	AVG	OBP	SLG	HR (per at bat)
1996	52	113	.312	.468	.730	8.134
1997	58	123	.274	.388	.646	9.310

A likely scenario with McGwire's homers per at-bat is that he will pass Ruth for a while and then fall back again as his "decline years" set in. This is analogous to what happened with the winning percentage race between Whitey Ford and Juan Marichal in the early 1970s. For a brief time, Marichal passed Ford's .690 winning percentage but then fell behind when his percentage dipped over his last seven seasons. One thing seems sure: McGwire will remain ahead of the third place hitter in homers per at-bat. Ralph Kiner hit one every 14.22 at-bats and McGwire would have to hit a steep decline to fall back to that ratio.

While McGwire's recent achievements seem staggering, he served notice early on that he was capable of great things. He won Rookie of the Year in 1987, hitting 49 homers in 557 at bats, a homer every 11.36 ABs. He led the league in homers and slugging (.618). He hit 30-plus the next three years but dropped to 22 in 1991. After hitting 42 in 1992, he missed 250 games over the next two seasons with foot injuries before bouncing back with 39 in 1995 in just 104 games and 317 at-bats (his best ratio, at one every 8.128 at-bats). By now he has hit 30-plus eight times and 40-plus four times.

Despite his achievements, one must bear in mind that McGwire and other long ballers have all the manufactured benefits of the nineties. The strike zone is small, the 30-teams water down talent and the league ERAs, which resemble mid-Western zip codes, are the highest since the 1930s when entire teams hit .300 and several teams averaged better than six runs per game. In addition, the parks are smaller and the ball more tightly wound. The result of this engineered, home run offense is that records are falling. The team record for home runs, 240 by the Yankees in 1961, was shattered by not one, but three teams, in 1996. That year Baltimore hit 257 long balls, Seattle hit 245 and Oakland 243. In 1997, Seattle did it again, hitting 251.

McGwire's totals are definitely aided by poor pitching. That being said, he has the bat speed and power to have hit homers in any era. If he stays healthy enough to get 1,400 more at-bats – about three average years for him – he will most certainly get the 113 homers (about 38 per season) needed to reach 500. By then he will be 37 and he can set his sights on 550 to 600 homers.

Let us hope he stays healthy. An average glove man and a slow runner, the 6-foot-5-inch, 225-pound McGwire is nonetheless a pure slugger, a guy capable of hitting moon balls every time he steps up. He is unofficial king of the tape measure blow these days, hitting the ball over 500 feet with regularity. It will be the long ball, and the long ball alone, that carries McGwire past 500 and into the Hall of Fame.

Best 5-Year Average
1993-1997

R	H	D	T	HR	RBI	AVG	OBP	SLG
93	86	14	0	33	75	.286	.425	.667

Best 10-Year Average
1987-1996

72	104	17	1	33	85	.259	.380	.546

Lifetime totals

G	1,380	RBI	983
AB	4,622	BB	890
R	811	K	1,104
H	1,201	AVG	.260
D	198	OBP	.379
T	5	SLG	.556
HR	387	SB	10
HR %	8.4	CS	8

54
JOE CRONIN
Shortstop

Born: 10/12/06 San Francisco, CA, Died: 9/7/84 Osterville, MA
5 feet 11-and-a-half inches, 180 pounds
Debut: 4/29/26, Played 20 years: 1926-1945
1926-1927, Pittsburgh; 1928-1934, Washington;
1935-1945, Boston (AL)

So reliable was Joe Cronin's production and clutch hitting that
Philadelphia manager Connie Mack said, "With a man on third and one
out, I'd rather have Cronin hitting for me than anybody, anywhere. That
includes Cobb, Simmons and the rest of them."

Look at Joe Cronin's numbers without knowing where he played and
you might not be terribly impressed. He was a .301 hitter for his 20 years
with the Pirates, Senators and Red Sox. Plenty more .300 hitters populate
baseball history. Take his .468 slugging average – pretty good but nothing
spectacular. However, Cronin was a shortstop, a shortstop who was a fine
fielder and who hit well beyond the demands of his position.

His best years were with Washington and Boston between 1929 and
1941. In that 13-year run, Cronin hit .300 eight times. That's one thing.
But what really jumps out at you are the years he knocked in 100 runs.
Eight times Cronin topped the century mark. For the decade, he drove in
an outstanding 1,036 runs – behind only Jimmie Foxx, Lou Gehrig, Mel

Ott, Al Simmons and Earl Averill.

In addition, Cronin was the league's leading shortstop between 1928 and 1933, three times leading the league in putouts, assists and double plays. He was appointed player-manager by Senators' owner Clark Griffith in 1933, replacing the great Walter Johnson at that post. In his first season, the "Boy Manager" won 99 games and the pennant, but lost the Series in five games to the New York Giants.

The 1933 season was to be the first of 15 consecutive managing seasons for Cronin in the American League. But after his good managerial start in 1933, the Senators took seventh place, winning just 66 games in 1934. The brightest light in that dismal season was Cronin's marrying Griffith's adopted daughter Mildred Robinson. In fact, while Cronin and Mildred honeymooned, Red Sox' owner Tom Yawkey was looking to buy him. He offered Griffith a record $225,000 and another shortstop, Lyn Lary, for Cronin. No one could recall another instance in which an owner got rid of his shortstop, manager and son-in-law in one trade.

Cronin would play the next 11 years for the Red Sox and manage the next 13. When the dust had cleared on his career, Cronin had more than 800 extra base hits and averaged 90 runs batted in for his best 15-year run. Over that same stretch he hit .306. His best year was 1938. Then 31, Cronin posted 51 doubles, 17 home runs and 94 RBI. He hit .325, had an on-base percentage of .428 and slugged .536. *The Sporting News* named him the outstanding major league shortstop seven times.

He was elected to the Hall of Fame in 1956. As a manager he won 1,236 and lost 1,055 (.540) and led Boston to his second pennant in 1946, the year after he retired as a player. In one of the most memorable of all World Series, Boston lost in seven games to St. Louis, as Enos Slaughter dashed home from first base on a single with the winning run in Game Seven. So Cronin never got his World Championship. Ted Williams still called him, "The best manager I ever played for."

After he retired as Boston manager in 1947, he was a Boston executive 11 years and was then named American League president in 1959. In his 14 years as president, the league expanded from eight to 12 teams. He also ended his career in controversy when he vetoed the Yankees' attempt to sign the Oakland A's manager Dick Williams, while approving the Tigers' signing of former Yankees' skipper Ralph Houk.

He was elected to the Hall of Fame in 1956.

Best 5-Year Average
1937-1941

R	H	D	T	HR	RBI	AVG	OBP	SLG
100	165	39	5	19	103	.307	.402	.505

Best 10-Year Average
1932-1941

86	158	37	8	12	99	.303	.389	.478

Best 15-Year Average
1929-1943

78	144	33	7	10	90	.306	.391	.473

Lifetime totals

G	2,124	RBI	1,424
AB	7,579	BB	1,059
R	1,233	K	700
H	2,285	AVG	.301
D	515	OBP	.390
T	118	SLG	.468
HR	170	SB	87
HR %	2.2	CS	71

55
JACKIE ROBINSON
Second Base

Born: 1/31/19 Cairo, GA, Died: 10/24/72 Stamford, CT
5 feet 11 inches, 204 pounds
Debut: 4/15/47, Played 10 years: 1947-1956, Brooklyn

Most everyone knows about the immense social importance of Jackie Robinson's career. By contrast, very few know about the statistical significance of his 10 years with the Dodgers. Because Robinson didn't debut in the major leagues until the age of 28, he had little chance of a 15 or 20-year career.

Ballplayers usually hit the major leagues at about 21 years of age, so one must use Robinson's 10-year totals to infer what he might have achieved had he played the additional seven years stolen by the color line. Robinson brought a new look to the game, a full-throttle aggressive style that made him a dangerous and exciting player. He won Rookie of the Year in 1947, scoring 125 runs, collecting 175 hits, hitting .297 and leading the league with 29 steals. Teammate Pete Reiser was second with 14.

Robinson also gave second base play a new all-around look. Not only did he lead the league in fielding in three of his first five years, he also put up RBI totals of 85, 124, 81 and 88 during that time. Further evidence of his heavy hitting were the five years he slugged above .500.

In his third year, 1949, Robinson hit .342 and won the batting title.

He knocked in a personal best 124 runs that season and slugged .528. He won the MVP and the Dodgers again met the Yankees in the Series. In 1947 the two teams squared off in a classic full of last second rallies, like Cookie Lavagetto's game-winning double to break up Bill Bevens' no-hitter; and great catches, like Al Gionfriddo's grab of Joe DiMaggio's 415-foot drive. New York needed Joe Page's sterling relief effort in Game Seven to win.

The 1949 Series didn't live up to its billing. Robinson hit .188 and, as a team, the Dodgers hit .210. The Yankees won in five games.

But Robinson and the Dodgers would have other chances. Between 1947 and 1956 Brooklyn would play in six World Series. Brooklyn versus New York was thus established as the greatest rivalry in baseball history. For his part, Robinson hit only .234 in 137 World Series at bats. The Dodgers went up three games to two in 1952, but failed to close out the Series in Games Six and Seven at Ebbets Field. They wasted four homers and eight RBI by Duke Snider. Johnny Mize hit three homers and Mantle and Berra chipped in two apiece for the Yankees. Mantle's sixth inning homer off Joe Black in Game Seven proved to be the game winner.

After the Dodgers lost four games to two in 1953, despite hitting .300 as a team (Robinson hit .320), their fans had a right to wonder if they would ever beat New York.

The answer would come in 1955. Snider hit four homers again and Johnny Podres pitched an eight-hit shutout in Game Seven for his second Series win to close out the Yankees in front of 62,465 at Yankee Stadium.

Six homers between Berra and Mantle – and a perfect game by Don Larsen in game five – helped the Yankees to win the 1956 Series in seven games. In the six Series battles since Robinson's rookie year, the two clubs had fought to an agonizing seven-game limit four times.

Robinson had a fair year in 1956, hitting .275. But he was 37 years old and the Dodgers actually traded him to the New York Giants. Robinson announced his retirement before the start of the 1957 season.

He finished with a .311 average and a .410 on-base average. What made his career greater was its very brevity. Any calculation of his totals must include the eight youthful seasons he lost due to the color barrier. If Robinson had played those eight years at the same pace that he played his last ten years – years between 28 and 37 years old – he would have ended up with 2,732 hits, 1,705 runs, 1,321 runs batted in and 355 stolen bases. Those are fine totals for any player and remarkable totals for a middle infielder. Viewed in his light, Robinson's election to the Hall of Fame in 1962, in his first year of eligibility, was certainly justified. Robinson used his retirement to turn more attention to become a spokesperson for the NAACP and an activist for civil rights and labor. But illness was also taking its toll. Robinson was suffering from diabetes, a disease he may have had since his playing days. By the early 1970s, he had also developed heart disease, was blind in one eye, and going blind in the other. Robinson, at 53, was now blind and hardly able to walk as a result of the diabetes. On Oct. 15, 1972, 25 years after he had integrated baseball, Robinson threw out the first ball to start the second game of the World Series. He said he longed to see a "black manager on the third base line." Nine days later he was dead, having suffered a massive heart attack at his Stamford, Connecticut, home.

Best 5-Year Average
1949-1953

R	H	D	T	HR	RBI	AVG	OBP	SLG
108	175	32	7	16	93	.329	.422	.502

Career Average
1947-1956

| 95 | 152 | 27 | 5 | 14 | 73 | .311 | .410 | .474 |

Lifetime totals

G	1,382	RBI	734
AB	4,877	BB	740
R	947	K	291
H	1,518	AVG	.311
D	273	OBP	.410
T	54	SLG	.474
HR	137	SB	197
HR %	2.8		

56
GEORGE SISLER

First Base

"Gorgeous George"
Born: 3/24/1893 Manchester, OH, Died: 3/26/73 Richmond
Heights, MO
5 feet 11 inches, 170 pounds
Debut: 6/28/15, Played 15 years: 1915-1930 (missed 1923)
1915-1927, St. Louis (AL); 1928, Washington;
1928-1930, Boston (NL)

George Sisler played 15 years between 1915 and 1930 (missing 1923 due to poisonous sinusitis that produced double vision) and left his mark on the game in amazing ways. In 1920 he collected 257 hits, a record which still stands. That year he hit .407 and two years later he hit .420. He was so flawless around first base, so good with a bat and quick on the bases, that people called him "Gorgeous George," "The Perfect Ballplayer" and "The Sizzler."

It must also be said here that when *The Sporting News* picked their all-time greatest team in 1960 and made Sisler the first baseman instead of Gehrig (whom they referred to as "old biscuit pants") – or Foxx for that matter – the grown men who voted must have taken leave of their senses. Sisler was the equal of neither player whose slugging and runs batted in far eclipse his. Since the fielding demands at first base are less than those of the other positions, first base is considered a hitting position. So whether or not he caught more ground balls than Gehrig or Foxx is none to the point. Gehrig hit 493 homers and slugged .632. Foxx hit 534 homers and slugged .609. Sisler hit 102 homers – 19 was his personal best – and slugged .468. Next.

But then *The Sporting News* is written in St. Louis and Sisler spent his "perfect" years playing for the St. Louis Browns, a team ever in quest of, but never approaching, perfection.

Ample evidence exists that Sisler was a great player.

Leonard Koppett pointed out in the *New York Times* that, "Like Ruth, Sisler started out as a pitcher, scoring notable 2-1 and 1-0 victories over Walter Johnson." What he doesn't say is that Sisler had a 5-6 lifetime record as pitcher, not exactly a Ruthian mark (Ruth was 94-46 and won 65 games in a three-year period). Victories over Johnson or not, the record shows that he was a mediocre pitcher. The evidence also shows that he could hit.

Born in March, 1893, in Nimisila, Ohio, Sisler earned a degree in mechanical engineering from the University of Michigan in 1915. At Michigan the baseball coach was Branch Rickey, who became manager of the St. Louis Browns in 1913. As a senior, Sisler was the outstanding player in the country. Upon graduating, he turned down a $5,200 offer from the Pirates and signed with the Browns for $7,400.

His success as a pro came quickly. He hit .285, .305 and .353 in his first three years. But he made a permanent mark in 1920, his sixth season. That year he led the league with his 257 hits and hit .407. It was a great year, but it was also the same season Babe Ruth was changing the face of the sport. Sisler had hits and batting average; Ruth led the league in runs (158), homers (54), RBI (137), walks (148), on-base average (.530), and the highest slugging mark in baseball history (.847). He also hit .376. The gap between Ruth and Sisler, the first place and second place finishers in home runs, was 35 – the largest gap ever between a home run winner and the runner-up.

The next year Sisler hit .371 and hit 12 homers, the last time he ever saw double-digits in that category. In 1922 he hit .420, scoring 134 runs and dealing out 246 hits – 178 of them singles. He also hit in 41 consecutive games that year and took MVP honors, the first time the award was given in the American League. But the Browns lost the pennant by a single game and he never again came close to playing in the World Series.

Then came the eye affliction that resulted from poisonous sinusitis, which kept him out for the 1923 season. Sisler never thought himself the same player after 1923. Now 31, he returned in 1924 as player-manager of the Browns, receiving $25,000 at a post that he would hold for three years.

He finished his career with Washington and the Boston Braves. In 15 years he never played on a team good enough to make the World Series.

He spent most of the 1930s in the printing and sporting goods business. In 1943, he rejoined Rickey in Brooklyn, taking on the duties of special instructor and scout. One of his students was Duke Snider. He followed Rickey to Pittsburgh in 1951, where one of his pupils would be a rookie named Roberto Clemente.

He was voted into the Hall of Fame in 1939, nine years after he retired. Sisler was no Gehrig or Foxx, but he did hit .340 lifetime and is one of the greatest ever to play the position. He once told *Baseball Magazine* that he wanted to "hang up a higher average than Ty Cobb's," and his .41979 average in 1922 did nip the .41962 Cobb had in 1911. Cobb called him "the nearest thing to a perfect ballplayer."

Best 5-Year Average
1918-1922

R	H	D	T	HR	RBI	AVG	OBP	SLG
112	211	36	16	10	91	.381	.423	.559

Best 10-Year Average
1917-1927 (missed all of 1923)

| 98 | 204 | 31 | 13 | 9 | 85 | .351 | .387 | .494 |

Career Average

| 86 | 187 | 28 | 11 | 7 | 78 | .340 | .379 | .468 |

Lifetime totals

G	 2,055	RBI	 1,175
AB	 8,267	BB	 472
R	 1,284	K	 327
H	 2,812	AVG	340
D	 425	OBP	379
T	 164	SLG	468
HR.	 102	SB	 375
HR%	. . . . . . 1.2		

57
GOOSE GOSLIN
Left Field

Born: 10/16/1900 Salem, NJ, Died: 5/5/71 Bridgeton, NJ
5 feet 11-and-a-half inches, 185 pounds
Debut: 9/16/21, Played 18 years: 1921-1938
1921-1930, Washington; 1930-1932, St. Louis (AL);
Washington, 1933; 1934-1937, Detroit; 1938, Washington

Let's talk about baseball's "all-forgotten team." To qualify for this team you must be a great player, but a special kind of great player. You must be a great player who everyone has managed to forget. Stan Musial plays left field on the all-forgotten team, while Eddie Mathews mans third base. Gabby Hartnett might be the starting catcher for the all-forgottens. But a place must be reserved for Washington Senators' outfielder Goose Goslin.

If you don't know much about Goslin, you've proved my point. Chalk up the next 10 minutes to education. One of the great unsung players in history, Goose Goslin was simply one of the most outstanding run producers who ever lived. Before launching ahead into Goslin's achievements, I want to note that he's not completely forgotten about. In his book *The Glory of Their Times*, Lawrence Ritter tells the personal side of Goslin's story.

Here are Ritter's first two paragraphs, told by Goslin himself.

Heck, let's face it, I was just a big ol' country boy havin' the time of his life. It was all a lark to me, just a joy ride. Never feared a thing, never got nervous, just a big country boy from South Jersey, too dumb to know better. In those days I'd go out and fight a bull without a sword and never know the difference.

Why, I never even realized it was supposed to be big doin's. It was just a game, that's all it was. They didn't have to pay me. I'd have paid them to let me play. Listen, the truth is it was more than fun. It was heaven.

Goslin was born in Salem, New Jersey on October 16, 1900. He explains that he rode his bike 10 miles to get to the sandlots where he could play ball. He'd play all day long and get spanked when he arrived home again, since he was invariably too late to milk the cows. Playing semi-pro ball one day, he met Bill McGowan, who would later become an American League umpire. Goslin was a pitcher and after finding that the Rochester, New York, team didn't need pitchers, McGowan found him a job in the Sally League, in Columbia, South Carolina.

Of his pitching exploits, Goslin recalled, "The harder I threw the ball, the harder they hit it." His manager, Zinn Beck, who also played third base, showed some ingenuity. "If you keep this up I'll never make it," his manager said one day, walking to the mound from third base, "cause the way they're hitting I'll get killed out there for sure." In short order the manager made Goslin an outfielder. Goslin hit .390 the following year and Clark Griffith, the Senators' owner, bought him.

Following two part-time seasons, Goslin became a full-time outfielder in 1923. He hit .300 and knocked in 99 runs. As good a showing as that was, it turned out to be a warm-up by Goslin's standards. In 1924 Goslin led the league in RBI with 129 and he hit .344. He would have walked off with the MVP award, but his teammate Walter Johnson took it with the pitcher's "triple crown," winning 23, striking out 158 and posting a 2.72 ERA. In the Series they had to face the New York Giants, winners of four consecutive pennants. It was one of the great World Series, with four of the seven games decided by one run.

With homers by George Kelly and Bill Terry, the Giants beat Johnson in Game One, 4-3. Washington won by an identical score in Game Two, with Goslin hitting a homer and Roger Peckinpaugh knocking in the winning run with a double in the bottom of the ninth. Back at the Polo Grounds, the Giants won Game Three, but the Senators rebounded to take Game Four, with Goslin hitting a three-run homer.

The Giants got the better of Johnson again in Game Five, winning 6-2, despite Goslin's third homer of the Series. Back in Griffith Stadium for Game Six, the Senators beat the Giants' ace Art Nehf, but were behind 3-1 going into the eighth inning of Game Seven. Then Bucky Harris' grounder to third hit a pebble and bounced over Freddie Lindstrom's head for a two-run single.

Pitching on one day's rest, Johnson came on in relief in the ninth and held the Giants scoreless, all the way through the twelfth, striking out five. After Hank Gowdy stepped on his catcher's mask and missed Muddy Ruel's foul pop, Ruel had another life and doubled to open the Senators' half. Walter Johnson reached base on shortstop Travis Jackson's error, which would have been the third out. Earl McNeely then hit a bouncer to Lindstrom and again the ball bounded over his head and Ruel, who usually ran like he was carrying a full safe of coins on his back, slid home with the winning run. For one year at least, Washington was not "first in war, first in peace and last in the American League."

Walter Johnson, then 36 and pitching in his 17th year, had won his World Championship, winning Game Seven in relief. But the hitting star was Goslin, who picked up 11 hits, batting .344 with three homers and 11 RBI.

Goslin knocked in 113 runs in 1925, and the Senators lost in seven games to the Pirates. Washington lead the series three games to one. But Pittsburgh won Game Five at Griffith and took Game Six at Forbes Field.

In Game Seven, Washington had leads of 4-0, 6-3 and still led 7-6 into Pittsburgh's half of the eighth. Johnson allowed 15 hits and five earned runs in a losing effort, after allowing just one run total in Games One and Four. But Roger Peckinpaugh was the Washington goat. In an inept fielding performance that may never be duplicated, Peckinpaugh made seven errors in the Series. He dropped a pop and threw wildly on another play to give Pittsburgh four unearned runs in the seventh and eighth innings. Though Washington lost, Goslin hit well again, banging three homers, knocking in six and hitting .308.

The Goose would not return to the Series again until 1933. But by then Goslin had become a star. He hit .379 to lead the league in 1928. On June 13, 1930, he was in St. Louis to play against the Browns when his teammate Sam Rice said, "You're in the wrong hotel." What Rice meant was that Goslin had been traded to St. Louis for Heinie Manush (and General Crowder) without his knowing it.

After finishing three years in St. Louis with RBI totals of 138, 105 and 104, he was traded back to Washington in December 1932. Goslin was now teammates with Manush and a hot shortstop, Joe Cronin. It wasn't enough to beat the Giants, who steamrolled them in five games, behind two victories by Carl Hubbell. Goslin had a sub-par season and was traded in December 1933, this time to Detroit. "The Senators have won only three pennants," Goslin later explained. "1924, 1925 and 1933 – and I was there each time. Come to think of it, they've never played a World Series game I didn't play every single inning of."

He proved to his new employers that they'd made the right decision by giving them three solid seasons in a row, knocking in 100, 109 and 125 runs. In 1934, the Tigers lost in seven games to St. Louis but Detroit rebounded in 1935 to beat the Cubs in seven. Goslin won Game Seven, singling home Mickey Cochrane with two out in the bottom of the ninth to win it, 3-2. "A lucky hit," was Goslin's humble take on the matter.

Goose had 2,735 of those lucky hits by the time his career ended three years later. More impressive, he was an RBI automaton, knocking in 100 or more runs in 11 seasons – one of only nine players to get 100 RBI ten times. He slugged .500 nine times. He said he got a bigger charge out of playing the Yankees because Babe Ruth was his hero and idol. "He was a picture up there at the plate. What a ballplayer. And such a sweet guy, too," Goslin recalled. "I tried to copy everything he did. But I still loved to beat him."

Back in Washington for the 1938 season, Goslin remembers swinging at a low outside pitch, wrenching his back. Manager Bucky Harris had to send in a pinch hitter, since Goslin could not finish his at-bat. "That was the last time I ever picked up a bat in the big leagues," Goslin said. "It was also the first and only time a pinch hitter was ever put in for the ol' Goose."

Goslin retired to little fanfare in 1938. The baseball world was following DiMaggio and Gehrig, who were smack in the middle of a Yankees' dynasty. It was 1968 – 25 years after his first year of eligibility – that he was elected to the Hall of Fame. He was, after all, the forgotten man.

Best 5-Year Average
1924-1928

R	H	D	T	HR	RBI	AVG	OBP	SLG
99	194	35	15	15	114	.348	.408	.548

Best 10-Year Average
1924-1933

| 99 | 184 | 34 | 12 | 20 | 107 | .326 | .393 | .509 |

Best 15-Year Average
1922-1936

| 96 | 178 | 33 | 11 | 17 | 104 | .319 | .385 | .509 |

Lifetime totals

G	2,287	RBI	1,609
AB	8,656	BB	949
R	1,483	K	585
H	2,735	AVG	.316
D	500	OBP	.387
T	173	SLG	.500
HR	248	SB	175
HR %	2.9	CS	89

58
JOHNNY MIZE

First Base

"The Big Cat"
Born: 1/17/13 Demorest, GA, Died: 6/2/93 Demorest, GA
6 feet 2 inches, 215 pounds
Debut: 4/16/36, Played 15 years: 1936-1953
1936-1941, St. Louis (NL); 1942-1948, New York (NL)
(missed 1943-45 due to WWII); 1949-1953, New York (AL)

Johnny Mize was a great offensive player. Despite missing three prime years while serving in the Navy during World War II – 1943 through 1945, beginning when he was 30 years old – he still posted eight 100-RBI seasons in a nine-year stretch. The streak stopped in 1946 when he broke his hand and missed 53 games.

The greatest skill of the "Big Cat" wasn't quickness but his ability to crunch a ball. He hit three homers in a game six times, the first player ever to do so. In 1936, his rookie season with the Cardinals, he hit for power right out of the box, slugging .577. He increased that average each of the next four years, slugging .595, .614, .626 and .636. Max Lanier, who began pitching with the Cardinals in 1938, recalls, "Joe Medwick was in his heyday when I joined the club. So was Johnny Mize, one of the greatest left-hand hitters. He and Medwick were as good a pair of hitters as I've seen."

Mize also hit above .300 each of his first nine years in the majors.

After "dropping off" to 16 homers, 100 RBI and a .317 average, the Cardinals traded him to the New York Giants after the 1941 season.

In his first year with New York, he led the league in RBI (110) and slugging (.521). He would go on to lead the league in slugging four times, in home runs four times and in RBI three times.

He posted two of his best years at the ages of 34 and 35. In 1947, he hit 51 homers and knocked in 138 runs, leading the league in both categories. He batted .302. Mize also led the circuit in runs with 137. It was the fourth time Mize had edged over .600 in slugging. He did not win the MVP that season, finishing behind the Boston Braves third baseman Bob Elliott (22 homers, 113 RBI, .317 average) and Cincinnati pitcher Ewell Blackwell, who led the league with 22 wins.

In 1948 he led in homers again, hitting 48 and knocking in 125. When his numbers declined to start the 1949 season, the Giants gave him to the Yankees for $40,000 in August. Now 36, Mize found a fortunate home for the last five years of his career. He became a part-time first baseman with New York, but from 1949 through 1953 he played in the World Series and New York won each time. In 1950, at age 37, he hit 25 homers in 274 at-bats and slugged .595. He struck out only 24 times. From 1951 through 1953, he led the league in pinch-hits.

Sportswriter Dan Parker wrote: "Your arm is gone; your legs likewise But not your eyes, Mize, not your eyes."

The Yankees beat Brooklyn, Philadelphia and New York from 1949 through 1951. But Mize didn't have a strong World Series either time. In 1952, the Big Cat roared one last time. It took the Yankees seven games to beat the Dodgers and Mize hit .400 with three homers – including a homer off Joe Black to win game four – and knocked in six runs.

Forty years old, Mize retired after the 1953 season. He hit 359 homers and his slugging average is eighth best ever, at .562. After being passed by in the voting in 13 different years between 1960 and 1973, the Veterans Committee inducted Mize into the Hall of Fame in 1981. He died on June 2, 1993.

Best 5-Year Average
1937-1941

R	H	D	T	HR	RBI	AVG	OBP	SLG
93	182	38	12	28	112	.337	.417	.562

Best 10-Year Average
1937-1949

| 94 | 165 | 30 | 7 | 30 | 107 | .319 | .402 | .597 |

Career Average (entire 15-yr career)

| 75 | 134 | 24 | 6 | 24 | 89 | .312 | .397 | .562 |

Lifetime Totals

G	1,884		RBI	1,337
AB	6,443		BB	856
R	1,118		K	524
H	2,011		AVG	.312
D	367		OBP	.397
T	83		SLG	.562
HR	359		SB	28
HR%	5.6			

205

59
RALPH KINER
Left Field

Born: 10/27/22 Santa Rita, NM
6 feet 2 inches, 195 pounds
Debut: 4/16/46, Played 10 yars: 1946-1953, Pittsburgh; 1953-1954,
Chicago (NL); 1955, Cleveland

To this day, no one has broken one of Ralph Kiner's records. Kiner began
his career with Pittsburgh in 1946, the year he started a streak of seven
consecutive home run titles. After that run of years he had 294 homers –
an average of 42 per year. Kiner said, "Home run hitters drive Cadillacs
and single hitters drive Fords." So we know what Kiner was driving
when he wasn't driving the ball.

Ralph Kiner's career is Harmon Killebrew's without the mileage.
Killebrew hit a homer once every 14.22 at-bats, while Kiner did it once
every 14.11 at-bats. But while Killebrew belted `em for 22 years, Kiner
did it for 10. That said, it's no shame taking a back seat to Killebrew in
the homer department.

And as Bill James points out in his *Baseball Historical Abstract*, Kiner
was very effective in hitting homers and drawing walks. After Kiner hit
51 homers in 1947, he drew 112 walks, then 117, then 122, then 137,
then 110, then 100 in consecutive years. He walked far more than he
struck out (1,011-749) – Sammy Sosa, are you listening? – and finished

with an impressive line: .279 average, .398 on-base average, and .548 slugging average.

Born in Santa Rita, New Mexico, in October, 1922, Kiner took flight right away, hitting 23 homers to lead the National League in his first year, the first rookie to do so since Harry Lumley in 1906. Then he got a little tutoring from Hank Greenberg in 1947. "Hank put me in a better position in the batter's box," said Kiner, "which enabled me to pull outside pitches, and changed my stance and whole approach to hitting, getting me not to swing at bad pitches." The result was 51 homers in 1947, including a staggering total of 48 after June 1.

Kiner peaked two years later, hitting 54 and leading the league in slugging for the second time with a .658 mark. While the Pirates hovered near the basement of the National League like a mother bird hovers near the nest, Kiner was drawing customers to Forbes Field. The distance to the left field fence had been shortened from 365 to 335 in 1947, but too much has been made of this fact. The 6-foot-2-inch, 195-pound Kiner had awesome power and 335 is a fair enough poke, about an average distance for major league parks then. Kiner followed that season with 47, 42 and 37 homers, to end his run of seven titles.

By then Kiner had surpassed Stan Musial in the salary department, reaching $90,000 in 1951. Despite this legacy of long balls, Branch Rickey was not impressed. After hearing Kiner tell about his home run totals, Rickey said, "Where'd we finish?" When Kiner replied 'last,' Rickey said, "We could have finished last without you." Rickey had a point: in Kiner's seven full seasons in steel town, the team won 442 and lost 635, a winning percentage of .410.

Losing was as much a Pittsburgh tradition in the forties and early fifties as Kiner's homers were. Four times in his first six years, the Pirates lost more than 90 games. In his seventh season, 1952, they didn't lose 90 games, however. That's because they lost 112 and won only 42. The rear ends in the seats dwindled to 686,673 that season, down from 1,517,021 in 1948. In a 10-player deal, Kiner was shipped to Chicago in June, 1953, a team slightly better than Pittsburgh since it finished 65-89. Chicago went 64-90 and Kiner was traded to Cleveland in November, 1954. After playing just 113 games in 1955, Kiner retired, a back sprain forcing him from baseball at the age of 32.

He had played an even 10 years, averaging 37 homers, 101 walks, 97 runs and 102 RBI. Neither his fielding, throwing, nor base running were worthy of note. Bill James mentions how Enos Slaughter once said "I could score on a fly ball to Kiner 30 feet behind third base." Then James turns the tables on ol' "Country," stating that the most runs Slaughter ever scored was 100, while Kiner scored 118, 104, 116, 112 and 124 in consecutive seasons. "Who you gonna take?" James asks.

I'd take Kiner in a New York minute. The only problem with his career is that the greatest hitters have 15 or 20 years or more, while Kiner played only 10. Twenty years after his retirement, the Baseball Writers of America recognized the magnitude of his achievement, inducting him in the Hall of Fame in 1975. By then, Kiner had even found a team more inept than the `52 Pirates. Kiner has been one of original broadcasters of the Mets, with them since their first season in 1962, the year they won 40 and lost 120.

Kiner's name surfaced recently when Mark McGwire passed him in home runs per at-bat. At the close of the 1997 season McGwire had 387 homers in 4,622 at-bats, or one every 11.94 at-bat. So Kiner stands third. If only one slugger surpassed his mark in more than 40 years, then don't hold your breath waiting for too many more to pass him.

Best 5-Year Average
1947-1951

R	H	D	T	HR	RBI	AVG	OBP	SLG
115	161	23	5	47	121	.294	.418	.609

Career Average
1946-1955

| 97 | 145 | 22 | 4 | 37 | 102 | .279 | .398 | .548 |

Lifetime totals

G	1,472	RBI	1,015
AB	5,205	BB	1,011
R	971	K	749
H	1,451	AVG	.279
D	216	OBP	.398
T	39	SLG	.548
HR	369	SB	22
HR%	7.1		

60
FRANKIE FRISCH
Second Base

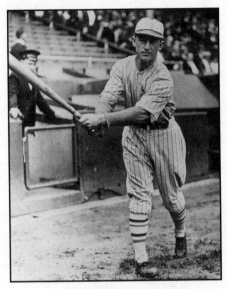

"The Fordham Flash"
Born: 9/9/1898 Bronz, NY, Died: 3/12/73 Wilmington, DE
5 feet 11 inches, 165 pounds
Debut: 6/14/19, Played 19 years: 1919-1926, New York (NL);
1927-1937, St. Louis (NL)

Frank Francis Frisch was more known by his nickname "The Fordham Flash" to those who watched him. He got the name because of his speed on the bases. In his 19 years as a second baseman and player-manager, he was part of four world championship teams, four more pennant winners and contributed mightily to all of them. The Bronx, New York, native could hit, run and field and by the time the dust settled, his record showed some impressive numbers: 2,880 hits and a .316 lifetime average.

Playing with Frisch on the 1921 Giants, Casey Stengel gushed when he recalled him. "Then there was Mr. Frisch which went to a university and could run fast, besides," Casey said. "He was the first second baseman that didn't pedal backwards when they hit the ball down the line. He'd put his head down and commenced running like in a race, and he'd beat the ball there."

Born in 1898, the running had started by the time he hit Fordham University. He was a sports legend on the Rose Hill campus, the captain of the baseball, football and basketball teams. He joined the New York Giants of John McGraw in 1919 and immediately became the kind of all-out player McGraw loved. He hit .341, collected 211 hits and led the league with 49 stolen bases in 1921. In the World Series, the Giants played the other inhabitants of the Polo Grounds, the New York Yankees. Ruth bashed 59 homers that year, 35 ahead of second place Ken Williams. Ruth hit .313 in the series but McGraw kept him in the park with just one homer as the Giants won five games to three. Frisch hit .300, stole three bases, scored five runs.

Frisch hit .327 the next year and this time the Giants swept the Yankees. McGraw – who ordered his pitchers to throw Ruth an assortment of slow stuff and brush backs – stifled The Babe completely, holding him to a .118 average and one RBI. Over the next two seasons, the Yankees and the Senators took the measure of the Giants, though Frisch hit .400 and .333 and totaled 20 hits in the two Series. McGraw's scrappers had won four pennants in a row. For the 1923 and 1924 seasons, Frisch hit .348 and .328.

Before the Mel Ott-Carl Hubbell Giants of the 1930s saw the post-season, Frisch was out of town. Frisch could bait an umpire and argue with the best of them. As a manager, he was once ejected for arguing and drew a five-day suspension the next day for arguing again. But he argued with McGraw, too. After taking a tongue lashing from McGraw one day, he disappeared for a while and was soon traded to the Cardinals for Rogers Hornsby. It was 1927, the year after Hornsby led the Cardinals to a surprise seven-game victory over the powerful Yankees. The trading of Frisch shocked the Giants' faithful, who assumed that he would one day succeed McGraw as manager. But the two men's fiery dispositions collided and they couldn't co-exist.

The change of scenery hardly slowed the 28-year-old flash. He helped the Redbirds to pennants in 1928, 1930 and 1931. Hornsby escaped St. Louis in time, because the Yankees trotted out the big lumber and avenged the Series loss to the Cardinals by sweeping them in 1928. In the most awesome one-two display in World Series history, Ruth and Gehrig combined for 16 hits, seven homers and 13 runs batted in, hitting .593. Waite Hoyt won two games and the Cardinals could muster only 10 runs in the four games.

In 1930, Frisch tried his hand against another dynasty in the making. The Philadelphia A's boasted a devastating lineup that included Jimmie Foxx, Al Simmons and Mickey Cochrane. On the mound they were led by Lefty Grove and George Earnshaw. The Cardinals lost Games Five and Six and the A's had their second consecutive championship.

In 1931 the Cardinals got revenge, with Burleigh Grimes beating Grove in Game Three and Earnshaw in Game Seven. Pepper Martin completely stole the show, getting 12 hits in 24 at-bats.

In 1934, Frisch hit .300 for the 13th time in 14 years. He was named manager of the team still known as the Gas House Gang, a rough and tumble bunch led by Martin, Paul and Dizzy Dean, Joe Medwick, Leo Durocher and Frisch. With the Dean brothers combining for all four wins and Martin and Medwick carrying the sticks, the Cardinals won in seven. Game Seven turned out to be the very essence of anti-climax, with the Birds winning 11-0. After Joe Medwick slid hard into Detroit third baseman Marv Owen, the frustrated Tiger fans turned ugly, pelting Medwick with bottles and food and halting the game for 20 minutes until Commissioner Landis ordered Medwick from the game.

Frisch was still the player-manager in 1937 when he decided to call it quits. He was on second and Terry Moore on first when a line drive found the left-center field gap. The 39-year-old had to huff and puff to get home and Moore slid in right behind him. "When they start to climb up the back of old Flash, I know it's time to quit," said Frisch. "I'll never play again." He never did.

He continued managing with the Cards through 1938, piloted the Pirates starting in 1940 and joined the Cubs in 1949. He stopped managing in 1951, his lifetime record at 1,138-1,078. He then became a radio voice for the Giants known for his wail, "Oh, those bases on balls!"

Frisch rates high among all who ever played second base. He had 200 or more hits three times and scored 100 runs seven times.

He walked 728 times and struck out just 272 times in more than 9,000 at-bats. He stole 419 bases and led the league in steals three times. He led the league in fielding three times and even banged out 709 extra-base hits.

Above all, Frisch was a member of more championship teams than any other National Leaguer, playing on four pennant winners with the Cardinals and four with the Giants. No wonder the scrappy player reached the Hall of Fame in 1947.

Frisch died at the age of 74 on March 13, 1973, in Wilmington, Delaware, about a month after he was critically injured in an auto accident.

Best 5-Year Average
1921-1925

R	H	D	T	HR	RBI	AVG	OBP	SLG
110	193	28	12	9	76	.336	.383	.471

Best 10-Year Average
1921-1930

| 106 | 187 | 31 | 11 | 8 | 78 | .331 | .383 | .468 |

Best 15-Year Average
1920-1934

| 94 | 176 | 29 | 9 | 7 | 76 | .321 | .371 | .443 |

Lifetime totals

G	2,311	RBI	1,244
AB	9,112	BB	728
R	1,532	K	272
H	2,880	AVG	.316
D	466	OBP	.369
T	138	SLG	.432
HR	105	SB	419
HR%	1.2		

61
BROOKS ROBINSON
Third Base

Born: 5/18/37 Little Rock, AK
6 feet 1 inch, 190 pounds
Debut: 9/17/55, Played 23 years: 1955-1977, Baltimore

Robinson lead the league in putouts eight times and assists eight times. He ended up with more putouts, assists, chances and double plays than any third baseman in history. He earned the nickname "Hoover," since he vacuumed everything around third. "He plays the bag like he came down from a higher league," umpire Ed Hurley once said.

Brooks Robinson led the American League in fielding 11 times in 16 years. Fielding average doesn't by itself indicate a great fielder; even an infielder with no range can make all the plays a few feet to either side of him. But Robinson was not a rangeless fielder. Gold Gloves are a subjective measure, determined by vote only, but he didn't get 16 straight Gold Gloves from 1960 through 1975 for not being a great fielder.

Aside from his fielding exploits, Robinson was a reliable clutch hitter and RBI man for the Birds. He won the MVP award in 1964, hitting 28 homers, knocking in 118 runs and hitting .317. His most memorable season was 1970, when he dominated the World Series in the field, spearing balls to his left, to his backhand and by scooping up slow rollers in front. "I'll become a left-handed hitter to keep the ball away from that guy," Johnny Bench said later. Robinson also hit .429, belting two homers and knocking in six.

It took Robinson until 1960 to secure the regular third base job in Baltimore. That year he hit 14 homers, knocked in 88 runs and hit .294. He also won the first of 16 consecutive Gold Gloves. Robinson became a fixture on a Baltimore team that would win four pennants between 1966 and 1971.

In 1966 Robinson hit 23 homers and knocked in 100 runs. But this fine season was a mere preamble to a most unexpected result – Baltimore's sweep of Los Angeles in the Series. In Baltimore it was the year of Robinson, mostly another Robinson – Frank Robinson. The versatile outfielder had come to the Orioles in exchange for Milt Pappas and promptly won the Triple Crown.

Three years later and the Birds were flying again. Brooks Robinson had hit only .214 in the 1966 Series and 1969 proved even worse. He could manage just one hit in 19 at-bats – an .053 average – against the likes of Tom Seaver, Jerry Koosman and Gary Gentry. The powerful Orioles were completely stymied by the Mets, hitting just .146 for the Series. The upset was nearly as surprising as the football Jets upsetting the Colts, who were 18-point favorites in Super Bowl III, nine months earlier. Few gave the Mets, a ninth place finisher in 1968, any chance of beating the Birds, who had won 109 and lost 53. After the Orioles won the first game, the Mets swept the next four.

The Orioles won 108 in 1970 and resolved not to end the season with the same embarrassment. The 1970 Series will forever be known as the Brooks Robinson series. Before game four, Reds' manager Sparky Anderson said, "I'm beginning to see Brooks in my sleep. If I dropped this paper plate, he'd pick it up on one hop and throw me out at first."

In 1971 Baltimore won 101 games, bringing their three-year total to 218 – an incredible average of 106-56. But they blew a two-games-to-none lead as the Pirates, led by Roberto Clemente playing like a man possessed, won in seven games. Robinson hit .318 in his last Series, bringing his career World Series average to .263.

It was the last year the 34-year old Robinson would hit double digits in homers. He played six more years, four of them good enough to win his last four Gold Gloves, but he had lost his hitting ability. "I could field as long as I could remember," he said, "but hitting has been a struggle all my life." He was more self-denigrating about his foot speed. "I have only one speed and it has never changed. That speed is very slow."

When he retired in 1977, he had played each of his 23 years in Baltimore. "I've been fortunate to have a very long career," he told the largest-ever crowd at Memorial Stadium on "Thanks Brooks Day" Sept.

18, 1977. "I really can't imagine how it could have been better. But it's over now and it's time for something else."

The depth of feeling for Robinson in Baltimore is hard to appreciate in a time when hardly anyone spends an entire career with one club. But sportswriter Gordon Beard captured it best. "Brooks Robinson never asked anyone to name a candy bar after him. In Baltimore, people name their children after him."

The man who started 15 straight All-Star games from 1960 through 1974 was elected to the Hall of Fame in 1983. He now broadcasts Baltimore games.

Best 5-Year Average
1962-1966

R	H	D	T	HR	RBI	AVG	OBP	SLG
80	173	30	4	21	90	.288	.341	.453

Best 10-Year Average
1962-1971

78	165	28	4	20	87	.274	.332	.435

Best 15-Year Average
1960-1974

72	164	28	4	18	83	.275	.331	.423

Lifetime Totals

G	2,896	RBI	1,357
AB	10,654	BB	860
R	1,232	K	990
H	2,848	AVG	.267
D	482	OBP	.325
T	68	SLG	.401
HR	268	SB	28
HR %	2.5	CS	22

62
PIE TRAYNOR
Third Base

Born: 11/11/1899 Framingham, MA, Died: 3/16/72 Pittsburgh, PA
6 feet, 170 pounds
Debut: 9/15/20, Played 17 years: 1920-1937
(missed 1936) Pittsburgh

The Dodgers' Hall of Fame second baseman Billy Herman recalls third baseman Pie Traynor as having the "most marvelous pair of hands you'd ever want to see." The opinion accords with what we know about Traynor, who played from 1920 through 1937 with the Pittsburgh Pirates.

Playing third, he led the league in assists three times, double plays four straight years and in putouts seven times. He could charge bunts flawlessly and he could go deep into the hole between third and short. He was also known for a strong arm.

When Harold Traynor was a boy, he wanted to play for the Sommerville, Massachusetts, parish team, coached by one Father Nangle. He couldn't and so he helped the team by chasing balls. When the priest took him to a grocery store for a reward, he usually said, "I'll take Pie, Father." Thus his nickname.

When he came up with the Pirates, he played short, but he made too many errors at the outset and they replaced him with Rabbit Maranville.

He found his niche at third and even hit better when Rogers Hornsby urged him to try a 42-ounce bat.

Traynor hit .320 and batted in 106 runs in 1925, when the Pirates won the pennant. It was the second of seven seasons that he went over 100 RBI. The Pirates won the pennant and beat the Washington Senators, the defending World Champions. Traynor hit .346 in the Series and even belted a homer off Walter Johnson in Game One. The Senators led the Series three-games-to-one but the Pirates, behind the hitting of Kiki Cuyler, Max Carey and Traynor, rallied to win.

By the 1927 Series the Pirates had added "Big Poison" and "Little Poison," Paul and Lloyd Waner, who hit .380 and .355 respectively, and accounted for 460 hits between them. But Traynor, after hitting .342 during the season, batted only .200 for the Series and the singles of the Waner brothers did not help the Pirates avert a four-game sweep. Ironically, the 1927 Yankees, famous for their "Murderer's Row" lineup, won the Series with pitching. Waite Hoyt, Wilcy Moore, Herb Pennock and George Pipgras held the Pirates to a total of 10 runs.

Traynor didn't play in another Series, but his best seasons still lay ahead. From 1928 through 1930 he hit .337, .356 and .366, while knocking in 351 runs. His arm was broken in 1934 when Philadelphia catcher Jimmie Wilson fell on it. He was a player-manager from 1934 through 1936 and then retired after the 1937 season.

In 1938, with Traynor still managing, the Pirates suffered a bitter loss in fighting for the pennant. They were well ahead of the second-place Cubs when they suddenly dropped six of their last seven games. The final blow to their hopes came when Gabby Hartnett hit a homer in the dark at Wrigley Field – the famous "Homer in the Gloamin'" – that gave the Cubs the pennant. Many thought that Traynor was too much of a gentleman, and far too even tempered, to make a very good manager.

After he made the Hall of Fame in 1948, one of his proudest moments came in July 1969, when, as part of baseball's centennial celebration, he was named the greatest third baseman of all-time.

He wasn't the greatest all-time third baseman in 1969 – someone named Eddie Mathews was – and it certainly isn't true nearly 30 years later, not since Mike Schmidt, Brooks Robinson, George Brett and Wade Boggs have come along.

Still, Pie Traynor did enough glove work and bat work as a third baseman to merit greatness. He finished with a .320 lifetime average.

Best 5-Year Average
1926-1930

R	H	D	T	HR	RBI	AVG	OBP	SLG
90	189	29	12	5	110	.343	.380	.465

Best 10-Year Average
1923-1932

| 91 | 185 | 29 | 13 | 5 | 101 | .329 | .371 | .455 |

Best 15-Year Average

| 78 | 160 | 25 | 11 | 4 | 85 | .321 | .361 | .436 |

Lifetime totals

G	1,941	RBI	1,273
AB	7,559	BB	472
R	1,183	K	278
H	2,416	AVG	.320
D	371	OBP	.362
T	164	SLG	.435
HR	58	SB	158
HR%	0.8		

63
HARRY HEILMANN
Right Field

"Slug"
Born: 8/30/1894 San Francisco, CA, Died: 7/9/51 Southfield, MI
6 feet 1 inches, 195 pounds
Debut: 5/16/14, Played 17 years: 1914-1932 (missed 1915, 1931)
1914-1929, Detroit; 1930, 1932, Cincinnati

He was known as the best right-handed hitter in the American League in
the 1920s. Harry Heilmann is another of those players who did extraordi-
nary things but is forgotten. Perhaps his deeds are overlooked because he
last played nearly 70 years ago beginning in 1914 with the Tigers and ending in 1932 with the Reds. He spent part of 1915 in the Pacific Coast
League and missed the rest on the disabled list and was ill in 1931.
Heilmann won four batting titles, 1921, 1923, 1925 and 1927 with averages
of .394, .403, .393 and .398. The rumor was that he won them in odd-num-
bered years because his effort surged at the end of each two-year contract.

He wasn't too bad in the even-numbered years, either. He hit .356 in
1922, .346 in 1924 and .367 in 1926. Hitting .300 or better 12 times in a
row from 1919 through 1930, Heilmann finished his career with an average of .342. While the right-handed hitter's style was to send liners all
over the field, he also hit for power, slugging over .500 10 times and over
.600 three times.

Ted Lyons, a righty who won 260 games as a White Sox' pitcher, recalled Heilmann's style in the book *Baseball When the Grass was Green*:

Harry Heilmann was one of the most marvelous men I ever met in baseball and one of the greatest right-handed hitters. He was a different type of hitter than, say, Hornsby; Hornsby has a smooth stroke with a beautiful follow-through; Harry had a choppy stroke, but powerful. He was a tough man to pitch to. That whole Tiger ball club was tough to pitch to in those days. I remember one year, until about June, they had three .400 hitters in the lineup. Heilmann, (Heinie) Manush and (Bob) Fothergill. Cobb couldn't even get in the lineup. I'd call that hitting, wouldn't you? Keeping Cobb on the bench! Fothergill came to the White Sox a few years later and he'd love to tell about that. "Remember the time Cobb couldn't get in the lineup?" he'd say, and he'd laugh and laugh.

One of the problems for Heilmann and his other mates – as far as recognition and slugging titles went - was the presence of Ruth and Gehrig in the American League. Their considerable shadow was cast over everyone else in the 1920s. So a run through the history of baseball tends to leave out steady and often great players like Heilmann. He had 100 RBI eight times and 200 hits four times.

Heilmann was not known as a great fielder, but he still won the right field job, throwing well enough that Heinie Manush moved to left field to accommodate him. When Ted Williams hit .406 in 1941, he was the first in baseball to hit .400 since Heilmann's .403 in 1923. Heilmann closed out his career with Cincinnati in 1932 and was elected to the Baseball Hall of Fame in 1952, in his 13th year of eligibility.

Best 5-Year Average
1921-1925

R	H	D	T	HR	RBI	AVG	OBP	SLG
106	206	39	12	16	119	.379	.446	.585

Best 10-Year Average
1921-1930

| 98 | 191 | 15 | 10 | 15 | 114 | .367 | .436 | .572 |

Best 15-Year Average
1916-1930

| 84 | 170 | 35 | 10 | 12 | 101 | .347 | .410 | .526 |

Lifetime totals

G	2,148	RBI	1,539
AB	7,787	BB	856
R	1,291	K	550
H	2,660	AVG	.342
D	542	OBP	.410
T	151	SLG	.520
HR	183	SB	113
HR%	2.4		

64
SAM CRAWFORD
Right Field

"Wahoo Sam"
Born: 4/18/1880 Wahoo, NE, Died: 6/15/68 Hollywood, CA
Played 19 years: 1899-1917
1899-1902, Cincinnati; 1903-1917, Detroit

Sam Crawford is the all-time leader in triples (309). He made the most of a "Dead Ball" era when it was difficult to hit homers. Crawford was a fleet-footed runner, in terrific physical condition and known as a great right fielder. He also managed to lead the league in homers twice, hitting 16 with Cincinnati in 1901 and seven with Detroit in 1908. He is thus the only player in this century to lead both leagues in homers.

As Lawrence Ritter recounts in *The Glory of their Times*, most baseball writers of the period agree that Crawford was the outstanding power hitter of his era. That can't be literally true, however, because Ty Cobb slugged .512, far better than Crawford's .458. A sportswriter of the time who covered the Tigers, H.G. Salsinger, said, "I have seen right fielders, playing against the fence, catch five fly balls off Crawford's bat in one game, balls that would have cleared the fence any time after the season of 1920, when the jackrabbit ball was introduced."

Born in April 1880, in Wahoo, Nebraska, Crawford first earned a salary of $150 a month with Cincinnati in 1899. Despite "Wahoo Sam's" 16 homers and 104 RBI in 1901, the Reds finished dead last. After he hit 22 triples in 1902, he jumped to the Detroit Tigers, where he led the American League with 25 triples.

Not until the Tigers were joined by Cobb in 1905 did they start to rise in the American League. Crawford finished second to Cobb in batting in 1907 and 1908 as the Tigers won the pennant each year. They won the pennant again in 1909. But neither Cobb nor Crawford hit particularly well: Cobb batted .262 in the three Series and Crawford hit .243. The Cubs won in 1907 and 1908 and then the Tigers faced Pittsburgh in 1909.

It was Crawford's opinion that Cobb, the left fielder he played with for 13 years, was not the best player of the time. He thought that Wagner was, especially after the 1909 Series, which was billed as a head-to-head competition between the game's two best players. Wagner hit .333 and stole six bases; Cobb hit .231 and stole two. "Honus was one of those natural ballplayers," Crawford said. "You know what I mean? Like Babe Ruth and Willie Mays. Those fellows do everything by pure instinct."

Besides being the triple king, Crawford also led the league in RBI three times, got more than 100 RBI six times and finished with an impressive 1,525.

Crawford recalls the competition between him and Cobb got to the point where Cobb couldn't stand if Crawford had a good day and he didn't. After a while, they only spoke when one was calling another off a fly ball.

Crawford finished with 2,961 hits and a .309 batting average. A controversy arose about whether he should have been given 87 additional hits which he got in 1899 while playing Grand Rapids in the Western League. The National Commission agreed that any player from the old Western League would be given his statistics when he entered the American League or National League. But the records do not credit Crawford with the 87 hits, otherwise he would have finished with 3,048.

Crawford ended his career in 1917. Despite his incredible achievements, he was passed up in Hall of Fame voting seven times between 1936 and 1946. Cobb campaigned the hardest for his old teammate's election and in 1957, 40 years after he retired, Crawford was selected by the Veteran's Committee.

Crawford died at the age of 88 in 1968.

Best 5-Year Average
1912-1916

R	H	D	T	HR	RBI	AVG	OBP	SLG
71	168	27	20	5	90	.310	.372	.464

Best 10-Year Average
1907-1916

| 83 | 178 | 30 | 18 | 5 | 94 | .317 | .371 | .464 |

Best 15-Year Average
1901-1915

| 89 | 181 | 29 | 18 | 6 | 93 | .314 | .365 | .458 |

Lifetime Totals

AB	9,570	RBI	1,525
R	1,391	BB	760
H	2,961	AVG	.309
D	458	OBP	.362
T	309	SLG	.452
HR	97	SB	366
HR%	1.0		

65
LUKE APPLING
Shortstop

"Old Aches and Pains"
Born: 4/2/07 High Point, NC, Died: 1/3/91, Cumming, GA
5 feet 10 inches, 183 pounds
Debut: 9/10/30, Played 20 years: 1930-1950
(missed 1944) Chciago (AL)

He was known as "old aches and pains" because he was baseball's greatest hypochondriac. Never mind that he lived to 83 years old and hit a towering homer at an Old Timer's Game in Washington D.C. at the age of 75. Besides the homer off Spahn at the age of 75, there was a greater honor in 1970: he was named the greatest player in the history of the White Sox by local baseball writers.

Appling was sure that he was injured everyday of his career. Despite his persistent groaning, he could always hit.

In his 20 years as a White Sox shortstop he hit .300 16 times. In fact, in one stretch he hit .300 in 16 of 17 years. When his average declined to .262 in 1942, he attributed the drought to his being completely healthy all year. When his maladies returned the next year, he hit .328 to lead the league.

His league leading .388 average in 1936 was the highest ever by a shortstop. He led the league again in 1943, hitting .328. Then he missed all of 1944 due to military service and all but 18 games in 1945. Had he played those two seasons he almost certainly would have gotten the 251 hits he needed to reach 3,000. Even with the layoff he was recognized as one of the greatest hitting shortstops ever, hitting .310 for his career and drawing nearly three walks for every time he struck out.

Among the maladies he said afflicted him over the years were indigestion, a stiff neck, fallen arches, a sore throat, dizzy spells, torn leg tendons, insomnia, symptoms of gout, astigmatism, a throbbing kneecap, and even mal de mer after a ferry ride. Appling could not have gotten away with it all if he couldn't play. He routinely complained to White Sox' manager Jimmy Dykes, "Honest, Jimmy, I'm dying." His only real injuries were a broken finger and a broken leg. He got the name "old aches and pains" only after rooming with Chicago's trainer.

When he broke his leg in 1938 he was robbed of speed and range. But two years later he finished second to DiMaggio in batting, hitting .348 to DiMaggio's .352. Appling was a spray hitter whose liners found the lines and gaps enough to net him 440 doubles and 102 triples. Appling was also legendary for his ability to foul off pitches. He could even foul off strikes that were not to his liking. Some say he averaged about 15 fouls a game, which, aside from costing Chicago an estimated $3,200 in lost balls a year, wore out opposing pitchers.

Ted Lyons, a Chicago pitching ace during Appling's tenure, recalled one game vividly. "I remember when Luke ran Charlie Ruffing of the Yankees right out of the game. It was a steaming hot day and when Appling was up in the first inning with two on and two out, Charlie got three balls and two strikes on him. Then Luke stood there and fouled off 14 pitches in a row. Finally he walked and the next batter hit one for a homer. It wasn't long before Ruffing was taken out."

Another time, after he fouled 10 balls into the stands, he said, "That's $27.50 and I'm not done yet. (balls cost about $2.75 each then).

Besides "old aches and pains" he was also known as "fumblefoot" and "old tanglehoof." But he set an American League record by leading the league in assists seven years in a row. Luis Aparicio – a better fielding but poorer hitting shortstop – eventually broke his records for games, double plays, putouts, assists and total chances by a shortstop.

Not only was Appling the first American League shortstop ever to win the batting title, but in 1949, at age 42, he was the oldest regular shortstop in baseball. That was his last .300 season and he retired the next year.

A managing stint in 1967 proved disastrous: he won 10 and lost 30 as the Kansas City A's finished last. That's all right. After Appling failed to get the necessary number of votes for seven different times, baseball brains finally figured in 1964 that he belonged in the Hall of Fame.

Best 5-Year Average
1933-37

R	H	D	T	HR	RBI	AVG	OBP	SLG
94	176	33	5	4	84	.328	.416	.430

Best 10-Year Average
1932-41

| 85 | 165 | 27 | 6 | 2 | 72 | .320 | .406 | .402 |

Best 15-Year Average
1933-1948 (missed 1944)

| 75 | 157 | 25 | 5 | 2 | 63 | .318 | .406 | .402 |

Lifetime totals

G	2,422	RBI	1,116
AB	8,856	BB	1,301
R	1,319	K	528
H	2,749	AVG	.310
D	440	OBP	.399
T	102	SLG	.398
HR	45	SB	179
HR %	0.5	SB	108

66
CAP ANSON
First Base

"Pops" "Old Anse"
Born: 4/11/1852 Marshaltown, IA, Died: 4/14/22 Chicago, IL
6 feet, 227 pounds
Debut: 5/6/1871, Played 27 years 1871-1897
1871, Rockford, National Association; 1872-1875, Philadelphia;
1876-1897 Chicago (AL); 1876-1897 Philadelphia (NL)

Commissioner Kenesaw Mountain Landis, when informed of Cap Anson's death, exclaimed, "Not Pop Anson. You don't mean my old friend Pop is dead. Oh, I just can't say anything." It was April, 1922, and no one knew then how the two would be linked in baseball history. In 1883 Anson refused to play in an exhibition game at Toledo because Toledo's roster included Moses Fleetwood Walker, a black catcher. Though Anson backed down when threatened with forfeiture of the gate, he used his standing and popularity in the game to ban black pitcher George Stovey in 1887 when John Montgomery Ward tried to sign him to the Giants. Landis would become as staunch an opponent of integration later on, not allowing black players a chance at playing major league baseball. The "gentleman's agreement" stood. Landis' died in November 1944, and the color line was broken in 1947.

Aside from his views on race, Anson's talent as a ballplayer was beyond doubt. In a career that began in 1871, when he was 19, he would lead the league in RBI eight times, batting average four times and on-base percentage four times. A strapping 6-foot, 227-pounder, Anson was a slick first baseman who led the league in fielding five times. He played his best ball with the Chicago White Sox, then of the National League, between the ages of 29 and 39 and ended his career in 1897, the first player ever to reach 3,000 hits, finishing with exactly that number.

His lifetime batting average was .329, a figure he was so proud of that he wanted his tombstone to read, "Here lies a .300 hitter."

Anson was born in Marshalltown, Iowa, in April 1852, and he became a good enough player to be sought by the Forest Citys of Rockford, Illinois, a semi-professional organization in the National Association. By 1872 he was playing with the Philadelphia Athletics and he played for the A's through 1875.

He was playing mostly third base when he joined Chicago in 1876 and brought the pennant to the Chicago White Sox. By the time he took over as manager in 1879 he played first base. He managed Chicago to pennants from 1880 to 1882, 1884 and 1885, and was responsible for several innovations, like rotating his pitchers and using signals to his hitters and fielders. Platooning and spring training, so common a part of modern baseball, were originated by Anson.

While Anson's stance on black ballplayers was unyielding, he was an affectionate figure on his own club and called "Cap" (because he was captain of the team) or "Pop" by his players.

After Chicago's period of dominance was over, however, Anson heard murmuring from fans and friends that the club would have been better served with him playing less and just managing. When his contract ended in 1897 it was not renewed.

Andrew Freedman signed him to manage the Giants but his term there was only 25 days. He turned down a donation of $50,000 from the Chicago fans, opened a billiard parlor in Chicago which was successful, but a semi-pro team he organized to tour the country was not. He organized a rival major league in 1899, the American Association, but this venture failed. He starred in a vaudeville act with his family and failed, and even served one term as city clerk of Chicago.

Aside from the .329 batting average, Anson finished with a 1,879 RBI and 1,719 runs. He was elected to the Hall of Fame in 1939.

Best 5-Year Average
1884-1888

R	H	D	T	Hr	Rbi	Avg	Obp	Slg
107	166	31	9	11	109	.342	.398	.513

Best 10-Year Average
1880-1889

R	H	D	T	Hr	Rbi	Avg	Obp	Slg
89	150	30	7	7	97	.341	.394	.488

Best 15-Year Average
1876-1890

R	H	D	T	Hr	Rbi	Avg	Obp	Slg
80	134	25	6	5	83	.338	.393	.469

Lifetime totals

G	2,276	RBI	1,879
AB	9,101	BB	952
R	1,719	K	294
H	3,000		(incomplete)
D	528	Avg	.329
T	124	Obp	.395
Hr	97	Slg	.446
Hr %	1.1	Sb	247

67
CARLTON FISK
Catcher

"Pudge"
Born: 12/26/47 Bellows Falls, VT
6 feeet 2 inches, 220 pounds
Debut: 9/18/69, Played 24 years: 1969-1993 (missed 1970)
1969-1980, Boston; 1981-1993, Chicago

Carlton Fisk is one of those few players who played in four decades. He began his career in 1969, several months after Woodstock, and finished in 1993, just in time to surf the net. In between, he broke records for games caught (2,226) and homers by a catcher (351).

Fans of the great Boston-New York rivalry that resurfaced in the 1970s will remember the animated debate about who was a greater catcher, Fisk or Thurman Munson. After Munson crashed his private plane and died in August 1979, Fisk was 31 years old. All he did was play 14 more years, retiring at 45 years old.

In his 24-year career Fisk played through injury upon injury. He adopted an extensive training program that kept him going. In the process, he surpassed Johnny Bench and then Bob Boone in games played behind the dish. In 1990 he became the oldest regular catcher in baseball history at 42, playing 137 games that year for the White Sox. He quit at 45 years old, retiring as one of only four catchers to hit 300 homers, score 1,000 runs and knock in 1,000 runs. The others were Johnny Bench, Yogi Berra and Gary Carter.

Born in December 1947, Fisk played three sports in high school in Charlestown, New Hampshire, and earned a scholarship to the University of New Hampshire. But he signed with the Red Sox and by 1972 became their full-time catcher. He took Rookie of the Year honors that season (the first to be chosen unanimously in the American League) and followed with even a better season in 1973. But he missed a combined 264 games due to injuries in 1974 (torn knee), 1975 (broken arm) and 1979 (injured elbow).

It was during those years that the Red Sox-Yankees rivalry became especially heated. The Red Sox drew first blood, winning the pennant in 1975 but losing to Cincinnati in the World Series, one of the best ever. It was Game Six, in the bottom of the 12th inning of a 6-6 game, that Fisk hit Pat Darcy's second pitch into the foul pole, with the help of some famous body English. But the Red Sox, in a script that has become their baseball legacy, blew a 3-0 lead in Game Seven, extending to 57 their streak of years without a World Series victory. They would also blow 2-run and 3-run leads in Games Six and Seven of the 1986 Series.

The Yankees won the Eastern Division in 1976, 1977 and 1978. They were no match for Cincinnati, being swept in the 1976 Series. But Cincinnati didn't return in 1977 and the Yankees returned with Reggie Jackson, who hit five homers to sink the Dodgers. In 1978, Boston led by 14-and-a-half games in July. Boston had pitching and an awesome lineup of Jim Rice, Fred Lynn, George Scott, Rick Burleson, Carl Yastrzemski and Fisk. The Yankees didn't have the same power up and down but had Graig Nettles, Thurman Munson and Jackson. And on the mound they had Ron Guidry, who finished 25-3, and Goose Gossage in the bullpen.

Both Fisk and Munson were acutely aware of the argument about the league's best catcher. One day, Munson noticed something in the press notes, prepared by Yankees' public relations man Marty Appel. It said, "AL Assist Leaders, Catchers: Fisk 27, Munson 25." Munson became incensed. "What's the idea of showing me up like this?" he demanded of Appel. "You think he's got a better arm than me? What a stupid statistic." Munson walked away. During the game he dropped third strikes three different times, throwing to first to complete the out with each one. Appel knew what he was doing: by game's end, Munson had 28 assists; Fisk, 27.

The Yankees caught up with Boston and both teams finished at 99-63. A one-game playoff ensued. The Yankees won (see section on Carl Yastrzemski) and beat the Dodgers in six games in the World Series. But as satisfying as another World Championship was, the best baseball of

1978 was played by two American League teams. The rivalry died a little the following year when Munson was killed, and has never been the same since.

Fisk, who had hit 20 homers and knocked in 88 runs in 1978, had a mediocre season in 1979 and a good one in 1980, before becoming a free agent, signing with the White Sox in 1981. He had played 11 years in Boston and was 33 when he was traded. So it must have appeared like the familiar ballplayer-leaves-to-play-his-last-few-years-with-new-team scenario. Who would have thought that Fisk had 13 more seasons in him and that he would hit more homers in Chicago than he had in Boston?

When he changed his Sox from Red to White, he also changed his number. Fisk had worn 27 in Boston but flip-flopped to 72 in Chicago, because it was a "turn around in my career." He slumped in early 1983 and, hitting .136, was replaced in both games of a July doubleheader by skipper Tony LaRussa. Fisk was enraged and went nose-to-nose with LaRussa. LaRussa hardly minded the confrontation, saying, "He came out fighting, the way a winner reacts to a challenge." Over the next 71 games Fisk hit 16 homers, drove in 49 runs, and raised his average 100 points, finishing with 26 homers, 86 RBI, a .289 average and a .518 slugging average, helping the pale hose win the Western Division. The following season "Pudge" registered career highs with 37 home runs and 107 RBI.

By the time he retired in 1993, Fisk's totals were among the best ever for a catcher: 376 homers, 1,330 RBI and a .269 average. It won't be long before the Hall of Fame calls.

Best 5-Year Average
1972-1976

R	H	D	T	HR	RBI	AVG	OBP	SLG
60	105	19	4	17	53	.277	.344	.481

Best 10-Year Average
1972-1981

| 66 | 117 | 22 | 3 | 17 | 61 | .283 | .349 | .471 |

Best 15-Year Average
1972-1986

| 66 | 117 | 21 | 3 | 19 | 65 | .271 | .334 | .462 |

All time totals

G	2,499	RBI	1,330
AB	8,756	BB	849
R	1,276	K	1,386
H	2,356	AVG	.269
D	421	OBP	.343
T	47	SLG	.457
HR	376	SB	128
HR%	4.3	CS	58

68
GARY CARTER
Catcher

"Kid"
Born: 4/8/54 Culver City, CA
6 feet 2 inches, 215 pounds
Debut: 9/16/74, Played 19 years: 1974-1992
1974-1984, Montreal; 1985-1989, New York (NL);
1990, San Francisco; 1991, Los Angeles; 1992, Montreal

Gary Carter is one of four catchers to hit 300 homers (the other three are Bench, Berra and Carlton Fisk) and he laid claim to being the best catcher in the game for a time, after Johnny Bench started to decline. Carter didn't play as well as Carlton Fisk for as long a period of time. But during his peak period – lasting between 1977 and 1986 – Carter could be counted on to deliver between 16 and 32 homers and between 72 and 106 RBI. This is good production, but not Bench, Berra or Campanella production.

The Montreal organization converted Carter from a shortstop to a catcher before he entered the major leagues. "I was the worst catcher you ever saw, a real joke," he said. Gary Carter entered the major leagues in 1974, playing just nine games. He played 144 games in 1975 – 92 of them in the outfield – before playing the majority of his games at catcher the following year. He would end up winning three Gold Gloves at the position, leading the league in assists six times and in games and putouts six straight years. In 1978 he set a major league record by allowing only a single passed ball in 157 games.

By the 1981 strike season Carter was acknowledged as the best catcher in the game. He helped that reputation in the All-Star Game, hitting two homers. Only Al Rosen, Ted Williams, Willie McCovey and Arky Vaughan had hit two homers in the All-Star Games before him. He won his second All-Star Game MVP in 1984, when he homered off Dave Steib.

Gary Carter drove in 100 runs four times in his career and seemed to provide the extra punch the New York Mets needed. With Carter's bat and leadership, the Mets challenged St. Louis in 1985 and then won it all in 1986. He hit 24 homers and knocked in 105 runs that season (and, like other Mets, appeared in many curtain calls made popular by fans after sacrifice flies). In the Series against Boston, he hit two homers and knocked in nine runs. He had driven in three runs in games Three and Four and then started the winning rally in Game Six, getting a single off Calvin Schiraldi with two outs and two strikes.

The Mets won 90 or more games each year from '84 through '88, and won 108 games in '86 and 100 more in '88. But the result – for a team that had Dwight Gooden, Darryl Strawberry, Keith Hernandez, and Len Dykstra – was a single World's Championship. Hernandez, Gooden and Strawberry battled addictions and the organization made some imprudent trades. The team with the most talent in baseball underachieved.

Carter's decline started in 1987, when he was 33. He hit 20 homers, drove in 83 runs and hit just .235 that year. In the 1988 League Championship Series against the Dodgers that everyone predicted the Mets would win, they lost in seven games. The turning point was Game Four when Dwight Gooden held a 3-1 lead in the ninth inning. Had the Mets won, they would have had a three-games-to-one lead. But Gooden surrendered a two-run homer to Mike Sciosa and the Dodgers won in extra innings. Carter, who had hit 11 homers, driven in 46 and hit .242 for the season, hit poorly in the Series. He batted a weak .222 in 27 at-bats, knocking in 3 runs while failing to hit a home run. He did hit his 300th homer in 1988.

After the Mets released Carter in 1989, he played a year each with the Giants, Dodgers and Expos. He then became a broadcaster with the Florida Marlins to begin the 1993 season.

Carter versus Fisk is very close. Carter slugged .439 to Fisk's .457 and Fisk was better longer than Carter. Carter's peak years are better than Fisk's, however, and he had better five, 10 and 15-year runs.

Both belong in the Hall of Fame.

Best 5-Year Average
1977-1981

R	H	D	T	HR	RBI	AVG	OBP	SLG
72	133	25	3	26	80	.268	.336	.486

Best 10-Year Average
1977-1986

R	H	D	T	HR	RBI	AVG	OBP	SLG
75	143	26	2	26	89	.274	.346	.480

Best 15-Year Average
1977-1991

R	H	D	T	HR	RBI	AVG	OBP	SLG
60	121	22	2	20	72	.265	.339	.454

Lifetime totals

G	2,296	RBI	1,225
AB	7,971	BB	848
R	1,025	K	997
H	2,092	AVG	.262
D	371	OBP	.338
T	31	SLG	.439
HR	324	SB	39
HR%	4.1	CS	42

69
OZZIE SMITH
Shortstop

"The Wizard of Ahs"
Born: 12/26/54 Mobile, AL
5 feet 11 inches, 150 pounds
Debut: 4/7/78, Played 19 years: 1978-1996
1978-1981, San Diego; 1982-1996, St. Louis

San Diego broadcaster Jerry Coleman once screamed, "Ozzie Smith just made another play that I've never seen anyone else make before, and I've seen him make it more than anyone else ever has!" Twisted logic notwithstanding, we know what he meant. Smith was nicknamed "The Wizard of Ahs" and he was all of that. He started out taking Gold Glove honors in 1980 and 1981 with San Diego and was still going with St. Louis by 1992. Smith got to balls that other great shortstops couldn't touch and made more acrobatic plays than anyone, anywhere.

He leads all National Leaguers in Gold Gloves with 13 and has a greater claim to be called the best fielding shortstop of all-time than anyone who ever lived. *Total Baseball*, which is responsible for the most thorough statistical calculations of any publication in the game, claims that Smith, in the course of his career, "has saved his teams 242 runs beyond what an average short-stop would have done, a mark unequaled at the position in this century."

In just his third year, 1980, he set an all-time record for assists by a shortstop (621). He was traded to St. Louis in December 1981, for Sixto Lezcano and Gary Templeton, and helped the Cards to win a pennant. They came back from being down three games-to-two to beat Milwaukee in the 1982 World Series, as Darrell Porter won the Series MVP.

Through 1982, Smith had never hit above .248. Starting with 1985, he put up an impressive 10-year run of averages: .276, .280, 303, .270, .273, .254, .285, .285, .288 and .262. He also became more adept at getting on base, keeping a two-to-one walks to strikeouts ratio. Combine this with his fielding; few shortstops in baseball were as valuable as Smith. He could steal bases right from the start. During the first 16 years of his career, from 1978-1993, he averaged 35 steals and nine times caught stealing per year. He retired having been successful on 80 percent of his steal/attempts.

He helped the Cardinals to their second and third World Series in 1985 and 1987, even hitting a decisive homer to beat the Dodgers in Game Five of the NLCS. Smith finished second to Andre Dawson in the MVP voting that season and reached .300 (.303) for the only time in his career.

He again helped his team to the post-season in 1996. The Cardinals swept the Division Series against San Diego and met the Braves in the NLCS. After losing Game One, the Cardinals stormed back to beat Greg Maddux, Tom Glavine and Greg McMichael in succession. Then the Braves bombed them 14-0, 3-1 and 15-0 to take the pennant. Ozzie Smith had played his last game.

He recorded 500 or more assists eight times, a record for shortstops. He could range far to his left or right and could dive then and pop right up and throw in time to get runners. Playing shortstop full-time for a major league team certifies that the player is adept at defense. But Smith went beyond others at the position. He made plays that others couldn't, all the while maintaining a high fielding percentage. In 1991, he set a record for NL shortstops, committing just eight errors in 150 games, winning his 13th consecutive Gold Glove, to break a National League tie with Roberto Clemente and Willie Mays. Because he finished with 1,257 runs and 2,460 hits, he also contributed at the plate. He is a cinch to go into the Hall of Fame.

Best 5-Year Average
1985-1989

R	H	D	T	HR	RBI	AVG	OBP	SLG
81	158	30	4	2	57	.274	.356	.350

Best 10-Year Average
1983-1992

R	H	D	T	HR	RBI	AVG	OBP	SLG
76	147	27	4	2	53	.263	.340	.330

Best 15-Year Average
1979-1993

R	H	D	T	HR	RBI	AVG	OBP	SLG
72	141	24	4	1	47	.262	.339	.328

Lifetime Totals

G	2,573	RBI	793
AB	9,396	BB	1,072
R	1,257	K	589
H	2,460	AVG	.262
D	402	OBP	.339
T	69	SLG	.328
HR	28	SB	580
HR%	0.3	CS	148

70
LUIS APARICIO
Shortstop

Born: 4/29/34 Maracaibo, Venezuela
5 feet 9 inches, 160 pounds
Debut 4/17/56, Played 18 years: 1956-1973
1956-1962, Chicago (AL); 1963-1967, Baltimore; 1968-1970,
Chicago (AL); 1971-1973, Boston

The story goes that Cleveland GM Hank Greenberg had a choice between
two promising shortstops. He didn't think Luis Aparicio deserved a
$10,000 bonus and instead made a trade for another Venezuelan, Chico
Carrasquel. Carrasquel played 10 pretty good seasons with four teams.
Luis Aparicio led the league in stolen bases nine consecutive seasons and
in fielding eight consecutive seasons. Greenberg made the wrong choice.

Luis Aparicio's father was the best shortstop in Venezuela for 25 years.
Luis then took his father's position on the town team and was signed by
the White Sox organization in 1954. In his first season in the majors he
led the American League in stolen bases and won the 1956 Rookie of the
Year Award. Several patterns were already set.

Aparicio would team with Nellie Fox, the 5-foot-9-inch second sacker
with a bottle-handled bat and a chaw of tobacco. The duo won more fielding
titles together than any other double play combination: 14 between them.
Aparicio was always a slick fielding shortstop, known for using a heavier

glove during infield practice so that his own glove would feel lighter during the game. He won nine gold gloves and still holds the major league record for most games at shortstop (2,581), assists (8,016) and double plays (1,553). On offense Fox batted second and Aparicio first, usually getting 150 hits and winning the stolen base title during his first nine years in the league.

Aparicio was a key part of the "Go Go White Sox" in 1959, stealing 56 bases and scoring 98 runs. Fox won the MVP award that year, with Aparicio second in the voting, leading in putouts, assists and fielding average. In that Series, the White Sox were led by Aparicio's eight hits and Fox's nine, but the Dodgers won in six games behind Larry Sherry's two victories.

Aparicio continued his pattern as the best base stealer and fielding shortstop in the league. He once had 26 consecutive steals. For a leadoff batter, however, he had a very poor on-base percentage of .313.

He was involved in a big trade in January, 1963. Aparicio and Al Smith went to Baltimore in exchange for Hoyt Wilhelm, Pete Ward, Ron Hansen and Dave Nicholson. Several years later the Orioles, with Frank Robinson winning the Triple Crown, were World Series winners, sweeping the Dodgers. So inept were the Dodgers that they committed more errors (six) than they scored runs.

Aparicio, now 33, was traded back to the White Sox in November, 1967, with Baltimore getting, among others, Don Buford, an outfielder who would help them win a World Series in 1969. In 1970 Aparicio had his best offensive season, hitting .313. He was traded to Boston in 1971, where he played his final three years, retiring in 1973. He had played 18 years and played every one of his 2,599 games at shortstop.

In 1984 he was elected to the Baseball Hall of Fame. He was no doubt pleased that his infield mate Nellie Fox, who had died in 1975, was elected to the Hall of Fame in 1996. Aparicio imitated Fox in his career, hollering like him, spitting tobacco juice like him and even naming his son for him. Now Fox had imitated him.

Best 5-Year Average
1958-1962

R	H	D	T	HR	RBI	AVG	OBP	SLG
84	156	21	6	5	47	.263	.309	.341

Best 10-Year Average
1957-1966

R	H	D	T	HR	RBI	AVG	OBP	SLG
83	154	21	7	6	44	.259	.307	.344

Best 15-Year Average
1956-1970

R	H	D	T	HR	RBI	AVG	OBP	SLG
78	154	22	6	5	44	.261	.310	.343

Lifetime totals

G	2,599	RBI	791
AB	10,230	BB	736
R	1,335	K	742
H	2,677	AVG	.262
D	394	OBP	.313
T	92	SLG	.343
HR	83	SB	506
HR%	0.8	CS	136

71
BILLY WILLIAMS
Left Field/First Base

Born: 6/15/38 Whistler, AL
6 feet 1 inch, 175 pounds
Debut: 8/6/59, Played 18 years: 1959-1976
1959-1974, Chicago (NL); 1975-1976, Oakland

Billy Williams is one of those players whose career totals could sneak up on you. Unless you were at Wrigley, checking his accomplishments day in and day out, you might not notice what Williams was steadily accomplishing in the sixties and seventies; many of us just missed it.

Bill James points out that, "His offensive totals were unquestionably helped by playing at Wrigley Field." Indeed, of the 392 homers the lefty batter hit while playing for the Cubs, 231 – 59 percent – came at Wrigley. Ernie Banks, a right-handed hitter, hit 56 percent of his at Wrigley. Williams went to the Oakland Coliseum and hit his final 34 homers in 1975 and 1976. James takes this decline as evidence that Williams couldn't hit in Oakland. But he played at the age of 37 and 38 in Oakland and missed 42 games in his last season, factors which at least contributed to his decline.

Of greater interest are his 15 seasons from 1961 (when he won Rookie of the Year) to 1975, when Williams was a full-time player. He hit 413 homers over those years, an average of 28 per year. He hit .300 five times, slugged .500 five times and .600 once and hit 30-plus homers five times. He didn't have peaks like Ernie Banks, but he sure did age well for a 15-year run. Banks' best 15-year run was from 1954 through 1968, when he hit 453 homers, an average of 30 per year. That's not much of a difference, if we just isolate home run hitting and forget that Banks was a shortstop.

Williams had his best year in 1970 – a bust out year when he hit 42 homers, drove in 129 runs, hit .322 and slugged .586 – and 1972, when he hit 37 homers, knocked in 122, hit .333 and slugged .606. 1970 was also the third time he reached 200 hits. Five times he knocked in 100 runs and seven more times 90-plus.

Loafing wasn't his thing, either: In the eight seasons from 1963 to 1970 he played between 161 and 163 games every year! He set a National league record by playing in 1,117 consecutive games (later broken by Steve Garvey). Williams' even demeanor contributed to his steadiness as a player.

Williams played with Ferguson Jenkins, Ernie Banks and Ron Santo on good Cub teams that never quite made it. He was traded to Oakland after the 1974 season and at least one player was glad to see him go. "No more Hank Aaron, Billy Williams or Bobby Bonds – I like that," Steve Carlton said about the three sluggers who were dispatched to the American League. Williams hit his 400th homer with Oakland in 1975. He was elected to the Hall of Fame in 1987.

Best 5-Year Average
1968-1972

R	H	D	T	HR	RBI	AVG	OBP	SLG
102	190	32	7	30	107	.307	.372	.524

Best 10-Year Average
1963-1972

| 101 | 189 | 32 | 7 | 30 | 101 | .300 | .366 | .514 |

Best 15-Year Average
1961-1975

| 91 | 175 | 28 | 6 | 27 | 95 | .294 | .364 | .496 |

Lifetime Totals

G	2,488	RBI	1,475
AB	9,350	BB	1,045
R	1,410	K	1,046
H	2,711	AVG	.290
D	434	OBP	.364
T	88	SLG	.492
HR	426	SB	90
HR %	4.6	CS	49

72
ANDRE DAWSON
Right Field

"The Hawk"
Born: 7/10/54 Miami, FL
6 feet 3 inches, 195 pounds
Debut: 9/11/76, Played 21 years: 1976-1996
1976-1986, Montreal; 1987-1992, Chicago (NL);
1993-1994, Boston; 1995-1996, Florida

Andre Dawson, a little like Don Sutton, piled up some very big statistics without the luxury of frequent greatness. Sutton won 20 games once and Dawson had one magnificent season. Nonetheless, Sutton made the Hall of Fame and Dawson belongs there, too.

In 1987 Dawson was voted the MVP of the National League for hitting 49 homers, knocking in 137 runs and slugging .568. It was the third of only five seasons in his 21-year career when he would slug .500. But he did hit 438 lifetime homers, knock in 1,591 runs and get 2,774 hits in a very good career. More than 1,000 of his hits were for extra bases – 1,039 to be exact – and he also stole 314 bases. Four more times Dawson knocked in 100, and three more times he knocked in 90.

There is a very good 15-year run here, starting in 1978 and running through 1992. In those 15 years, he hit 380 homers (25 per year) and knocked in 1,360 runs (91 per year). He also hit .300 or better five times.

His 1,039 extra-base hits is one of the highest totals among those players not in the Hall of Fame.

Best 5-Year Average
1987-1991

R	H	D	T	Hr	Rbi	Avg	Obp	Slg
74	156	24	5	30	99	.286	.326	.517

Best 10-Year Average
1981-1990

R	H	D	T	Hr	Rbi	Avg	Obp	Slg
79	154	28	5	26	91	.287	.332	.504

Best 15-Year Average
1977-1991

R	H	D	T	Hr	Rbi	Avg	Obp	Slg
79	156	28	6	25	89	.284	.326	.492

Lifetime Totals

G	2,627	RBI	1,591
AB	9,927	BB	589
R	1,373	K	1,509
H	2,774	AVG	.279
D	503	OBP	.327
T	98	SLG	.482
HR	438	SB	314
HR %	4.4	CS	109

73
JIM RICE
Left Field/Designated Hitter

Born: 3/8/53 Anderson, SC
6 feet 2 inches, 200 pounds
Debut: 8/19/74, Played 16 years: 1974-1989, Boston

Bill James wrote that ballplayers tend to establish their "peak value" in their twenties and you don't find out their "career value" until they are well into their thirties. This is certainly true in the case of Jim Rice. At the ages of 24, 25 and 26, Rice, with bat cocked high, was a menacing figure and devastating hitter, totaling 124 homers and 383 RBI in a three-year period. He was the best hitter in the American League.

It is also true that Rice was astounding at Fenway during those three years, hitting 82 homers at home and only 42 on the road. But after 1983, the year he turned 30, he never again hit 30 homers in a season. While he was accustomed to slugging as high as .600 in his twenties, after 30 his highest average was .490.

It's hard to figure how Rice's power game fell off a cliff. Whatever the reason, it certainly diminishes him as a player. Still, he did enough, long enough, to put up some impressive totals. Although Rice didn't achieve one of the ultimate measuring sticks of a great career – a 15-year run – his 14-year run from 1975 through 1988 makes for a good average.

In those 14 seasons he had 378 homers and 1,410 RBI, which averages out to 27 homers and 101 RBI per year.

Rice started his assault early, hitting 22 homers and knocking in 102 runs in his rookie season. Fred Lynn, the Sox' brilliant center fielder, won Rookie of the Year and Most Valuable Player.

Lynn would go on to win four Gold Gloves. One of the crueler aspects of that year for Rice – who finished third in the MVP voting – and the Red Sox was that an injury to Rice kept him out of the 1975 Series. In a series decided by one run, the Sox lost in seven games to the Reds.

Rice didn't like being the DH and eventually was moved to left field. He established himself as a power hitter in 1977, hitting 39 homers and knocking in 114. It was the first of three 200-hit seasons for Rice.

Rice had his career year in 1978, winning the MVP by clubbing 46 homers, knocking in 139 runs and hitting .315. That was the season of Boston's 14-and-one-half-game lead in July. When Rice slumped, so did the team and the Yankees overcame the deficit, finishing in a tie. New York won the playoff game on yet another day in Red Sox history when they came tantalizingly close to taking the prize, only to fall back.

Rice followed his 1978 season with a stellar 1979 season, hitting another 39 homers, knocking in 126 runs and hitting .305. In 1980 Rice broke his wrist and missed 31 games, then came the 1981 strike season and in 1982 he snapped back with 24 homers and 97 RBI.

In all, Rice had eight 100-RBI seasons. He suffered his third cruel defeat as a Red Sox' player in 1986. The Sox came from being down three-games-to-one against California to beat them and win the pennant. Against the Mets, they led two-games-to-none in the Series and then three-games-to-two. Rice contributed, hitting .333 in 27 at-bats, though he hit no homers and collected just one RBI. In Game Six they were ahead by two runs with none on base and two outs and two strikes on Gary Carter. But Carter and the next two batters singled, then a wild pitch and Bill Buckner's error brought in the winning run. In Game Seven they led 3-0. But Bruce Hurst, who had won two games in the Series, could not hold the lead and the Mets rallied to win.

In his third year of Hall of Fame eligibility in 1997, Rice was turned away. His credentials – 382 homers, 1,451 RBI and .298 average – should be enough to get him in.

Best 5-Year Average
1976-1980

R	H	D	T	HR	RBI	AVG	OBP	SLG
100	186	28	10	35	111	.308	.356	.559

Best 10-Year Average
1975-1984

| 92 | 179 | 27 | 7 | 30 | 106 | .303 | .352 | .526 |

Best 15-Year Average
1974-1988

| 82 | 160 | 24 | 5 | 25 | 95 | .300 | .353 | .506 |

Lifetime Totals

G	 2,089	RBI	 1,451
AB	 8,225	BB	 670
R	 1,249	K	 1,423
H	 2,452	AVG	 298
D	 373	OBP	 356
T	 79	SLG	 502
HR.	 382	SB	 58
HR %	...... 4.6	CS	 34

74
TONY PEREZ
First Base

Born: 5/14/42 Camaguey, Cuba
6 feet 2 inches, 205 pounds
Debut: 7/26/64, Played 23 years: 1964-1986
1964-1976, Cincinnati; 1977-1979, Montreal; 1980-1982, Boston;
1983, Philadelphia; 1984-1986, Cincinnati

Tony Perez was the RBI linchpin on the axle of the "Big Red Machine."
He had 1,652 RBI – 18th on the all-time list. Every player with more is
either in the Hall of Fame or on the way. Perez drove in more than 90
runs all 11 years from 1967 through 1977 and then again in 1980. Seven
times he drove in more than 100 runs.

Tony Perez is oft disrespected in these kinds of surveys, perhaps
because he was more consistent than spectacular and because he was
one of several players swallowed up in the Reds' loaded lineup of the
1970s. Perez was the number five man in the lineup, a position reserved
in the order for RBI men.

To get a larger picture, Perez knocked in 1,414 runs in a 15-year period, an average of 94 per year. Take the 12-year slice from 1967 through
1978 and he averaged 100 RBI for those dozen years! In fact, the only
players with more lifetime RBI than Perez who are not in the Hall are
Dave Winfield and Eddie Murray, both currently ineligible. Winfield and

Murray each collected 3,000 hits and are guaranteed to make the Hall of Fame. When players reach either 300 wins, 500 homers or 3,000 hits, they are ultimately inducted. No comparable established plateaus exist for RBI. Besides the RBI totals, Perez has enough other distinctions to merit his inclusion. He had 2,732 hits, 963 for extra bases, including 505 doubles, 79 triples and 379 homers. For the life of me, I cannot see why Perez does not get more respect. He has been getting votes every year since 1992, but hasn't hit the magic number in six consecutive years. In his book *The Politics of Glory: How the Hall of Fame Really Works*, Bill James notes that Perez is the only eligible player with more than 900 extra base hits (963) not in the Hall of Fame (at the time James wrote, Dwight Evans and Dave Parker, both of whom have 900 extra base hits, were not eligible). The only player with more extra base hits who is not in the Hall is Andre Dawson, who had 1,035. Dawson is not yet eligible.

James compares the best-qualified eligible players at certain positions who are not in the Hall of Fame, with the worst-qualified who are in. At first base he lists Tony Perez, and Frank Chance (of Tinkers-to-Evers-to-Chance poetry fame). Chance who was inducted in 1946. Here are their numbers:

	G	AB	R	H	2B	3B	HR	RBI	SB	AVG.	SLG AVG.
Perez	2777	9778	1272	2732	505	79	379	1652	49	.279	.463
Chance	1286	4295	798	1274	199	80	20	596	405	.297	.394

The comparison shows that some players, because of reputations deserved or undeserved, are swept into the Hall by the force of popular opinion, which is easy enough to sway.

Best 5-Year Average
1969-1973

R	H	D	T	HR	RBI	AVG	OBP	SLG
84	172	29	4	30	107	.295	.367	.516

Best 10-Year Average
1969-1978

| 79 | 161 | 31 | 4 | 25 | 100 | .286 | .354 | .488 |

Best 15-Year Average
1967-1981

| 75 | 156 | 29 | 4 | 23 | 94 | .282 | .345 | .475 |

Lifetime Totals

G	2,777	RBI	1,652
AB	9,778	BB	925
R	1,272	K	1,867
H	2,732	AVG	.279
D	505	OBP	.344
T	79	SLG	.463
HR	379	SB	49
HR %	3.9	CS	33

75
JOE CARTER
Left Field

Born: 3/7/60 Oklahoma City, OK
6 feet 3 inches, 215 pounds
Debut: 7/30/83, Played 15 years: 1983-1997
1983, Chicago (NL); 1984-1989, Cleveland; 1990, San Diego; 1991-1997, Toronto

Toward the close of the 1997 season Joe Carter achieved a distinction enjoyed by only eight other players in the long history of baseball: he had his 10th 100 RBI season. He now has 1,382 career RBI. Across the last 12 seasons he has driven in 1,281 runs – an average of 107 per season.

Carter has done enough other things, too. He has hit 20 or more homers in each of the last 12 years and now has 379 for his career. He has slugged over .500 three times. He had two of his best seasons – hitting 34 and then 33 homers – while playing on Toronto's World Championship teams in 1992 and 1993.

In each Series he hit two homers and his 1993 homer off Mitch Williams ended the Series in six games. It reminded some viewers of Bill Mazeroski's homer to break a tie and beat the Yankees in the seventh game of the 1960 Series. But Carter's blast was the first time ever that a batter ended a Series with a homer when his team was behind.

On his RBI seasons alone, Carter should be put into the Hall of Fame.

Best 5-Year Average
1992-1996

R	H	D	T	HR	RBI	AVG	OBP	SLG
83	147	29	4	30	105	.259	.306	.482

Best 10-Year Average
1986-1995

R	H	D	T	HR	RBI	AVG	OBP	SLG
85	154	31	4	30	107	.256	.301	.470

Best 15-Year Average
1983-1997 (entire career)

R	H	D	T	HR	RBI	AVG	OBP	SLG
75	139	27	3	25	92	.259	.302	.464

Lifetime Totals

G	2,063	RBI	1,382
AB	8,034	BB	503
R	1,119	K	1,326
H	2,083	AVG	.259
D	410	OBP	.303
T	52	SLG	.464
HR	378	SB	227
HR %	4.7	CS	68

Some deserving players who just missed making the top 100:

Richie Allen
Richie Ashburn
José Conseco
Max Carey
Orlando Cepada
Ed Delehanty
Bill Dickey
Dwight Evans
Nellie Fox
Steve Garvey
Billy Hamilton
Gil Hodges
Joe Jackson
Willie Keeler
Chuck Klein
Don Mattingly
Fred McGriff
Joe Medwick
Dale Murphy
Al Oliver
Kirby Puckett
Tim Raines
Sam Rice
Ron Santo
Rusty Staub
Bill Terry
Zack Wheat

Up and Coming

In time, these players may take their place among the all-time greats.

Roberto Alomar
Jeff Bagwell
Albert Belle
Craig Biggio
Nomar Garciaparra
Juan Gonzalez
Derek Jeter
Chipper Jones
Chuck Knoblauch
Tino Martinez
Mike Piazza
Alex Rodriguez
Sammy Sosa
Moe Vaughn
Larry Walker

IV
The Top 25 Pitchers

1
WALTER JOHNSON

"Big Train"
Born: 11/6/1887 Humbolt, KS, Died: 12/10/46 Washington DC
6 feet 1 inch, 200 pounds
Debut: 8/2/07, Played 21 years: 1907-1927 Washington

Next to Walter Johnson's name in *Total Baseball* is enough bold black ink to make people with light clothes nervous. He led the league in wins six times, in complete games six times, in innings five times, in strikeouts 12 times, in ratio (walks plus hits divided by innings) four times and in ERA five times. The "Big Train" won between 20 and 36 games every year from 1910 to 1919. Then he won 20 twice more at the ages of 36 and 37. In the 21 years Johnson pitched for the Washington Senators, opposing hitters batted just .227 against him. He won 417 games, an average of 20 per season for two decades.

The 6-foot-1-inch, 200-pound "Big Train" started pitching in 1907. In his judgment, a four-day period in 1908 in which he pitched three shutouts, ranked at the top of his achievements. In those three games, the Humboldt, Kansas, native blanked New York 3-0, 6-0 and 4-0, allowing only 12 hits in the three contests.

Starting in 1910 he went on a streak in which he won 25 or more for seven consecutive seasons. He won 16 consecutive games in 1912. His peak season was 1913, when he finished 36-7 with a 1.14 ERA to take the

MVP Award. Personal excellence for Johnson was rarely matched by his team, however. Over his first 13 years in the league, in which he won 20 eleven times, all the American League pennants were won by Detroit, Philadelphia, Boston and Chicago. Despite Johnson's Herculean efforts, the Senators were the very definition of mediocrity. "Washington: First in War, First in Peace and Last in the American League," while not always true, wasn't far from true either. Johnson lost 27 games by the score of 1-0 and he lost 65 games in which his team failed to score a single run.

When he failed to win 20 for the first time in 10 years in 1920, it looked as if he wouldn't get the chance to play in a World Series. But in 1924, at 36 years old, he led the league in wins with a 23-7 mark and in ERA (2.72). He was awarded his second MVP. The Senators edged New York by two games and Johnson pitched in relief in Game Seven, holding the Giants scoreless from the ninth through the twelfth. The Senators scored on a bad-hop single in the bottom of the inning and Johnson had his first World Championship in 18 years.

The following season he won 20 again and two more in the World Series. But this time Washington squandered a three-games-to-one lead to Pittsburgh.

Johnson had such a gentlemanly bearing that he would never "loosen up the hitters" by throwing at them. Ty Cobb admitted that he took advantage of Johnson's good nature. He crowded the plate, safe in the knowledge that Johnson wouldn't brush him back. "He was one of the finest, most decent men in baseball," Cobb once remarked, "and he was too much a gentleman ever to dust me off at the plate although I deserved it." So Cobb crowded the dish, his knees and chin well out over it. Johnson pitched him outside, instead of driving him away from the plate as he should. Johnson was never too effective against Cobb.

Johnson pitched his 21st and last season in 1927. He managed the Senators from 1929 through 1932, then retired. But he returned in the summer of 1933 to manage Cleveland and resigned that post in August, 1935.

He drew much publicity on Feb. 22, 1936, for still having the arm strength to hurl two silver dollars 272 feet across the Rappahannock River at a celebration of Washington's Birthday. Later that year he was one of the five original players elected to the Hall of Fame, the others being Babe Ruth, Ty Cobb, Honus Wagner and Christy Mathewson.

Johnson pitched to Ruth at an Aug. 23, 1942, exhibition between games of a Senators-Yankees doubleheader at Yankee Stadium. 69,136 came to witness the two come out of retirement and their appearance benefited the Army-Navy Relief Fund by more than $80,000.

Johnson died on Dec. 10, 1946. At the time of his death he was first in strikeouts (3,508) and first in shutouts with 110. One more note: Johnson's Senators played .492 over his 21 seasons, while he pitched .599, 107 points better than his team.

Best 5-Year Run and Average 1911-1915

	W	L	PCT.	IP	H	BB	K	Ratio	ERA
Totals	149	63	.703	1744	1328	314	1181	8.5	1.79
Average	30	13		349	266	63	236		

Best 10-Year Run and Average 1910-1919

	W	L	PCT.	IP	H	BB	K	Ratio	ERA
Totals	265	143	.650	3425	2604	661	2219	8.6	1.72
Average	27	14		343	260	66	222		

Best 15-year Run and Average 1910-1924

	W	L	PCT.	IP	H	BB	K	Ratio	ERA
Totals	345	202	.631	4650	3783	1029	2833	9.3	2.10
Average	23	13		310	252	69	189		

Career

W	L	PCT	G	GS	CG	SH	SV	IP	H	HR	BB	K	Ratio
417	279	.599	802	666	531	110	34	5914	4913	97	1363	3509	9.9

ERA	Opponent's Avg
2.17	.227

2
CHRISTY MATHEWSON

"Big Six"
Born: 8/12/1880 Factoryville, PA, Died: 10/7/25 Sarana Lake, NY
6 feet 1 inches, 195 pounds
Debut: 7/17/1900, Played 17 years: 1900-1916
1900-1916, New York (NL); 1916 Cincinnati

He was called the "Big Six," named after New York's fastest fire engine,
known for putting out fires all over Manhattan. Christy Mathewson was
just as effective at putting out baseball fires with his screwball or "fadeaway" pitch. All things considered – winning percentage (.665), ERA
(2.13) wins (373) ratio (9.6), control (walking one batter every 5.9
innings) and endurance (completing 434 out of 551 starts) – he is right
at the top of the greatest pitchers who ever lived. As good as the Giants
were, winning at a .591 clip during the years Mathewson pitched, Matty's
winning percentage was still 74 points above the team.

He became a full-time starter for the Giants at 20 years old, in 1901.
Over the next 14 years, he won 358 games, an average of 26 a season. He
won 30 games four times, peaking in 1908 with a 37-11 record. He won
the ERA title five times, with miserly totals like 1.28, 1.43 and 1.14. He
led in strikeouts five times, in shutouts four times and in ratio five times.

But he may have been proudest of his ability to put the ball where he
wanted it. "He could throw a ball into a tin cup at pitching range," said

Johnny Evers. "A pitcher's speed is worth nothing," Matty said, perhaps making a statement to the fireballers, "if he cannot put the ball where he wants to. To me, control is the first requirement of good pitching." Greg Maddux, meet Christy Mathewson.

The image of Mathewson as a clean-cut, heroic man endures. He was an All-American football player at Bucknell. He headed two literary societies at the college and was elected class president. He was nationally known as a checkers expert, a passion that persisted when he was too ill to do much else. He didn't normally pitch on Sundays.

Beginning in 1903 he won 30 or more three straight times – winning 94 and losing 33 over that span. In the 1905 World Series he turned in a pitching performance for the ages, hurling three shutouts (two of them four-hitters) in five days against the Philadelphia A's and beating Eddie Plank and Chief Bender in the process. Mathewson allowed 14 hits in 27 innings, striking out 18 and walking just one. The Giants won in five games.

Mathewson won 20 every year right through 1914. His winning became so monotonous that New York sportswriter Damon Runyon described it this way: "Mathewson pitched against Cincinnati yesterday. Another way of putting it is that Cincinnati lost a game of baseball. The first statement means the same as the second."

In 1916 John McGraw, the Giants' manager and Matty's best friend, traded "The Big Six" to Cincinnati so that he could manage the Reds. He joined a chemical warfare unit in France during WWI, and was accidentally "gassed." His lungs were weakened and he later contracted tuberculosis. Living in the quiet village of Saranac Lake, New York, he followed baseball in the papers and played checkers with experts from all over the country who came to see him.

He died of tuberculosis pneumonia on Oct. 7, 1925, the opening day of the World Series. John McGraw praised his repertoire of pitches. Three Finger Brown remembered his lordly entrance. "He'd always wait until about 10 minutes before game time, then he'd come from the clubhouse across the field in a long linen duster, like auto drivers wore in those days, and at every step the crowd would yell louder and louder."

Mathewson was one of the original five Hall of Famers in 1936.

Best 5-Year Run and Average 1904-1908

	W	L	PCT.	IP	H	BB	K	Ratio	ERA
Totals	148	56	.725	1676	1355	314	983	9.0	1.88
Average	30	11		335	271	63	197		

Best 10-Year Run and Average 1903-1912

	W	L	PCT.	IP	H	BB	K	Ratio	ERA
Totals	279	109	.719	3252	2774	560	1858	9.22	1.90
Average	28	11		325	277	56	186		

Best 15-Year Run and Average 1901-1915

	W	L	PCT.	IP	H	BB	K	Ratio	ERA
Totals	370	181	.672	4668	4107	794	2468	9.25	2.10
Average	25	12		311	274	53	165		

Career

W	L	PCT	G	GS	CG	SH	SV	IP	H	HR	BB	K	Ratio
373	188	.665	635	551	434	79	28	4780	4218	91	844	2502	9.6

ERA	Opponent's Avg
2.13	.236

3
TOM SEAVER

"Tom Terrific" "The Franchise"
Born: 11/17/44 Fresno, CA
6 feet 1 inch, 206 pounds
Debut: 4/13/67, Played 20 years: 1967-1986   ·
1967-1977 New York (NL); 1977-1982, Cincinnati; 1983, New York
(NL); 1984-1986, Chicago (AL); 1986, Boston

He was know as "Tom Terrific" and "The Franchise." When the New York
Mets held Tom Seaver Day in 1988, Seaver stood at the microphone and
said, "I have thought what I would do today to show my appreciation..."
With that, he walked from home plate to the mound then bowed in each
direction: to the fans in left, in right and behind home plate. He thanked
them from his place. It was one of the simplest yet most profound ges-
tures of appreciation ever from an athlete.

The Mets and their fans had much for which to thank Seaver. He had
taken them from darkness to light. Over his career, Seaver pitched for
teams that played .502 baseball. He pitched .603, 101 points better than
those teams. He has the highest winning percentage (.603) of any 300-
game winner in the last half century. That impressive list includes
Warren Spahn, Gaylord Perry, Don Sutton, Phil Niekro, Early Wynn,
Nolan Ryan and Steve Carlton. He struck out 200 or more batters a
record nine straight years and led the league in whiffs five times. He led

the circuit in ERA three times. In the sixties and seventies, only Sandy Koufax (2.76) had a lower ERA than Seaver (2.86), but Koufax (2,324) didn't even pitch half as many innings as Seaver (4,782). Only Whitey Ford (2.75), of those post-World War II hurlers who pitched 15 years or more, had a lower ERA than Seaver.

The Indians, Phillies and Mets all wanted to sign Seaver. Commissioner William Eckert picked his name out of a hat for New York on April 3, 1966. The Mets signed him to a $50,000 bonus and assigned him to Jacksonville. When he joined the Mets in 1967, Seaver didn't think it was so cute to play for a team whose identity was that of lovable losers. "There are two places in this league," he said, "first place and no place." He posted a 25-7 record in 1969, winning his first of three Cy Young awards. He lifted a team to first that finished ninth the year before. The Mets then swept the Braves in the first League Championship Series.

Then an incredulous city tuned in on their transistors and stopped before store front televisions as the Mets finished one of the most amazing sports stories in history. After losing Game One to the heavily favored Baltimore Orioles, they used flawless fielding and timely hitting and swept the next four games. The Orioles hit just .146 for the Series.

On April 22, 1970 Seaver fanned 19 Padres, including the last 10 in a row. But the Mets had a problem scoring runs. So even as Seaver led the league in strikeouts (283) and ERA (2.82), his record slipped to 18 and 12. He won 60 games over the next three years, winning two ERA titles and two strikeouts titles in the process.

In 1971, Seaver was miffed that he didn't win the Cy Young Award for a second time. He finished 20-11 and led the league with personal bests in ERA (1.76) and strikeouts (289). The Cubs' Ferguson Jenkins finished 24-13 with 263 strikeouts and an ERA of 2.77 – a full run per game more than Seaver. When Jenkins got the award, Seaver and his wife Nancy named their cat Ferguson Jenkins, just so they would be reminded.

His 19-10 season in 1973 was good enough for his second Cy Young. He led the league in five categories: ERA (2.08), complete games (18), strikeouts (251), ratio (8.9) and opponents' batting average (.206). The Mets rallied at the close of the season to win the Eastern Division and then beat the Reds in five games. But with a three-games-to-two lead on Oakland in the World Series, Seaver lost Game Six to Catfish Hunter, 3-1. Holtzman then beat Matlack in Game Seven and the A's had back-to-back titles.

Seaver got his third Cy Young Award in 1975, winning 22 games and posting a 2.38 ERA. After a contract dispute with Mets' Chairman of the Board M. Donald Grant in 1977, Seaver was traded to the Reds. In exchange for their "franchise," the Mets got four undistinguished players: pitcher Pat Zachary, infielder Doug Flynn and outfielders Dan Norman and Steve Henderson. Seaver finished the year 21-6 for his fourth 20-win season. The following year he threw his first no-hitter.

He might have won his fourth Cy Young Award for finishing 14-2 and leading the league in wins in the strike-shortened 1981 season. But the country was swept up in "Fernando Mania" and the 13-7 Valenzuela was given the award.

Seaver returned to the Mets in 1983 but they left him unprotected before the draft and the White Sox picked him up for the 1984 season. Seaver turned in two good seasons at the ages of 39 and 40. In 1984 he won 15 and lost 11 for the White Sox. In 1985 he won 16 and lost 11, including his 300th victory at Yankee Stadium.

For anyone who still had doubts, Seaver showed in that game he was not just a thrower but a pitcher. He knew ahead of time that the opportunity for his 300th win would come on a Sunday in New York, against a potent hitting Yankee team battling for the pennant. "I knew I wanted to keep (Rickey) Henderson off base and (Dave) Winfield and (Don) Mattingly in the ballpark, and somewhere in there I knew Winfield would be coming up as the tying run or winning run in the last three innings," he said. "And sure enough, Winfield came up in the eighth with runners on first and third and two out." The Yankees trailed 4-1.

"What I wanted to do was get the count to 3-2 and use Winfield's aggressiveness against him," Seaver recalled. The count went 3-2. Pitching from the stretch, Seaver looked at first and stepped off the rubber. "I'm sure people were thinking, 'Why would he be concerned with the runner at first?' I was priming the pump. I was getting Winfield anxious." Seaver threw a change-up and Winfield, way out in front, struck out.

Seaver finished 7-13 with Chicago and Boston in 1986. After the season he retired.

He had 311 wins, was fourth in strikeouts with 3,640 and seventh in shutouts with 61. Besides the numbers, the image of Seaver will endure. He took the mound every fourth day and, with that powerful leg drive that made his right knee drag in the dirt, dominated hitters for many years.

Best 5-Year Run and Average 1969-1973

	W	L	PCT.	IP	ERA	H	BB	Ratio	K
Totals	103	51	.669	1410	2.35	1076	367	9.2	1280
Average	21	10		282		215	73		256

Best 10-Year Run and Average 1969-1978

	W	L	PCT.	IP	ERA	H	BB	Ratio	K
Totals	187	102	.647	2717	2.52	2120	762	9.5	2381
Average	19	10		272		212	76		238

Best 15-Year Run and Average 1967-1981

	W	L	PCT.	IP	ERA	H	BB	Ratio	K
Totals	259	143	.644	3794	2.60	2997	1074	9.7	3075
Average	17	10		253		200	72		205

Career

W	L	PCT	G	GS	CG	SH	SV	IP	H	HR	BB	K	Ratio
311	205	.603	656	647	231	61	1	4782	3971	380	1390	3971	10.2

ERA	Opponent's Avg
2.86	.226

4
LEFTY GROVE

Born 3/6/1900 Lanaconing, MD, Died: 5/22/75 Norwalk, OH
6 feet 3 inches, 190 pounds
Debut 4/14/25, Played 17 years: 1925-1941
1925-1933, Philadelphia (AL); 1934-1941, Boston

After Lefty Grove died on May 22, 1975, Red Smith wrote a column with a headline, "The Terrible Tempered Mr. Grove." He took the mound with a hair-trigger temper that could explode into rage at any moment, especially when a fielder made an error behind him. The record shows that opposing batters should have been the enraged ones.

Between 1927 and 1933 – when the twin towers of baseball were the Yankees and Grove's Philadelphia A's – Lefty won 20, 24, 20, 28, 31, 25 and 24 games, going 172 and 54. That's an average of 25-8, the kind of record great pitchers post in their single best year. Grove averaged that record seven years. Better yet, during the A's glory years from 1929 through 1931, he won 79 and lost 15!

Among 200-game winners in this century, Lefty Grove is second to Whitey Ford (.690) in winning percentage. Robert Moses (.680) "Lefty" Grove led the league in ERA an astounding nine times, in strikeouts seven times, in winning percentage five times and in wins four times. Lefty Grove, with Bob Feller and Carl Hubbell, were baseball's best pitchers between 1925 and 1950. Grove won 300 games and lost 141. In the process, his Philadelphia A's, who interrupted the Yankees' World Series run in 1929, won three pennants and two World Series.

Talking about Grove's fastball, Philadelphia sportswriter Bugs Baer said that Grove, "could throw a lamb chop past a wolf." One day at Yankee Stadium the A's were leading 1-0 when Mark Koenig led off the Yankees' ninth with a triple. Nine pitches later, Grove had struck out Babe Ruth, Lou Gehrig and Bob Meusel. Another time he relieved Jack Quinn with the bases loaded and none out; threw just 10 pitches to strike out Ruth, Gehrig and Lazzeri.

On August 23, 1931, Grove proved he could be both great – and grouchy. He had won 16 straight games, tying an American League record shared by Smokey Joe Wood and Walter Johnson. He was pitching against the Browns in St. Louis. Grove and Dick Coffman were locked in a scoreless tie. Goose Goslin got a bloop single off Grove and scampered home when Jimmy Moore, a substitute for Al Simmons in left, mis-judged an ordinary fly ball by Jack Burns. The A's lost 1-0. "After I lost that game, I came back and won six or seven in a row," Grove recalled in Donald Honig's *Baseball When the Grass Was Green*. "Would have won about 24 straight except for that loss. After that game I went in and tore the clubhouse up. Threw everything I could get my hands on – bats, balls, shoes, gloves, benches, water buckets; whatever was handy. Giving Al Simmons hell all the while. Why Simmons? Because he was home (with an injury) in Milwaukee, that's why. Still gets me mad when I think about it."

Connie Mack, needing money to support the A's, sold Grove to the Red Sox for $125,000 after the 1933 season, when Grove won 24. Mack had gotten the best of Grove's career and made a cash profit in the bargain: before the 1925 season Mack bought Grove from Jack Dunn, the owner of the International League Orioles, for $100,600 – $600 more than the Yankees paid the Red Sox for Ruth in 1919. Grove didn't win his first game until he was 25 years old.

After a bad arm in 1934, Grove finished his last seven years, all win-ning seasons. At the time he said, "I'm throwing just as hard as I ever did, the ball's just not getting there as fast."

In 1941, at age 41, he beat Cleveland 10-5. It was his last win and his 300th.

He was elected to the Hall of Fame in 1947 and died in 1975.

Best 5-Year Run and Average 1928-1932

	W	L	PCT.	ERA	IP	H	BB	Ratio	K
Totals	128	34	.790	2.57	1406	1297	346	10.5	925
Average	26	7			281	259	69		185

Best 10-Year Run and Average 1927-1936

	W	L	PCT.	ERA	IP	H	BB	Ratio	K
Totals	217	87	.714	2.90	2578	2483	670	11.0	1507
Average	22	9			258	248	67		151

Best 15-Year Run and Average 1925-1939

	W	L	PCT.	ERA	IP	H	BB	Ratio	K
Totals	286	129	.689	2.97	3649	3535	1095	11.4	2150
Average	19	9			243	236	73		143

Career

W	L	PCT	G	GS	CG	SH	SV	IP	H	HR	BB	K	Ratio
300	141	.680	616	457	298	35	55	3940	3849	162	1187	2266	11.6

ERA	Opponent's Avg
3.06	.255

5
WARREN SPAHN

Born: 4/23/21 Buffalo, NY
6 feet, 175 pounds
Debut: 4/19/42, Played 21 years: 1942-1965 (missed 1943-1945)
1942-1952, Boston (NL); 1953-1964, Milwauke (NL); 1965, New
York (NL); 1965 San Francisco

Warren Spahn was 25 years old when he won his first game in 1946. Yet he went on to become the winningest left-hander in baseball history, notching 363 victories. He got 342 of those victories in a 17-year period from 1947 through 1963 – an amazing 20 per season.

No other post-World War II pitcher has won games at near the same clip as Spahn. He won 20 or more game 13 times, the last time when he was 42 years old in 1963. Said Stan Musial: "I don't think he'll ever get into the Hall of Fame – he'll never stop pitching."

Warren Spahn started his career with the Boston Braves in 1942, pitching 16 innings without a decision. He enlisted in the Army, suffered shrapnel wounds in a battle along the Rhine and was awarded a bronze star and a Purple Heart. Spahn returned after being away from baseball for three years to win eight games in 1946. After that, it was off to the races.

"Hitting is timing," said Spahn. "Good pitching is upsetting timing." The proof was in the pudding. Without an overwhelming fastball, Spahn reeled off the following victory totals: 21, 15, 21, 21, 22, 14, 23, 21, 17, 20, 21, 22, 21, 21, 21, 18 and 23. Dizzy? Not half as dizzy as National League hitters were chasing Spahn's screwball. The man's favorite number seemed to be 21. "A pitcher needs two pitches," the master deceiver said. "One they're looking for and one to cross `em up."

In 1951, after Willie Mays' 0-21 drought against the National League, he blasted a Spahn offering over the roof at the Polo Grounds. "For the first 60 feet it was a hell of a pitch," Spahn joked after the game. Thinking back on Mays' slump, he said, "I'll never forgive myself. We might have gotten rid of Willie forever If I'd only struck him out."

Spahn anchored the Braves staff in two cities for 20 years. In Milwaukee's pennant winning seasons, 1957 and 1958, he led the league in wins, first with 21 and then with 22. In 1957 the Braves beat the defending champion Yankees in seven games. Despite two wins by Spahn in the 1958 Series, the Braves gave back a three-games-to-one lead and lost.

In 1960, then 39 years old, Spahn had won 267 major league games by the start of the season. He hadn't pitched a no-hitter. On Sept. 15, he changed that, striking out 15 Phillies in the process.

He won his 300th at the age of 40 in 1961 and pitched a second no-hitter that season. By the time he had been traded to the Mets in 1965, he had led the league in wins eight times, in complete games nine times, in strikeouts four times, in ERA three times and in ratio four times.

Having played for Casey Stengel on the Boston Braves in the late 1940s and now again for the Mets, Spahn made one of the best cracks ever, saying, "I'm probably the only guy who worked for Stengel before and after he was a genius." Coming out of retirement to catch Spahn in 1965, Yogi Berra said, "I don't think we're the oldest battery, but we're certainly the ugliest."

After the 1965 season and 21 years of pitching in the National League, Spahn retired. He still stands fifth in wins (363), eighth in innings pitched (5,244) and sixth in shutouts (63).

Best 5-Year Run and Average 1957-1961

	W	L	PCT.	ERA	IP	H	BB	Ratio	K
Totals	106	60	.636	3.09	1382	1270	358	10.6	673
Average	21	12			276	254	72		135

Best 10-Year Run and Average 1954-1963

	W	L	PCT.	ERA	IP	H	BB	Ratio	K
Totals	205	118	.635	3.03	2758	2519	665	10.4	1267
Average	21	12			276	252	67		127

Best 15-Year Run and Average 1949-1963

	W	L	PCT.	ERA	IP	H	BB	Ratio	K
Totals	306	189	.618	2.98	4218	3802	1114	10.5	2104
Average	20	13			281	253	74		140

Career

W	L	PCT	G	GS	CG	SH	SV	IP	H	HR	BB	K	Ratio
363	245	.597	750	665	382	63	29	5243	4830	434	1434	2583 2,583	10.8

ERA	Opponent's Avg
3.09	.244

6
BOB FELLER

Born: 11/3/18 Van Meter, IA
6 feet, 185 pounds
Debut: 7/19/36, Played 18 years: 1936-1956,
(missed 1942-1944) Cleveland

Warren Spahn lost three years to service in World War II; Bob Feller missed nearly four years. He missed all of 1942, 1943, 1944 and pitched only nine games in 1945. What would he have done had he not missed those years? We cannot say exactly; but we can use inductive inference to answer the question. In the three years before the War and the one year after, Feller won 102 games and lost 48, for an average of 25 wins and 12 losses per year. Give Feller that same average for the nearly four years he missed (subtract his 5-3 record in 1945), and you add 97 wins and 45 losses to his career totals. Feller then finishes with 363 wins and 207 losses (.637) instead of his present record of 266 and 162 (.621).

Even with a four-year hole in his career, Feller's ledger is astounding. In his last four years before the War (1938-1941) and his six year after (1946-1951) he won 211 games and lost 118 – an average of 21 and 12 over a 10-year period. "Rapid Robert" led the league in wins six times (getting 25 or more three times, in 1940, 1941 and 1946), in shutouts four times, in strikeouts seven times and in ERA once. Batters hit .231 against him for his career.

Bob Feller lived out as much a storybook career as any pitcher. He came to the Indians in July 1936, when he was 17. He grew up on a farm in Van Meter, Iowa, in the kind of rural setting that rivals the hamlet in the Field of Dreams. The blazing fastball that was his calling card he developed doing chores on the family farm and by throwing a ball into a backstop his father fashioned from two-by-fours and chicken wire.

Before Feller's major league debut, he had struck out eight Cardinals in three innings of exhibition work. In his first Major League start, he struck out 15 St. Louis Browns. Several games after that he struck out 17 Philadelphia Athletics to tie Dizzy Dean's record. Then he went home to Van Meter to finish high school.

"I was a bonus baby," Feller said, recalling his start. His bonus? "I got two autographed baseballs plus a scorecard from the 1935 All-Star Game." He wasn't complaining, though. "I'm glad I didn't get a (cash) bonus," said Feller, "you're supposed to get paid after you do your job."

Feller threw as hard as anyone before him or since. In 1946, in Washington, D.C., he was paid $700 to throw several balls through an opening in a photoelectric measuring device. Senators' owner Clark Griffith promoted the event and about 31,000 fans showed up to see the results. His highest average speed – which is what Jugs machines measure today – was about 107 miles per hour. The highest speed crossing the plate, which is what the 1946 machine measured, was 98.6.

Feller used that blinding speed to stymie American league hitters for almost two decades. He spun 12 one-hitters and a no-hitter. Feller set what was then a record when he struck out 18 Tigers in 1938. "Go on up there and hit what you can see," the Senator's manager Bucky Harris once instructed his players. "If you can't see it, come on back."

Of the many amazing things about Feller's career, none is more impressive than this fact: the only event that stopped his stranglehold of league leading totals in wins, innings and strikeouts was his service in World War II.

What he didn't get was a World Series victory. In 1948 the Indians beat the Braves, four games to two. Feller lost both his starts. He threw a four-hitter in Game One but lost to Johnny Sain, 1-0. In Game Five he pitched poorly, was relieved in the seventh and lost to Spahn, 11-5.

In 1954 the Indians posted an American League record, winning 111 and losing 53, breaking the Yankees' string of five consecutive pennants. Feller, then 35, contributed to the Tribe's record with a 13-3 season. But Cleveland manager Al Lopez passed up Feller, pitching Bob Lemon (23-7) in Game One and Game Four, Early Wynn (23-11) in Game Two and Mike Garcia (19-8) in Game Three. Each had better ERAs than Feller, too. "I never was sure why Lopez didn't use me in that Series," said

Feller. "I pitched 100 more innings than (reliever Hal) Newhouser and I certainly knew the Giants' hitters. I had been pitching against them for 16 years. Leo Durocher, the Giants' manager, said he's wondered the same thing." Lemon lost two and the Indians were swept. Feller wouldn't have helped Cleveland's bats, however. The Giants outscored Cleveland 21-9. The Indians hit .190 as a team.

After 4-4 and 0-4 seasons, Feller retired in 1956 and took his place in the Hall of Fame in 1962.

Best 5-Year Run and Average 1939-1947 (not including 1942-1945)

	W	L	Pct.	ERA	Ip	H	Bb	Ratio	K
Totals	122	59	.674	2.69	1629	1263	734	11.0	1311
Average	24	12			326	252	147		262

Best 10-Year Run 1938-1951

	W	L	Pct.	ERA	Ip	H	Bb	Ratio	K
Totals	211	118	.641	3.12	2893	2410	1361	11.7	2053
Average	21	12			289	241	136		210

Best 15-Year run 1936-1954

	W	L	Pct.	ERA	Ip	H	Bb	Ratio	K
Totals	257	151	.630	3.24	3609	3087	1696	11.9	2479
Average	17	10			241	206	113		165

Career

W	L	PCT	G	GS	CG	SH	SV	IP	H	HR	BB	SO	Ratio
266	162	.621	570	484	279	44	21	3827	3271	224	1764	2581	12.0

ERA	Opponent's Avg
3.25	.231

7
GROVER CLEVELAND ALEXANDER

Born: 2/26/1887 Elba, NE, Died: 11/4/50 St. Paul, NE
6 feet 1 inch, 185 pounds
Debut: 4/5/11, Played 20 years: 1911-1930, 1911-1917,
Philadelphia (NL); 1918-1926, Chicago (NL);
1926-1929, St. Louis (NL); 1930, Philadelphia (NL)

Grover Cleveland Alexander had to overcome small ballparks, epilepsy and an unwavering devoted love of alcohol and he still won 373 games. If Christy Mathewson, that other 373-game winner, was the picture of virtue and clean living in the early years of the century, Alexander was the anti-Christy. His closest companion during and after his career was booze.

He enjoyed his drinking straight, but his pitching was mixed. Alexander was known for blending hard ones, sharp breaking curves, outstanding control. And pitching quickly. When asked why he worked so fast on the mound he replied, "What do you want me to do – let those sons of bitches stand up there and think on me?"

Like many greats, Alexander's reputation gets connected to a single moment in time, the time being Oct. 10, 1926. But that moment came after Alexander the Great's conquering period. Prior to that memorable World Series game against the Yankees, old Alex had won 20 games eight times and 30 games three times.

He began in 1911 with the Philadelphia Phillies. In seven years for a club that usually played around the .500 mark, Alexander won 30 games in three consecutive seasons. The achievement is all the more staggering, considering Philadelphia's phone booth of a ballpark called Baker Bowl. The right field fence was 272 feet away and right-center just 300 feet! The Phillies won 90 games in 1915 – Alex won 31 of them – and captured the pennant. But they were dispatched in five games by the Red Sox. Alex won the Phils' only Series game. In 1916 he won 33, including 16 shutouts. He followed this with 30 in 1917, including complete game victories in both ends of a Labor Day doubleheader. The achievement was miraculous – 94 wins against 35 losses in three years. Further, he won the "pitcher's Triple Crown" – leading the NL in ERA, strikeouts and wins – all three seasons. He won 190 games and lost 88 for an average of 29 and 13. After the Phils' December 1917 trade of Alexander to the Cubs – for two players and the considerable sum of $55,000 – they finished last seven times in the next 11 years.

Even in 1918, the Cubs were 10 years removed from their last championship. Across nine years in Wrigley, Alexander won the ERA title twice – with microscopic markers of 1.72 and 1.91 – and had seasons of 22 and 27 wins.

But midway through the 1926 season, the 39-year-old was waived by Chicago and picked up by St. Louis. Little was expected of him: he had only a 3-3 record with Chicago. St. Louis was battling for a pennant and Alexander won nine games, two games more than he lost, which was their margin of victory over second place Cincinnati.

Against the Yankees and Ruth, who would hit four homers in the Series, little chance was given to St. Louis. The Yankees were going home to New York with a three-games-to-two lead. Alexander, who had won Game One, 6-2, over Urban Shocker, beat Bob Shawkey in Game Six and, figuring his season over, began a rousing celebration after the game.

Rogers Hornsby said later, "Hell, I would rather have him pitch a crucial game for me drunk than anyone I've ever known sober. He was that good." Jesse Haines nursed a 3-2 lead while Alexander nursed his hangover in the bullpen. But Haines tired in the seventh and the Yankees loaded the bases with two out when Hornsby summoned Alexander.

Alexander said he would give Tony Lazzeri "a fastball well inside on the first pitch." "You can't do that," Hornsby said, knowing that Lazzeri loved hard stuff. Alexander insisted that he would foul the pitch and then have to deal with curves on the outside that he, "won't touch." Hornsby relented. "Who am I to tell you how to pitch? Go ahead. Do it your way." As Alex predicted, Lazzeri hit a long one that whizzed just to the left of the foul pole. Then he fanned him on consecutive curve balls.

The Yankees mustered nothing until a Ruth walk – his 11th of the

Series – with two outs in the ninth. But Ruth was caught stealing and the Series was over. Alex had allowed three earned runs in 20 innings. Alluding to Lazzeri's long foul, Alexander said, "Less than a foot made the difference between a hero and a bum." Asked how he felt about striking out Lazzeri, Alex said, "Ask Lazzeri how he felt striking out."

Forty years old the following season, Alexander won 20 for the last time. "Old Pete" retired at the age of 43, after his 20th season, in 1930.

In October, 1950 he was standing for three innings in the back of the mezzanine at Yankee Stadium during the Yankees-Phillies World Series when a reporter spotted him and led him to the press box. The 63-year-old was happy to sit down. Watching DiMaggio and the Yankees, Alex told of the difficulty he had pitching to Hornsby and how he held Babe Ruth to a lone single in 16 times at bat in five games of the 1926 and 1928 Series. Alexander died a month later.

With a lifetime percentage of .642, Alexander pitched an amazing 112 points better than the .530 teams for which he played. Among the 25 great pitchers listed here, only Roger Clemens has a larger differential (.644-.518 +126)

Best 5-Year Run and Average 1913-1917

	W	L	PCT.	ERA	IP	K	H	BB	Ratio
Totals	127	63	.688	2.03	1714	981	1527	321	9.70
Average	25	13			343	196	305	64	

Best 10-Year Run and Average 1911-1920

	W	L	PCT.	ERA	IP	K	H	BB	Ratio
Totals	219	121	.644	2.32	3015	1712	2725	652	10.1
Average	22	12			302	171	273	65	

Best 15-Year Run and Average 1911-1925

	W	L	PCT.	ERA	IP	K	H	BB	Ratio
Totals	299	175	.631	2.61	4222	1937	4055	803	10.4
Average	20	12			281	129	270	54	

Career

W	L	PCT	G	GS	CG	SH	SV	IP	H	HR	BB	SO	Ratio
373	208	.642	696	600	437	90	32	5190	4868	164	951	2198	10.2

ERA	Opponent's Avg
2.56	.250

8
CY YOUNG

Born: 3/29/1867 Gilmore, OH, Died 11/4/55 Newcomerstown, OH
Played 22 years: 1890-1911
1890-1898, Cleveland (NL); 1899-1900, St. Louis (NL);
1900-1908, Boston (AL); 1909-1911, Cleveland (AL);
1911, Boston (NL)

"I can't understand these modern fellers," Cy Young remarked in his later years. "I just pitched every third day. `Twarn't nuthin' to it.

"All us Youngs could throw," said the country boy who was born on a farm. "When I was a kid I usta kill squirrels with a stone. And my grand-dad once killed a turkey buzzard with a rock." At the end of his career, he explained why he didn't warm up before games. "I figured the old arm had just so many throws in it," he said, "and there wasn't any use wasting them." Because of his rubber arm and longevity, Cy Young owns some records that will never be broken in these times of pitch-every-fifth-day hurlers.

He is first in wins (511), losses (316), complete games (750), games (906) and innings (7356). His 76 shutouts are fourth best all-time and his 906 games put him in ninth place.

Born in Gilmore, Ohio, on March 29, 1867, Denton True Young left home to try out for a Canton club in the Tri-State League in 1890. He started throwing to the team's star hitter who couldn't even tick the ball.

"I thought I had to show all my stuff, and I almost tore the boards off the grandstand with my fastball," he recalled. Noticing the splintered grandstand behind home plate, the batter told his manager, "Sign that kid, boss. He did more damage to your grandstand than a cyclone." One player shortened the name to "Cy," Young recalled, and it stayed that way.

Later that year he was rejected by Cap Anson, then player-manager for the White Sox, who thought the 6-foot-2-inch, 200-pound pitcher was just another "big farmer." He debuted for the National League Cleveland Spiders with a three-hit victory on Aug. 6, 1890, against Chicago. Anson now tried in vain to purchase him. He had won nine – including both ends of a doubleheader, 5-1 and 7-3 – by season's end.

After that appetizer, he won 20 or more for the next nine years, topping 30 victories three times. He pitched the Spiders to a Temple Cup Championship in 1895, winning 35 games during the season and three of Cleveland's four victories in the Cup Series. In 1897 he pitched the first of three no-hitters, this one against the Cincinnati Reds. By 1899 Young and other Cleveland stars were shipped to St. Louis. Turning 33 in 1900, he registered only 19 wins, his lowest total since his rookie season. By 1901 he had jumped to the upstart American League and won 33 games for the Boston Pilgrims. Young pitched in Game One of the first World Series game ever. He won two games, as Boston beat the Pirates five-games-to-three. He then won 32, 28 and 26 games in successive years, giving him over 400 wins by the end of 1904. He had pitched a perfect game against Rube Waddell and the Philadelphia Athletics on May 5. "Funny thing about that one," Young said later, "is that there wasn't even one hard chance —until Waddell came up for the final out. He hit a sizzler but it went right at an infielder."

At age 41, he pitched his third no-hitter in 1908. He notched his 500th win for the Cleveland Indians in 1910. In 1911, he was playing for the Boston Braves when he lost the last game he ever pitched, 1-0. "When the kids beat you, it's time to quit," Cy said. But this kid was Grover Cleveland Alexander. Young won 291 of his 511 games in the National League and 220 in the American League. His win total is 94 ahead of the second-place winner, Walter Johnson.

After his retirement, his appearance at ballparks turned even veteran players into little kids. "Is that him?" players would ask of their teammates and then they would surround Young. One day a young reporter asked him, "Pardon me, Mr. Young, were you a big league pitcher?" "Young feller," said Young, "I won more games than you'll likely see in your lifetime."

Best 5-Year run and Average 1892-1896

	W	L	Pct.	ERA	IP	H	BB	Ratio	K
Totals	159	74	.682	3.12	2066	2133	464	11.3	639
Average	32	15			413	427	93		128

Best 10-Year Run and Average 1892-1901

	W	L	Pct.	ERA	IP	H	BB	Ratio	K
Totals	283	151	.652	2.91	3839	3940	671	10.8	1212
Average	28	15			384	394	67		121

Best 15-Year Run and Average 1891-1905

	W	L	Pct.	ERA	IP	H	BB	Ratio	K
Totals	414	228	.645	2.68	5687	5590	1557	11.3	2105
Average	28	15			379	373	104		140

Career

W	L	PCT	G	GS	CG	SH	SV	IP	H	HR	BB	SO	Ratio
511	316	.618	906	815	749	76	17	7356	7092	138	1217	2803	10.4

ERA	Opponent's Avg
2.63	.252

9
STEVE CARLTON

"Lefty"
Born: 12/22/44 Miami, FL
6 feet 4 inches, 210 pounds
Debut: 4/12/65, Played 24 years: 1965-1988
1965-1971, St. Louis; 1972-1986, Philadelphia; 1986, San Francisco;
1986, Chicago (AL); 1987, Cleveland; 1987-1988, Minnesota

Steve Carlton's 15-year silent treatment of baseball writers led broadcaster Ernie Johnson to remark in 1983, "The two best pitchers in the National League don't speak English – Fernando Valenzuela and Steve Carlton." Steve Carlton's reticence over time was exceeded by his excellence as a pitcher. He won 329 games and lost 244 and is second in career strikeouts with 4,136. Sociable or not, Carlton had a dominant pitching style, relying on a hellacious slider and fastball. "I've never paced myself," he said. "I've always thrown everything as hard as I can for as long as I can." His unorthodox training included isometrics, kung fu and twisting his hands in three-foot deep buckets of rice. He went on the disabled list for the first time in 1985 – his 21st year in baseball! Describing Carlton's mysterious approach to training and pitching, his catcher Tim McCarver said "Carlton does not pitch to the hitter, he pitches through him. The batter hardly exists for Steve. He's playing an elevated game of catch."

It must have worked. He won 20 games six times and led the league in strikeouts and innings five times each. In a 12-year period from 1971 through 1982, he won 228 games, an average of 19 per year! "Sometimes I hit him like I used to hit Sandy Koufax," said Willie Stargell, "and that's like trying to drink coffee with a fork." After a 20-win season in 1971, Carlton was not given the money he demanded from the Cardinals and was traded to the Phillies for Rick Wise in Feb. 1972. Considering that Bob Gibson's career was winding down, the Cardinals made an awful blunder letting go of the awesome left-hander. The full extent of the mistake was apparent only a few months later.

Carlton won 27 games for the last-place Phillies, accounting for an astounding 45 percent of their 59 wins, a modern record. His ERA was 1.97 and Lefty completed the Triple Crown with 310 strikeouts. His first Cy Young Award led to a $167,000 salary, a record for pitchers. After losing 20 the next year, he ran off win totals of 16, 15, 20, 23, 16, 18, 24, 13 and 23 over the next nine seasons.

He ended up pitching in five League Championship Series, but in 1976, 1977 and 1978 the Phils couldn't get to the World Series, thwarted by the Reds once and by the Dodgers twice. In 1980 he won 24 and lost 9 to win his third Cy Young honor (he won his second in 1977). Lefty completed the Phillies' dream season by winning two series games – the Second and the clinching Sixth – striking out 17 Royals in 15 innings. It was the Phillies first World Championship. Mike Schmidt won the World Series MVP. On Sept. 23, 1983, Carlton won his 300th game against the Cardinals, who had traded him 11 seasons before. In the Series the Phils faced Baltimore but lost in five games. Carlton, then 38, had completed his last great season the year before, when he won 23 and lost 11 to take home his fourth Cy Young Award. He went 13 and 7 in 1984 and got his 4,000th strikeout.

Then 39, Carlton hung around for five more years, all losing campaigns. He was a combined 16-37 for the Phils, Giants, White Sox, Indians and Twins. Those decline years lowered his percentage from .602 to .574.

He still holds the NL record for strikeouts with 4,136. He was truly one of the dominant pitchers of his time and was elected to the Hall of Fame in 1994.

Best 5-Year Run and Average 1976-1980

	W	L	PCT.	ERA	IP	H	BB	Ratio	K
Totals	101	50	.669	2.89	1337	1126	403	10.3	1053
Average	20	10			267	225	81		211

Best 10-Year Run and Average 1971-1980

	W	L	PCT.	ERA	IP	H	BB	Ratio	K
Totals	190	116	.621	3.04	2795	2417	941	10.8	2191
Average	19	12			280	242	94		219

Best 15-Year run and Average 1969-1983

	W	L	PCT.	ERA	IP	H	BB	Ratio	K
Totals	268	177	.602	3.02	4052	3523	1375	10.9	3334
Average	18	12			270	235	92		222

Career

W	L	PCT	G	GS	CG	SH	SV	IP	H	HR	BB	SO	Ratio
329	244	.574	741	709	254	55	2	5217	4672	414	1833	4136	11.3

ERA	Opponent's Avg
3.22	.240

10
GREG MADDUX

Born: 4/14/66 San Angelo, TX
6 feet, 175 pounds
Debut: 9/3/86, Played 12 years: 1986-1997
1986-1992, Chicago (NL); 1993-1997, Atlanta

Greg Maddux, just 32 years old, is already worthy of Hall of Fame consideration. He was won 184 games, lost 108 (.630) and won four consecutive Cy Young Awards from 1992 to 1995. He has led the NL in ERA three times, innings pitched five times, shutouts twice and wins three times. Greg Maddux and Roger Clemens are the class of the current pitching corps, better than all the pitchers who started their careers in the last 20 years. They are the only active pitchers worthy of being ranked with the top 25 moundsmen of all-time. Maddux has posted an impressive .630 percentage over his career – 94 points better than the clubs for which he's pitched. His 2.80 ERA is the best in the last 20 years.

In 1997, he was an astounding 19-4. But this drew a yawn from those used to his exploits. And why not? Maddux previously put up marks of 15-11, 19-2, 16-6, 20-10 and 20-11. None of this is what makes Mr. Maddux most impressive, however. The undersold part of his work is how his ERA compares with the overall League ERA since 1992.

Greg Maddux' ERA versus League ERA Since 1992

Year	National League ERA	Maddux' ERA
1992	3.50	2.18
1993	4.04	2.36
1994	4.21	1.56
1995	4.18	1.63
1996	4.21	2.72
1997	4.20	2.20

Amazing to tell, but the chart shows that in 1994 Maddux was 2.65 runs per game better than the average pitcher in the league and in 1995 he was 2.55 runs better than the average pitcher. No other pitcher in history has been that far ahead of the league in ERA over a comparable period of time. For six years, Maddux has been pitching anywhere from 1.3 to 2.6 runs better than the league average. Not Addie Joss, not Ed Walsh, not Mathewson, not Johnson, not Hubbell, not Grove, not Koufax, not Marichal, not Seaver – none of the ERA leaders of the various eras in this century have been so far ahead of the league average ERA. Statistically speaking, it's as if two games are being played: the games pitched by others and the games pitched by Maddux. Maddux has done this despite playing 11 of 12 years in two launching pads: Wrigley Field and Fulton County Stadium.

Despite the amazing achievement of 1994, Maddux went "only" 16-6 that season, because the Braves played just 114 games due to the strike. Then too, while the Braves have been in every post-season since 1991, they haven't done this on the strength of their hitting. Maddux loses more than his share of 2-1 and 3-2 games, not to mention games where he exits with a lead only to see another Braves' reliever blow it.

To the undiscerning eye Maddux will always appear less than masterful. He doesn't have a great fastball. He sets up hitters by using the whole plate, moving the ball in and out, and by walking less than a man per eight innings over the last four years. It's his style and, like Ford and Spahn before him, he won't overwhelm hitters. But it's because of pitchers like him that the Braves are willing to spend more on arms than the Clinton Administration.

Best 5-Year Run and Average 1992-1996

	W	L	PCT.	ERA	IP	H	BB	Ratio	K
Totals	90	40	.692	2.13	1191	951	204	8.7	905
Average	18	8			238	190	41		181

Best 10-Year Run 1988-1997

	W	L	PCT.	ERA	IP	H	BB	Ratio	K
Totals	176	90	.662	2.59	2411	2077	524	9.7	1699
Average	18	9			241	208	52		170

12-Year career average

	W	L	PCT.	ERA	IP	H	BB	Ratio	K
	184	108	.630	2.80	2598	2302	609	10.1	1820
	15	9			217	192	51		152

Career

W	L	PCT	G	GS	CG	SH	SV	IP	H	HR	BB	SO	Ratio
184	108	.630	369	365	80	23	0	2598	2301	128	609	1820	10.1

ERA	Opponent's Avg
2.80	.238

11
ROGER CLEMENS

"The Rocket"
Born: 8/4/62 Dayton, OH
6 feet 4 inches, 215 pounds
Debut: 5/15/84, Played 14 years: 1984-1997
1984-1996 Boston; 1997, Toronto

Roger Clemens is praised by his teammates for his unfailing work ethic. It's paid off royally. Clemens has won four Cy Young Awards and owns the largest pitcher-team-differential of any of the 25 greats mentioned here. In his 14-year career, he has pitched .644 baseball – an amazing 126 percentage points above the teams on which he has played.

To those of us who started watching baseball in the nineteen-sixties, easily the most pitching-rich era in baseball history, we got used to pitchers who threw a lot of innings, won 18 to 25 games and struck out a lot of batters. Though precious few of those kind of dominating pitchers have taken the mound in the nineteen-eighties and nineteen-nineties, Roger Clemens is an exception, a refreshing throwback. Early on, the hard thrower was nicknamed "Rocket" or "Rocket Man" after the Elton John song of that title.

Clemens' fourth Cy Young came in 1997. His other Cy Young Awards came in 1986, 1987 and 1991. In 1991 he won just 18 and lost 10 but he led the league in shutouts, innings, strikeouts and ERA.

After being first in the June 1983, draft, he went 9-4 for the Red Sox in 1984 but suffered a strained tendon in his right arm that ended his season. The following season he was 7-5 before facing rotator cuff surgery in August. It didn't look promising for the 23-year-old, but the following April 29, he broke the records of three Hall of Fame caliber pitchers, striking out 20 Seattle Mariners at Fenway Park. Tom Seaver, Steve Carlton and Nolan Ryan had all struckout 19 in a game. That season was Clemens' most magnificent. He finished 24-4, leading in wins, percentage (.857), ratio (8.9), ERA (2.48), batting average (.195) and on-base percentage against (.253). Mark Langston edged him for the strike out title, 245 to 238. Clemens also won the MVP voting, getting 339 votes to Don Mattingly's 258.

The season was a magic ride. On three days rest and pitching with the flu, he notched the pennant-winning victory over California. In the World Series against the Mets he struck out 11 batters in 11 innings and exited two games with leads, including the devastating sixth game defeat the Red Sox suffered. After Bruce Hurst couldn't hold a sixth inning 3-0 lead in Game Seven, the Mets scored eight runs in their last three at-bats to win the Series.

Clemens followed his all-everything year by leading the league in victories (20), complete games (18) and shutouts (7) in 1987. In fact, in a seven-year run from 1986 through 1992, he won 136 games, an average of 19.4 during that stretch.

The following four years he hit the skids, winning 40 and losing 39. Shoulder and elbow problems were taking their toll. A highlight of his last year with Boston, 1996, was a 20-strikeout game against the Tigers in September. Despite his 10-13 record that season, signs of the old Clemens were peeking through the losses. For one, he struck out more than a batter per inning, fanning 257 in 243 frames. Three months later the Blue Jays signed him as a free agent.

At 35 years old, Clemens simply posted one of his best seasons ever. He went 21-7 and finished with a shrunken 2.07 ERA. He pitched with a larger repertoire than ever before, mixing five pitches: circle change, fork ball, fastball, slider and curve.

All in all, it was a great comeback season. He finished with 292 strike-outs and a 9.3 ratio. He has won 213, lost 118 and it seems like he'll get his 3,000th strikeout soon.

Best 5-Year Run and Average 1986-1990

	W	L	PCT.	ERA	IP	H	BB	Ratio	K
Total	100	42	.704	2.71	1280	1052	359	9.9	1224
Average	20	8			256	210	72		225

Best 10-Year Run and Average 1986-1995

	W	L	PCT.	ERA	IP	H	BB	Ratio	K
Total	166	89	.651	2.92	2298	1914	684	10.2	2133
Average	17	9			230	191	68		213

14-Year Career Average 1984-1997

	W	L	PCT.	ERA	IP	H	BB	Ratio	K
Total	213	118	.644	2.97	3040	2563	924	10.3	2882
Average	15	8			202	172	62		206

Career

W	L	PCT	G	GS	CG	SH	SV	IP	H	HR	BB	SO	Ratio
213	118	.644	418	417	109	41	0	3040	2563	211	924	2882	10.3

ERA	Opponent's Avg
2.97	.229

12
WHITEY FORD

"The Chairman of the Board"
Born: 10/21/28 New York, NY
5 feet 10 inches, 181 pounds
Debut: 7/1/50, Played 16 years: 1950-1967
(missed 1951-1952) New York (AL)

Pitchers like Whitey Ford tend not to get the credit they deserve. He couldn't throw the ball with the speed of people like Robert Feller and only completed about a third of the games he started. But hear this: all he did was win 69 percent of all the games he ever pitched, a higher percentage than any modern 200-game winner. Add to that pearl that his lifetime ERA (2.75), lowest of all post-World War II starting pitchers with more than 1,500 innings pitched. Is that enough? Try this: while the Yankees played .592 during Ford's tenure, he pitched 98 points above them.

That is already sufficient evidence to recommend this wonderfully deceptive pitcher, deservedly nicknamed "Chairman of the Board" by his catcher Elston Howard. Mickey Mantle called him "Slick." "I don't care what the situation was or how high the stakes were," Mantle said of his teammate. "The bases could be loaded and the pennant riding on every pitch, it never bothered Whitey. His pitched his game. Cool. Crafty. Nerves of steel." A little like Spahn and a little like Maddux, Ford won with moxie and smarts, seizing every advantage he could lay his hands on. While he was never overpowering, Ford didn't allow batters many healthy cuts. Over his career, opposing hitters hit just .235 against him. What he got, he got with guile and control and a memorable curve. He also stayed ahead of guessing batters. He once said, "You would be amazed how many important outs you can get by working the count to where the hitter is sure you're going to throw to his weakness and then you throw to his power instead."

Yet I can still hear the detractors. 'Sure, he pitched to a high percentage,' some will say, 'he pitched for the Yankees.' Yes, he pitched for a silver spoon organization if there ever was one. But of the greats on this list, only Roger Clemens (+126) Grover Cleveland Alexander (+112), Walter Johnson (+107) and Tom Seaver (+101) own a larger pitcher-team-differential. If you judge a man by the company he keeps, then Edward Charles Ford did just fine.

If people were looking for an early sign, Ford gave them a small one in 1950. The 21-year old finished 9-1 that first year and threw a shutout as the Yankees swept the Phils in the Series. Winning a high percentage of games and post-season appearances would become regular features on Ford's resume.

He then missed two years in the military before coming back to post 12 consecutive winning seasons. Along the way he led the league in wins three times, winning percentage three times and in ERA twice. In 10 of those seasons, the Yankees won the pennant. All told, Ford pitched in 11 World Series and the Yankees won six. Said Casey Stengel, "If you had one game to win and your life depended on it, you'd want him to pitch it." True to Casey's words, Ford hurled 29-and-two-thirds consecutive scoreless innings beginning in the 1960 Series.

The Yankees won 15 in a row to end the 1960 season and beat Baltimore by eight games in the standings. But for reasons unknown, Art Ditmar and not Ford started Game One of the 1960 Series. Ford won 10-0 and 12-0 massacres in Game Three and Game Six but New York lost to Pittsburgh in seven games despite outscoring them 55 to 27. Ford never got a third start. Casey Stengel was fired after the season.

After the 1961 fall classic, in which the Yankees beat the Reds four games to one, Ford's World Series record was 9-4. But he went one-and-four over the next three Series against the Giants, Dodgers and Cardinals. He had a 16-13 season for the declining Yankees in 1965 and then went 2-5 and 2-4 over the next two years.

The two members of the "Slick and Mick Show" went into the Hall of Fame side-by-side in 1974.

Best 5-Year Run and Average 1961-1965

	W	L	PCT.	ERA	IP	H	BB	Ratio	K
Totals	99	38	.714	2.86	1297	1178	324	10.4	892
Average	20	8			259	236	65		178

Best 10-Year Run and Average 1956-1965

	W	L	PCT.	ERA	IP	H	BB	Ratio	K
Totals	171	75	.695	2.92	2266	2015	677	10.7	1461
Average	17	8			227	202	68		146

Best 15-Year Run and Average 1950-1966 (missed 1951, 1952)

	W	L	PCT.	ERA	IP	H	BB	Ratio	K
Totals	234	102	.696	2.88	3126	2726	1077	10.9	1935
Average	16	7			208	182	72		129

Career

W	L	PCT	G	GS	CG	SH	SV	IP	H	HR	BB	SO	Ratio
236	106	.690	498	438	156	45	10	3170	2766	228	1086	1956	11.0

ERA	Opponent's Avg
2.75	.235

13
JUAN MARICHAL

"The Dominican Dandy"
Born: 10/20/37 Laguna Verde, Dominican Republic
6 feet, 185 pounds
Deput: 7/19/60, Played 16 years: 1960-1975
1960-1973, San Francisco; 1974, Boston; 1975, Los Angeles

For people who like baseball trivia questions, here's a good one: who won 25 games three times, yet never won a Cy Young Award? The answer is Juan Marichal and the answer tells a story. While Drysdale, Koufax and Gibson won six of the nine Cy Young Awards between 1962 and 1970, Marichal was better than all of them. Better than Koufax because he pitched well for 10 years, better than Gibson and Drysdale because he had far better won-lost records than both and a better ERA to boot.

Marichal won 191 games and lost 88 in the 1960s, more wins than any other pitcher in the decade. He did this with such an assortment of pitches and that high leg kick that one hitter was led to say, "Marichal had four different pitches at four different speeds; 16 pitches, really." In one 1969 game against the Mets, he pitched shutout inning after inning, finally losing to the Mets on a leadoff homer by Tommie Agee in the bottom of the fourteenth. It was not an isolated incident.

From 1964 through 1969 Marichal completed 146 games out of 210 starts – an average of 24 out of 35 starts for that period. We may never see complete game totals like that again and if Marichal could do it – as a strikeout pitcher – what does that tell us about the pitching talent these days?

In his *Historical Abstract*, Bill James makes several points about "The Dominican Dandy" that bear repeating. If you combine his won-lost record in 1963, 1964, 1966 and 1968, his overall record is better than that of the four Cy Young Award winners (Koufax, Dean Chance, Koufax and Gibson) for those years. Marichal was 97-31 over the four seasons; the Cy Young guys, 94-32.

James also points out that Marichal pitched a disproportionate number of games against the toughest teams in the league. Against Los Angeles he was 37-18 (.672), more than 40 percentage points above his record. He was 18-21 (.462), however, against the Cardinals, the other frequent pennant winner of his time.

Marichal's career versus Gibson's is clear. Marichal finished 243-142 (.631) with a 2.89 ERA versus Gibson's 251-174 (.591) and 2.91 ERA. ERA is a wash and Marichal finished 40 points ahead in winning percentage.

Koufax finished 165-86 (.655), but that's 78 less wins than Marichal's total. In fact, if you take Marichal's best 10-year run – from 1962 through 1971 – he won 202 and lost 97 (.676). So in 10 years he won 37 more games than Koufax won in his entire career. The assumption that Koufax and Gibson were better than Marichal must be based on their frequent appearances, and heroic appearances at that, in the World Series on national television. It is surely not based on regular-season records.

Since people now praise Greg Maddux for pinpoint control, Marichal deserves more praise. Marichal walked 709 batters in 3,509 innings – one every 4.94 innings. As great as Maddux' control has been, over his career he has walked 609 batters in 2,598 innings – one every 4.26 innings. If Marichal had better control than Maddux, then that tells you what kind of pitcher he was.

Marichal was voted into the Hall of Fame in 1983.

Best 5-Year Run and Average 1963-1967

	W	L	Pct.	ERA	Ip	H	Bb	Ratio	K
Totals	107	45	.704	2.36	1394	1147	246	9.0	1082
Average	21	9			279	229	49		216

Best 10-Year run and Average 1962-1971

Totals	202	97	.676	2.64	2802	2423	540	9.5	1940
Average	20	10			280	242	54		194

Best15-Year Run and Average 1960-1974

Totals	243	141	.633	2.87	3497	3033	713	9.6	2302
Average	16	9			233	202	48		153

Career

W	L	Pct	G	GS	CG	SH	SV	IP	H	HR	BB	SO	Ratio
243	142	.631	471	457	244	52	2	3507	3153	320	709	2303	10.0

ERA	Opponent's Avg
2.89	.237

14
CARL HUBBELL

"King Carl" The Meal Ticket"
Born: 6/22/03 Carthage, MO, Died: 11/21/88 Scottsdale, AZ
6 feet, 170 pounds
Played 16 years: 1928-1943 New York (NL)

"Getting under Hubbell's screwball is like trying to hit fungoes in a well," one National League hitter said out of frustration. He was nick-named "King Carl" and "the Meal Ticket," and he was all of that for the New York Giants from 1928 through 1943. Hubbell grew up on a pecan farm in Oklahoma and got the attention of the Detroit organization. But Detroit manager Ty Cobb thought that Hubbell's "butterfly pitch," or screwball, would blow out his left arm, so he forbade him to throw it.

Without use of his best pitch, Hubbell's performance suffered and his confidence eroded. After Hubbell pitched two poor seasons in the minors, Detroit released him in 1928, optioning him to Toronto. It would turn out to be a terrible decision.

Hubbell bounced around with five minor league teams before Giants' skipper John McGraw got him from Beaumont of the Texas League for $30,000, a record sum for that loop. Like Lefty Grove and Warren Spahn, Hubbell was 25 when he won his first Major League game.

In his first full season, 1929, he threw a no-hitter. He first topped 20 victories in 1933, leading the league with 23 wins, 308 innings, 10 shutouts and a 1.66 ERA. He also threw an 18-inning 1-0 shutout over the Cardinals at the Polo grounds. The Giants won the pennant, the first of three that Hubbell led them to. They then dumped the Senators in the World Series, four games to one. Hubbell won Game One and then Game Four, pitching 20 innings without allowing an earned run. He also took MVP honors.

While 1933 was Hubbell's best season, he is more often connected to 1934, when he performed a feat for the ages. He started the second All-Star Game on July 10, 1934, by giving up a single to Charlie Gehringer and walking Heinie Manush. He then struck out Babe Ruth, Lou Gehrig and Jimmie Foxx to end the first inning. In the second he whiffed Al Simmons and Joe Cronin. In succession he struck out three of the top 10 players of all-time and five Hall of Famers. Gabby Hartnett shouted down to players on the AL bench, "We gotta hit that all season!"

Summer classic aside, Hubbell was working on a different kind of string. In 1934 he won 21, then 23 in '35, 26 in '36 (Hubbell's second MVP season) and 22 in '37. In all, he won 115 and lost 50 in that five-year run. In the process he led the NL in ERA three times, in ratio four more times, and in wins three times. He was so accurate during his peak years that he averaged about one walk per nine innings.

The Yankees beat the Giants four games to two in 1936 and four games to one in the 1937 World Series. Hubbell won two of the Giants' three Series Games against the heavy hitting Yankees' squads. Despite the two disappointing World Series, Hubbell had finished 1936 with 16 straight wins, and won his first eight in 1937 for a 24-game winning streak.

In 1938, Hubbell was already 35 and had been throwing his unhittable screw ball for so many years that his left arm was actually curved. He underwent elbow surgery after the `38 season and was never the same, going 48 and 42 from 1939 through 1943.

He finished with 253 wins and was inducted to the Hall of Fame in 1947. He ran the Giants farm system, directing player development from 1943 through 1977 and scouting from 1978 through 1985, enjoying the development of fellow Hall of Famers like Willie Mays, Willie McCovey and Juan Marichal – the Giants' future meal tickets.

Best 5-Year Run and Average 1933-1937

	W	L	PCT.	IP	H	BB	K	Ratio	ERA
Totals	115	50	.697	1488	1382	245	706	9.8	2.49
Average	23	10		298	276	49	141		

Best 10-Year Run and Average 1929-1938

	W	L	PCT.	IP	H	BB	K	Ratio	ERA
Totals	195	106	.648	2708	2560	510	1395	10.2	2.76
Average	20	11		271	256	51	140		

Best 15-Year Run and Average 1928-1942

	W	L	PCT.	IP	H	BB	K	Ratio	ERA
Totals	249	150	.624	3524	3374	701	1646	10.4	2.93
Average	17	10		235	225	47	110		

Career

W	L	PCT	G	GS	CG	SH	SV	IP	H	HR	BB	SO	Ratio
253	154	.622	535	431	260	36	33	3590	3461	227	725	1677	10.6

ERA	Opponent's Avg
2.98	.251

15
JIM PALMER

Born: 10/15/45 New York (NL)
6 feet 3 inches, 196 pounds
Debut: 4/17/65, Played 19 years: 1965-1984 (missed 1968)
Baltimore

Jim Palmer was so reliable a pitcher for Baltimore that, beginning in 1970, he won 20 or more games eight times in nine years. His 186 wins were more than any pitcher in the 1970s. He won three Cy Young Awards (1973, 1975 and 1976) and finished with more wins (268), shutouts (53) and complete games (211) than any Oriole pitcher in history (268). Further, the only other American League pitchers to win 20 or more eight times were Walter Johnson and Lefty Grove. His career ERA (2.86) is the second best of his era and fifth among pitchers with 3,000 innings or more. His dominance was such that when Red's outfielder Merv Rettenmund was asked, "Would you rather face Tom Seaver or Jim Palmer," he replied, "that's like asking me If I'd rather be hung or go to the electric chair."

Baltimore won five pennants during Palmer's career – in 1966, 1969, 1970, 1971 and 1979 – and Palmer clinched the first four of them. At 20 years old, he shut out the Dodgers 6-0 on four hits, beating Sandy Koufax in Game Two of the 1966 World Series. It was Sandy Koufax' last game. Palmer developed a sore arm and pitched only nine games over the next two seasons. But in 1970 he began a streak of four consecutive 20-win seasons.

All told, Palmer was 8-2 in post-season play. The two losses came against the Mets, in Game Three of the 1969 Series, and against the Pirates, in Game Six of the 1979 Series.

With Frank Robinson, Brooks Robinson, Boog Powell, Paul Blair, Mark Belanger and a staff that also included Dave McNally and Mike Cuellar, the Orioles were a perennial power in the American League. Earl Weaver was their combustible manager. Palmer and Weaver were a comic duo, with Weaver constantly getting on Palmer about his minor (and perhaps imaginary) injuries and hypochondria and Palmer returning fire about Weaver's vertically challenged stature. Commenting on yet another of Weaver's many trips to the mound, Palmer once said, "Did you ever notice that Earl always goes to the highest spot on the mound when he comes out?"

At the age of 36, Palmer had one last roar. With Palmer winning 11 games in a row down the stretch in 1982, the Orioles mounted a furious comeback against the Milwaukee Brewers. With the teams tied at 94-67, Palmer faced Don Sutton, two pitchers with more than 500 wins between them. The winner would capture the AL East flag. Robin Yount smacked two homers off Palmer and Don Sutton was the better pitcher that day as the Brewers won.

Palmer finished 5-4 in 1983 and then retired after the 1984 season. Upon retiring he said, "It really bothers me to think I may never throw a home run pitch again." He surrendered 303 homers in his career. He immediately got what he deserved, being inducted into the Hall of Fame in 1990.

Best 5-Year Run and Average 1969-1973

	W	L	PCT.	ERA	IP	H	BB	Ratio	K
Totals	99	42	.702	2.48	1338	1069	453	10.2	848
Average	20	8			268	214	91		170

Best 10-Year Run and Average 1969-1978

	W	L	PCT.	ERA	IP	H	BB	Ratio	K
Totals	192	101	.655	2.53	2769	2262	882	10.2	1615
Average	19	10			277	226	88		161

Best 15-Year Run and Average 1969-1983

	W	L	PCT.	ERA	IP	H	BB	Ratio	K
Totals	245	134	.646	2.77	3578	3042	1127	10.5	1963
Average	16	9			239	203	75		131

Career

W	L	PCT.	G	GS	CG	SH	SV	IP	H	HR	BB	SO	Ratio
268	152	.638	558	521	211	53	4	3948	3349	303	1311	2212	10.7

ERA	Opponent's Avg
2.86	.230

16
BOB GIBSON

Born: 11/9/35 Omaha, NE
6 feet 1-and-a-half inches, 195 pounds
Debut: 4/15/59, Played 17 years: 1959-1975, St. Louis

The recurrent image of Bob Gibson is one of a pitcher who came right at you. It seemed he threw everything hard. If hitters dove out over the plate, he buzzed them inside, reminding them that the outside was the portion of the plate where he made his living. On the mound he was all purpose, little play. Said Dodgers' announcer Vin Scully, "Bob Gibson pitches as though he's double parked."

Like Don Drysdale, another hard throwing right-hander of his time, Gibson would hit batters to keep them off the plate. Notice this comment: "I never hit anybody in the head intentionally," Gibson said in 1981. "If a guy got hit on the head it was his own fault. The head is the easiest part of the body to get out of the way. I hit guys in the ribs. The ribs don't move."

The intimidating style was good enough for five 20-win seasons in six years between 1965 and 1970. He won Cy Young Awards in 1968 and 1970. In `68, he set the record for the lowest ERA (1.12) in 300 or more innings and led the league in shutouts (13) and strikeouts (268). His regular catcher, Tim McCarver, gave his opinion on Gibson's success. "Bob Gibson is the luckiest pitcher I ever saw," said McCarver. "He always pitches when the other team doesn't score any runs." Between 1963 and 1972 Gibson won 16 or more every year except for 1967, when a line drive off the bat of Roberto Clemente fractured his leg and put him on the disabled list for two months.

Then consider his World Series performances. In 1964, 1967 and 1968 he pitched nine Series games and won seven of them. In 1964 he lost Game Two to Mel Stottlemyre, 8-3. But in Game Five he rebounded and held a 2-0 lead when Tom Tresh hit a two-run homer in the bottom of the ninth to tie it. But Tim McCarver's three-run homer in the tenth gave St. Louis the victory as Gibson went the whole 10 innings and struck out 13 Yankees. He came back to throw Game Seven on two days rest. Though surrendering three Yankee homers, he held on for a 7-5 win.

Asked why he didn't take out his weary pitcher, who threw 27 innings in the Series, manager Johnny Keane said, "I never considered taking him out. I had a commitment to his heart."

He showed the Red Sox as much heart three years later. After missing eight weeks due to the leg fracture, Gibson returned to spoil Boston's "Impossible Dream" party. He allowed the Sox one run in Game One and shut them out in Game Four on three days rest. In Game Seven he topped Boston's ace, 22-game winner Jim Lonborg. He allowed three hits and St. Louis won 7-2. In 27 innings he had struck out 35 Red Sox and allowed a parsimonious 14 hits. It was probably the most dominant pitching in a Series since Christy Mathewson's three successive shutouts against the A's in 1905.

It looked awfully bleak for the Tigers the next year, as Gibson allowed four measly hits and struck out a record 17 in the opener. In Game Four he gave the Cardinals a three-games-to-one lead, beating Cy Young Award recipient and 31-game winner Denny Mclain, 10-1. St. Louis jumped out to a 3-0 lead against Mickey Lolich in Game Five. But Nelson Briles couldn't hold the lead and Detroit won 5-3. Following the first frame of Game Five, the Cardinals would score but two runs over the next 26 innings.

Pitching on two days rest in Game Seven, Lolich outpitched Gibson and the Tigers won 4-1. But in three World Series Gibson not only was seven-and-two, but posted a 1.89 ERA and struck out an amazing 92 batters in 81 innings.

Gibson won 43 games over the next two years, but the Cardinals didn't make it to the postseason. Several more milestones remained for Gibson, however. He won 16 in 1971, including his 200th win. And in 1974, now 38 and pitching on weak knees, he notched his 3,000th strikeout. But he went 14-23 over his last two seasons, bringing his lifetime percentage below .600. He retired in 1975 and it was automatic that he would be inducted into the Hall of Fame in 1981, his first eligible season.

Best 5-Year Run and Average 1968-1972

	W	L	PCT.	ERA	IP	H	BB	Ratio	K
Totals	100	53	.654	2.91	1435	1152	409	9.8	1204
Average	20	11			287	230	82		241

Best 10-Year run and Average 1963-1972

	W	L	PCT.	ERA	IP	H	BB	Ratio	K
Totals	191	105	.645	2.65	2730	2230	812	10	2295
Average	19	11			273	223	81		230

Best 15-Year Run and Average 1960-1974

	W	L	PCT.	ERA	IP	H	BB	Ratio	K
Totals	245	159	.606	2.85	3695	3122	1235	10.6	3009
Average	16	11			246	208	82		201

Career

W	L	PCT	G	GS	CG	SH	SV	IP	H	HR	BB	SO	Ratio
251	174	.591	528	482	255	56	6	3884	3279	257	1336	3117	10.9

ERA	Opponent's Avg
2.91	.228

17
SANDY KOUFAX

Born: 12/30/35 Brooklyn, NY
6 feet 2 inches, 210 pounds
Debut: 6/24/55, Played 12 years 1955-1966
1955-1957, Brooklyn; 1958-1966, Los Angeles

Sandy Koufax had two careers. In the first one, lasting the six years from 1955 through 1960, he was the picture of mediocrity, winning 36 and losing 40 while walking approximately six batters per nine innings. He did show signs: he tied Bob Feller's record by striking out 18 on August 31, 1959. But his ERA and ratio of runners-to-innings were stratospheric due to wildness.

In his second career, spanning the six years from 1961 through 1966, he was utterly magnificent, winning 129 and losing 47, including Cy Young Awards in 1963, 1965 and 1966. That he had six astounding years was his greatest asset. It was also his greatest liability, because most of the great pitchers here had runs of 10 or 12 or 15 impressive seasons. Some were impressive even longer.

Pointing this out is worthwhile, because some people believe that, "Koufax was the greatest pitcher in baseball for six years," and, "Koufax was the greatest pitcher ever," are somehow equivalent statements. They are not. He pitched 12 years and he was great for half of them.

Koufax turned around his mechanical problem of not locating the target and winding and throwing too hastily. In 1961 he was 18-13, leading the league with 269 strikeouts. The following year he was 14-7 with a league leading 2.54 ERA. Over the next four years Koufax really cranked it up. In 1963 he was 25-5, with 306 strikeouts, 11 shutouts and a 1.88 ERA – leading the NL in all three categories. In the World Series he won Game One and then Game Four as the Dodgers swept New York. In Game One he struck out a World Series record 15 batters. He allowed just three earned runs and struck out 23 in 18 total innings. "I can see how he won 25 games," said Yankee catcher Yogi Berra. "What I don't understand is how he lost five."

Koufax followed his 25-5 effort with a 19-5 season, this time leading the league with an even lower ERA (1.74). He also led the league in shutouts (seven) and percentage (.792). But the Dodgers, who had finished last in runs scored in 1963, were next to last in offense in 1964. They slid to fifth place with an 80-82 record. They hit .250 as a team and scored just 572 runs, a measly 3.5 per game. Adhesions in his pitching arm broke loose, leading to arthritis.

After he threw his third no-hitter in August, he had to stop pitching for the season. "What makes Sandy Koufax great is the same thing that made Walter Johnson great," said Los Angeles sportswriter Jim Murray. "The team behind him is the ghastliest scoring team in history. They pile up runs at a rate of one every nine innings. With the Babe Ruth Yankees, Koufax would have been the first undefeated pitcher in history."

The Dodgers scored only 521 runs and hit an anemic .245 in 1965. Following medical orders, Koufax didn't throw between starts in 1965 and went 26-8, finishing the regular season by tossing his fourth no-hitter, a perfect game against the Cubs on Sept. 9th. With Koufax' 26 and Drysdale's 23 wins, the Dodgers edged the Giants by two games.

In the Series, they faced the Twins, who scored a league leading 774 runs. Mudcat Grant beat Drysdale 8-2 in Game One. Walt Alston started Drysdale in Game One Oct. 6 because Koufax was observing Yom Kippur. Drysdale was roughed up and had to be replaced in the third inning. On the bench Alston said to Drysdale, "Why couldn't you be Jewish, too?" Jim Kaat beat Koufax 5-1 in Game Two. Then Osteen, Drysdale and Koufax won successive games in Los Angeles, with Osteen and Koufax throwing shutouts. Grant beat Osteen to tie the Series in Game Six but Koufax, pitching on two days rest, shutout Kaat and the Twins 2-0 in Game Seven. In 24 innings Koufax struck out 29 batters, giving up just 13 hits and allowing only one run for a Series ERA of 0.38!

In 1966 Sandy finished 27-9, leading the circuit in wins, complete games (27), shutouts (5), innings (323) and ERA (1.71). The Dodgers won 95, again edging the Giants by two games. Their offense hit rock bottom: they posted 490 runs for a league low.

This time it caught up with them. After the third inning of a 5-2 loss against Baltimore in Game One, they didn't score another run in the Series. Koufax, though allowing just one earned run, lost Game Two. Drysdale lost Game One and Game Four and the Dodgers were swept, posting a grand total of two runs in 36 innings!

Koufax had more to worry about than a lost World Series. The arthritis in his arm was worse. "If you had one good arm and one bad arm and somebody said you could buy back the use of your bad arm, I think you'd do it. In a sense, that's what I'm doing," he said as he announced his retirement.

In 1972, at 36, he became the youngest player ever inducted into the Hall of Fame. He was also named Player of the Decade in the 1960s, despite not playing a game between 1967 and 1969. Over his last six seasons Koufax struck out 1,713 batters in 1,633 innings– an average of 10.5 men every nine innings! It was proof of what Jim Murray once said about him: "Sandy's fastball was so fast, some batters would start to swing as he was on his way to the mound."

Best 5-Year run and Average 1962-1966

	W	L	PCT.	ERA	IP	H	BB	Ratio	K
Totals	111	34	.766	1.95	1376	959	316	8.3	1444
Average	22	7			275	192	63		289

Best 10-Year Run and Average 1957-1966

	W	L	PCT.	ERA	IP	H	BB	Ratio	K
Totals	161	81	.665	2.70	2221	1655	760	9.8	2336
Average	16	8			222	166	76		234

12-Year Average 1955-1966

	W	L	PCT.	ERA	IP	H	BB	Ratio	K
Totals	165	87	.655	2.76	2324	1754	817	10	2396
Average	14	7			193	146	68		200

Career

W	L	PCT.	G	GS	CG	SH	SV	IP	H	HR	BB	SO	Ratio
165	87	.655	397	314	137	40	9	2324	1754	204	817	2396	10.0

ERA	Opponent's Avg
2.76	.205

18
MORDECAI BROWN

"Three Finger"
Born: 10/19/1876 Nyesville, IN, Died: 2/14/1948 Terre Haute, IN
Played 14 years: 1903-1916
1903, St. Louis; 1904-1912, Chicago (NL); 1913, Cincinnati; 1914, St. Louis and Brooklyn, (Federal League); 1915, Chicago (Federal League); 1916, Chicago (NL)

His name was Mordecai Peter Centennial Brown, because he was born Oct. 19, 1876, in the year of the hundredth anniversary of America's independence. But not long after his arrival in the major leagues in 1903, people would know him as Three Finger Brown. His is one of the great stories in baseball.

When he was a boy in Nyesville, Indiana, he poked his right hand under a corn chopper on the farm. Half of his index finger was torn off and several weeks later he broke the third and fourth fingers while chasing a hog. The hand healed in a twisted mess. Despite his handicap Brown became a semi-pro infielder with a Coxville semi-pro team of miners. When the team's star pitcher fell and broke his arm, Brown took over and struck out 14 in five innings, using a curve that broke unusually because of the shape of his hand. The hand that was such a hindrance at third base, could be used to throw knucklers and "dip balls."

After reaching the big leagues with St. Louis at the age of 26, he was traded to Chicago in the off season. Beginning in 1904, when Brown arrived, the Cubs won 90 or more games for nine straight years. He played with the 1906, 1907, 1908 and 1910 pennant winning Chicago teams. In those four seasons, the Cubs won 426 games and lost 186 – a remarkable average of 107 and 47, for a percentage of .696.

The Cubs' staff included Ed Reulbach, Orval Overall and Jack Pfeister. To his Cub mates Brown was also called "miner," because he was a coal miner before his major league career.

The 1906 Cubs, who finished 116-36, still hold the record for most wins. In the Series, however, they lost to the infamous "Hitless Wonders," the light hitting White Sox, who scored a league low 460 runs (three per game) and batted .230 for the season. Brown lost two games in the Series as the Cubs lost in six.

In 1907 the Cubs rebounded with 107 wins for their second straight .700-plus season. They won four straight against the Tigers in the Series. Brown clinched the sweep with a seven-hit shutout. He was at it again in 1908, winning two. He won Game One as a reliever and shut out the Tigers on four hits in Game Four. Orval Overall shutout Detroit in Game Five for the Cubs' second straight World Championship.

Brown's five World Series victories tend to be overshadowed by a single playoff game in 1908. He had his first of six consecutive 20-win seasons that year, winning 26 and losing six. In a game on Sept. 23, Mathewson dueled Brown in a 1-1 tie. A two-out hit scored a runner from third and apparently gave the Giants the victory. But Fred Merkle, who was on first, failed to touch second base and was ultimately ruled out and the game ruled a tie.

Due to "Merkle's Boner," both teams finished at 98 and 55 and a play-off between New York and Chicago in the Polo Grounds ensued on Oct. 8. The match-up of Brown and Mathewson was repeated and this time Brown bested Mathewson 4-2. The Cubs captured the pennant and, soon after, the Series.

In that season, and the five that followed, Brown posted a combined 147 and 54 won-lost record – an average of 25 wins and 9 losses per year.

After 1912 he was traded to Cincinnati and later played on the Cardinals, the Dodgers and the Cubs before retiring in 1916. He finished with a 239-130 record and a stingy 2.06 ERA. Ty Cobb once said of Brown's curve ball, "It was the most devastating pitch I ever faced. Christy Mathewson's fadeaway was good, but it was nothing like that curve that Three-Fingered Brown threw at you." Asked if his wicked curve was aided by a deformed right hand, Brown replied, "To know for sure I'd have to throw with a normal hand, and I've never tried it."

He died in 1948 and was elected to the Hall of Fame the following year.

Best 5-Year Run and Average 1906-1910

	W	L	PCT.	ERA	IP	H	BB	Ratio	K
Totals	127	44	.743	1.42	1459	1094	267	8.4	689
Average	25	9			292	219	53		139

Best 10-Year Run and Average 1903-1912

| Totals | 195 | 96 | .670 | 1.82 | 2479 | 2057 | 495 | 9.3 | 1105 |
| Average | 20 | 10 | | | 248 | 206 | 50 | | 110 |

14-Year Run and Average 1903-1916

| Totals | 239 | 130 | .648 | 2.06 | 3172 | 2708 | 673 | 9.8 | 1375 |
| Average | 17 | 9 | | | 98 | 193 | 48 | | 98 |

Career

W	L	PCT	G	GS	CG	SH	SV	IP	H	HR	BB	SO	Ratio
239	130	.648	481	332	271	55	49	3172	2708	43	673	1375	9.9

ERA	Opponent's Avg
2.06	.233

19
NOLAN RYAN

Born: 1/3/47 Refugio, TX
6 feet 2 inches, 195 pounds
Debut: 9/11/66, Played 27 years: 1966-1993 (missed 1967)
1966-1971, New York (NL); 1972-1979, California;
1980-1988, Houston; 1989-1993, Texas

Nolan Ryan threw the famed "Ryan Express," the fastball to end all fast-balls. During his second no-hitter in 1983, Mickey Stanley walked back to the bench, saying, "Those were the best pitches I ever heard." Oscar Gamble didn't have many expectations hitting against Ryan. "A good night is 0-4 and don't get hit in the head," said the Cleveland DH. Ryan was at once the most awesome and enigmatic pitcher in baseball history.

He was utterly dominant on the mound, the all-time record holder in hits per game (6.56), opponents batting average (.204) and strikeouts (5,714). He is second behind Randy Johnson in strikeouts per game (9.55), fifth in innings pitched (5,386) tied for seventh with Tom Seaver in shutouts (61) and tied for 12th with Don Sutton in wins (324). Then again, he is the all-time leader in walks (2,795) and leads this century in losses (292).

So despite the awesome strikeout totals and seven no-hitters – the sixth and seventh with Texas in 1990 when he was 43 years old! – it must be said that Nolan Ryan was not a consistent winner. "He's not the best pitcher in baseball," said Jim Fregosi, Ryan's manager in California. "Never has been. I'll say this: he's the most exciting .500 pitcher in baseball."

Fregosi was right. Ryan won just 32 games more than he lost. Ryan defenders reply that he played for poor teams. Actually, he played for mediocre teams. From 1966 through 1993, Ryan's clubs won a total of 2,177 games and lost 2,147. That's a percentage of .503. Ryan, by comparison finished with a .526 percentage. In short, he was only slightly better (23 percentage points) than the teams he played on. Compare this differential with that of the other 24 great pitchers in this section.

GREAT PITCHERS VERSUS THEIR TEAMS

	Pitcher Pct.	Team's Pct.	Differential
Roger Clemens	.644	.518	+126
Grover Alexander	.642	.530	+112
Walter Johnson	.599	.492	+107
Tom Seaver	.603	.502	+101
Whitey Ford	.690	.592	+98
Cy Young	.619	.521	+98
Lefty Grove	.680	.583	+97
Greg Maddux	.630	.537	+93
Juan Marichal	.631	.547	+84
Sandy Koufax	.655	.573	+82
Carl Hubbell	.622	.545	+77
Christy Mathewson	.665	.591	+74
Eddie Plank	.627	.557	+70
Warren Spahn	.597	.528	+69
Mordecai Brown	.648	.584	+64
Bob Gibson	.591	.531	+60
Bob Feller	.621	.562	+59
Jim Palmer	.638	.580	+58
Robin Roberts	.539	.485	+54
Kid Nichols	.634	.584	+50
Steve Carlton	.574	.526	+48
Ferguson Jenkins	.557	.510	+47
Tim Keefe	.603	.560	+43
Gaylord Perry	.542	.516	+26
Nolan Ryan	.526	.503	+23

Ryan's differential is far less than any of the other greats listed here. Tom Seaver and Walter Johnson played for poorer teams than Ryan and both managed to rise above, pitching more than 100 percentage points better than their mediocre clubs. But throughout his career Ryan pitched only slightly better than the squads for which he played on.

It seems that for every magnificent statistic Ryan achieved, he hurt his performance with another statistic. He led the league in strikeouts 11 times, but eight times he led in walks. He led the circuit in opponents' batting average 12 times, but because of the walks his ratio of baserunners per nine frequently was above 12. Consider the first five times he led the league in opponents' batting average. Those years he posted amazingly low averages of .171, .190, .195, .193 and .212!. But those same years he allowed his opponents on-base percentages of .292, .314, .323, .331 and .314. These numbers explain why he didn't win more often.

That said, Ryan's greatest feats were still amazing. During an eight-day period in 1972 (his first year with California), he struck out 15 Rangers, 16 Red Sox and 16 A's. He won 19 and lost 16 that year, nine of his wins shutouts. He threw two no-hitters the following year, notched 21 victories (and 16 losses) and led the league with 383 strike outs, breaking Koufax' previous record.

On August 12, 1974, he struck out 19 Red Sox to tie the record of Tom Seaver and Steve Carlton. He got his third no-hitter later that season against the Twins and ended with 22 wins and 16 losses. He threw his fourth no-hitter in 1975 against the Orioles.

When he signed as a free agent with Houston in 1979, one pretty fair fastball hitter, Reggie Jackson, was glad to see him go. "Ryan's the only guy who put fear in me," said Mr. October when he was playing with the Yankees. "Not because he could get me out, but because he could kill me. Every hitter likes fastballs like everybody likes ice cream. But you don't like it by the gallon. That's how you felt when Nolan was throwing the fastball by you. You just hoped to mix in a walk, so you could have a good night and go 0-3."

A year after signing with the Astros, he got his fifth no-hitter to break Koufax' record. That year Ryan set the all-time walk record, notching his 1,776th. "I'd like to thank all the umpires," Ryan said of the record. "If it wasn't for them, it wouldn't have been possible." He posted his first ERA title that year, finishing with a 1.69 mark. He surpassed Walter Johnson's career strikeout record in 1983.

Miraculously, Ryan remained a power pitcher past the age of 40. Between 1987 through 1992, when he was 45, he had more strikeouts than innings pitched. He seemed to have a bionic arm. He finally retired in 1993, after 27 major league seasons.

Best 5-Year Run and Average 1972-1976

	W	L	PCT.	ERA	IP	H	BB	K	Ratio
Totals	93	78	.544	2.99	1424	970	836	1592	11.4
Average	19	16			285	194	167	318	

Best 10-Year Run and Average 1972-1981

	W	L	PCT.	ERA	IP	H	BB	K	Ratio
Totals	160	136	.541	3.04	2561	1824	1468	2756	11.6
Average	16	14			256	182	147	276	

Best 15-Year Run and Average 1972-1986

	W	L	PCT.	ERA	IP	H	BB	K	Ratio
Totals	224	188	.544	3.11	3600	2621	1933	3784	11.4
Average	15	13			240	175	129	252	

Career

W	L	PCT	G	GS	CG	SH	SV	IP	H	HR	BB	SO	Ratio
324	292	.526	807	773	222	61	3	5386	3923	321	2795	5714	11.5

ERA	Opponent's Avg
3.19	.204

20
EDDIE PLANK

"Gettysburg Eddie"
Born: 8/31/1875 Gettysburg, PA, Died: 2/24/26 Gettysburg, PA
Played 17 years: 1901-1917
1901-1914, Philadelphia (AL); 1915, St. Louis (Federal League);
1916-1917, St. Louis (AL)

Eddie Plank was a sly left-handed pitcher for the Philadelphia A's during a 10-year period when they won five pennants and three World Series. When the A's won the pennant in 1905, Plank won 24 games. They won the pennant and the Series in 1910 and Plank contributed 16 wins. They repeated as World Champions the following year and Plank won 23. Two years later they won again and Plank won 18. Their final pennant of the era came in 1914 and Plank won 15. In all, he won 96 games on five flag winning A's teams.

It was the Gettysburg native's manner to slow the game down and rattle hitters by talking to himself on the mound. He had precision control, walking just 1,072 in 4,503 innings. He could hit any spot with his curve or fastball. Said Hall of Famer Eddie Collins, "His motion was enough to give batters nervous indigestion."

Describing Plank in *The Glory of their Times*, teammate Rube Bressler placed pitchers in two categories – "power pitchers and manipulators." The former class, said Bressler, included guys like Grove, Feller and Johnson.

The latter class included guys like Plank, Herb Pennock, Alexander and Eppa Rixey who set up hitters with stuff. "Sad" Sam Jones recalled that Eddie Plank once urged him not to throw to first base to hold runners close. "There are only so many pitches in this old arm," Plank said. "And I don't believe in wasting them throwing to first base." Instead of throwing, Plank would just stop and stare at the runner. There was no need to throw.

Plank won 20-plus games seven times for the A's and once for the St. Louis Terriers of the upstart Federal League in 1915, where he won his 300th game. He was the first left-hander to reach that mark. Not bad for a pitcher who had spent two years in Gettysburg College and didn't toss his first Major League game until he was 25 years old.

He averaged 20 wins per year for 16 years – from 1901 through 1916. In World Series play Plank could have sued for non-support. He lost five of seven World Series decisions despite posting a 1.32 ERA in October ball. Playing for the St. Louis Browns in 1917, he retired after losing a 1-0 game to Walter Johnson. He opened a garage business but retired in 1923, having accumulated sufficient wealth to take life easy. He succumbed to a paralytic stroke on Feb. 24, 1926, just four months after the death of his great World Series rival of 1905, Christy Mathewson. When Plank died, Connie Mack called him the greatest left-hander he had ever known.

His ledger includes 326 wins (10th all-time), a 2.35 ERA and his 69 shutouts, the most ever by a left-hander. Believe it or not, it took sportswriters 29 years after his retirement to put him in the Hall of Fame in 1946.

Best 5-Year Run and Average 1903-1907

	W	L	PCT.	ERA	IP	H	BB	Ratio	K
Totals	116	67	.634	2.25	1593	1370	362	9.8	896
Average	23	11			319	274	72		179

Best 10-Year Run and Average 1903-1912

	W	L	PCT.	ERA	IP	H	BB	Ratio	K
Totals	214	117	.647	2.06	2867	2476	685	9.9	1545
Average	21	12			287	248	69		155

Best 15-Year Run and Average 1901-1915

	W	L	PCT.	ERA	IP	H	BB	Ratio	K
Totals	305	173	.638	2.37	4129	3650	967	10.1	2150
Average	20	12			275	243	64		143

Career

W	L	PCT	G	GS	CG	SH	SV	IP	H	HR	BB	SO	Ratio
326	194	.627	623	529	410	69	23	4495	3958	41	1072	2246	10.5

ERA	Opponent's Avg
2.35	.239

21
TIM KEEFE

"Smiling Tim" "Sir Timothy"
Born: 1/1/1857 Cambridge, MA, Died: 4/23/33 Cambridge, MA
Played 14 years: 1880-1893
1880-1882, Troy (NL); 1883-1884, New York (American Association);
1885-1891, New York (NL); 1891-1893, Philadelphia (NL)

"The Mets' first great pitcher wasn't Tom Seaver," it says in *Total Baseball*. "It was Tim Keefe, who won 41 games his first year and 37 in his second for the New York Metropolitans of the American Association." You can look it up. The years were 1883 and 1884. In 1884 the "Mets" won the American Association championship and that fall they lost in the first World Series, bowing to Providence of the National League.

Keefe was credited with being the first to employ a change-up and was perhaps the first to keep meticulous records of opposing batters, using shorthand notation. Before his success with the Metropolitans, Keefe broke in with the Troy Haymakers in 1880 after playing with several semi-pro and New England minor league teams.

In 1885 the right-hander joined the New York Giants. He won 32 that year, then 42, then 35 and 35 again in 1888. He also won a record 19 straight games that season, finishing with 35 wins, 12 losses and four ties. The streak began on June 23, when he beat the Quakers (later the Phillies). He went unbeaten for 45 more days before losing to the White

Stockings (Cubs) at the Polo Grounds. Amazingly, Keefe finished each game. He then went 4-0 in the World Series, helping the Giants beat the St. Louis Browns. For his regal bearing, he was given the name "Sir Timothy" by the Giants.

Keefe enjoyed one more good season before jumping to the Players League and finally ending his career in 1893 with the Phillies.

The Cambridge native died at the age of 75 in 1933.

The world next heard of Tim Keefe in 1964, when he was given an overdue honor of election to the Hall of Fame. He won 342 games, lost just 225 (.603) and led the league in ERA three times, including the lowest ERA ever —0.80 in 1880. He was voted Cambridge Massachusetts's All-Time Greatest Athlete in a poll taken in the Cambridge Chronicle in 1976.

Best 5-Year Run and Average 1883-1887

	W	L	PCT.	ERA	IP	H	BB	Ratio	K
Totals	187	96	.660	2.41	2513	2075	491	9.2	1406
Average	37	19			503	415	98		281

Best 10-Year Run and Average 1881-1890

	W	L	PCT.	ERA	IP	H	BB	Ratio	K
Totals	302	185	.620	2.56	4317	3746	983	9.9	2274
Average	30	19			432	375	98		227

14-Year Average 1880-1893

342	225	.603	2.62	5047	4432	1236	10.3	2560
24	16			361	317	88		183

Career

W	L	PCT	G	GS	CG	SH	SV	IP	H	HR	BB	SO	Ratio
342	225	.603	600	594	554	39	2	5047	4432	75	1236	2560	10.3

ERA	Opponent's Avg
2.62	.226

22
FERGUSON JENKINS

Born: 12/13/43 Chatham, Ontario, Canada
6 feet 5 inches, 210 pounds
Debut: 9/10/65, Played 19 years: 1965-1983
1965-1966, Philadelphia; 1966-1973, Chicago (NL);
1974-1981, Texas; 1982-1983, Chicago (NL)

In an eight-year period, from 1967 through 1974, Ferguson Jenkins won 20 games six times in a row and seven times in all. He managed the great run with the Chicago Cubs, who haven't been the class of the National League since Mordecai Brown pitched for them 90 years ago. Born in Chatham, Ontario, Canada, Jenkins stands ninth all-time in strikeouts with 3,192 and is the only pitcher to strike out 3,000 without walking 1,000.

With Jenkins, you knew two things: he was going to throw hard and he was going to be around the plate. He broke in with the Phillies in 1965 and pitched in relief for the Phils and the Cubs the following season. He didn't emerge as a regular starter until 1967. He served notice at the All-Star Game that he had special stuff. He struck out six to tie Carl Hubbell's All-Star Game record set in 1934. He won 20 that season and, despite pitching in Wrigley, a grave yard for pitchers, he followed the 1967 season by winning 20, 21, 22, 24 and 20. He won the Cy Young Award in 1971.

But he never received the accolades he deserved. The headline pitchers in the National League were Bob Gibson, Tom Seaver, Steve Carlton and

Juan Marichal. While not always getting star notoriety, Jenkins was not averse to speaking his mind. "I don't think these people at Wrigley Field ever saw but two players they liked," Jenkins said, "Billie Williams and Ernie Banks. Billy never said anything and Ernie always said the right thing." After Jenkins sagged to 14 and 16 in 1973, the Cubs traded him to Texas in the off-season for Bill Madlock. He promptly led the AL in wins with 25 the following year.

After the 1975 season Texas traded Jenkins to Boston, where he was 12-11 and 10-10 before they traded him back to Texas. It would be an understatement to say that he and Red Sox manager Don Zimmer didn't get along. "The man knows nothing about pitching or pitchers," Jenkins said. "He's a lifetime .230 hitter who's been beaned three times. He hates pitchers. We will never see eye to eye."

Back to Texas he flew, where he promptly went 18-8 and then 16-14 the following season. All told, in the 13 years from 1967 through 1979, when he was 35, Jenkins won 239 games, an average of 18.4 per season. That's quite a record for someone traded five times in his career.

For some reason unknown to this writer, he didn't get the needed support to get into the Hall of Fame in 1989 or 1990. But in 1991 he garnered 334 votes and was inducted.

In *The Politics of Glory* and his *Historical Abstract*, Bill James makes the point that Jenkins, and Catfish Hunter, belong in the, "Robin Roberts family of pitchers." The family markings of these pitchers are (a) outstanding control, (b) medium-range strikeouts, (c), very high number of home runs allowed and (d) an ability to pitch a large number of innings without arm trouble. James is right on the mark here. And just as Roberts and Hunter made the Hall of Fame, so Jenkins deserved his entry, too.

Best 5-Year Run and Average 1967-1971

	W	L	PCT.	ERA	IP	H	BB	Ratio	K
Totals	107	72	.598	2.97	1545	1338	316	9.63	1306
Average	21	14			309	268	63		261

Best 10-Year Run and Average 1967-1976

	W	L	PCT.	ERA	IP	H	BB	Ratio	K
Totals	195	141	.580	3.17	2912	2606	579	9.84	2184
Average	20	14			291	261	58		218

Best 15-Year Run and Average 1966-1989

	W	L	PCT.	ERA	IP	H	BB	Ratio	K
Totals	257	193	.571	3.26	3995	3696	840	10.2	2887
Average	17	10			266	246	56		192

Career

W	L	PCT.	G	GS	CG	SH	SV	IP	H	HR	BB	SO	Ratio
284	226	.557	664	594	267	49	7	4500	4142	484	997	3192	10.4

ERA	Opponent's Avg
3.34	.243

23
GAYLORD PERRY

Born: 9/18/38 Williamston, NC
6 feet 4 inches, 215 pounds
Debut: 4/14/62, Played 22 years: 1962-1983
1962-1971, San Francisco; 1972-1975, Cleveland; 1975-1977,
Texas; 1978-1979, San Diego; 1980, Texas; 1980, New York (AL);
1981, Atlanta; 1982-1983, Seattle; 1983, Kansas City

Don Sutton described an encounter he had with Gaylord Perry in 1979.
"He handed me a tube of vaseline," said Sutton. "I thanked him and gave
him a sheet of sandpaper." Before he abused baseball substances, Perry
became a full-time starter for the Giants in 1964, first won 20 in 1966,
and, 17 years and seven teams later, had 314 victories, retiring in 1983.
Upon retiring he said, "The league will be a little drier now, folks."

Seven times Perry had a below-3.00 ERA and he led the league in victories with three different teams – the Giants, the Indians and the
Padres. Gaylord Perry threw a lot of motion at hitters and had many of
them, like the Yankees' Bobby Murcer, psyched out before they ever got
to the plate. Aside from all the loaded balls Perry was accused of throwing, he could flat out pitch. Between 1966 and 1974 he won 174 games –
an average of 19 a year. The workhorse pitched more than 250 innings
nine times and over 300 innings five times.

But the mention of Perry will always bring to mind foreign substances. Don Sutton may have become a pupil after their meeting, because he began loading up his pitches. A reporter asked Sutton if he used a foreign substance and he replied, "No, Vaseline is manufactured right here in the United States of America." But Perry was the professor emeritus of the junk ball.

He used Elm throat lozenges to produce saliva and moved from there to K-Y when he wanted to grease 'em up. A Pillsbury flour and resin concoction produced his "puffball." When second baseman Julio Cruz fielded Willie Randolph's grounder for the last out of Perry's 300th victory in 1982, he said he ran the ball toward first to hide the fact that he was flipping it around in his hand "to find the dry side" before throwing it.

By that time Perry had already reached 3,000 strikeouts. He finished with 3,534, good enough for sixth place all time. To Perry, strikeouts were more strategic than normal. "Going for a strikeout is like showing off your drive in golf," he said. "They pay off on how you putt. I like to save my strikeouts for when I need them." He also had excellent control, walking only 1,379 batters in 5,351 innings.

Perry could laugh at himself and brought a good deal of drama to the encounter between hitter and pitcher. When he retired at the age of 45 in 1983, he told of one of his endorsement efforts. "I once called the president of Vaseline and told him he should use me in a commercial since I used his product all the time. He got a little upset when he found out what I used it for. He said, 'Vaseline is only for babies and fannies.'"

Best 5-Year Run and Average 1970-1974

	W	L	PCT.	ERA	IP	H	BB	Ratio	K
Totals	104	73	.588	2.76	1616	1345	447	10.0	1060
Average	21	15			323	269	89		212

Best 10-Year run and Average 1966-1975

	W	L	PCT.	ERA	IP	H	BB	Ratio	K
Totals	193	144	.573	2.75	3085	2635	791	10.0	2130
Average	19	14			309	264	79		213

Best 15-Year Run and Average 1966-1980

	W	L	PCT.	ERA	IP	H	BB	Ratio	K
Totals	266	200	.571	2.88	4270	3796	1096	10.3	2879
Average	18	13			285	253	73		192

Career

W	L	Pct	G	GS	CG	SH	SV	IP	H	HR	BB	SO	Ratio
314	265	.542	777	590	303	53	11	5350	4938	399	1379	3534	10.8

ERA	Opponent's Avg
3.11	.245

24
ROBIN ROBERTS

Born: 9/30/26 Springfield, IL
6 feet, 190 pounds
Debut: 6/18/48, Played 19 years: 1948-1966
1948-1961, Philadelphia; 1962-1965, Baltimore;
1965-1966, Houston; 1966, Chicago (NL)

Pitching for four teams that played only .485 baseball over his 19-year career, Robin Roberts won 286 games and pitched .539 baseball, 54 percentage points above the teams for which he toiled. Because of this pitcher-team-differential, Roberts – and not Early Wynn – deserves the nod for this place. Early Wynn's teams played .552, while he pitched .551 (-1).

Roberts will fondly be remembered for pitching on Philadelphia's "Whiz Kids," a team that won 91 games in 1950 and delivered the city its first pennant in 35 years. Roberts won 20 that year, his first of six consecutive 20-win seasons. The Philly workhorse led the league five times in complete games, five times in innings and never in ERA. Even during his best seasons he would surrender 35, 40, up to 46 homers. "In the long history of organized baseball, I stand unparalleled for putting Christianity into practice," Roberts said after surrendering a league leading 46 homers in 1956. "And to prove that I was not prejudiced, I served up home run balls to Negroes, Italians, Jews and Catholics alike. Race, creed, nationality made no difference to me."

Roberts could afford to laugh. He was a hard thrower who didn't mess with the edges of the plate. He put the ball over. The result was an unexceptional 3.41 ERA but a most exceptional 902 walks in 4,689 innings. That's one measly free pass every 5.2 innings. "I can neither understand this or explain it," he said to a writer wondering about his pinpoint control. "I can't comprehend why other pitchers are wild."

When he was 28-7 in 1952, he led the league by 10 wins. With a 2.59 ERA, a 9.3 ratio, and league leading totals in complete games (33) and innings (346), that was his greatest year.

He was also known for a quick wit. Asked about his greatest All-Star Game thrill, he said, "When Mickey Mantle bunted with the wind blowing out in Crosley Field."

He allowed 505 homers. But he will be remembered less for the homers and more for the wins. He took the ball every fourth day and didn't show up on the disabled list until 1961, his 14th year, when he was 34 years old.

After that season, he finished up the last five years of his career with the Orioles, Astros and Cubs. He retired at the age of 40 and was elected to the Hall of Fame 10 years later, in 1976.

Best 5-Year Run and Average 1951-1955

	W	L	PCT.	ERA	IP	H	BB	Ratio	K
Totals	118	67	.638	.292	1631	1481	279	9.7	818
Average	24	13			326	296	56		164

Best 10-Year Run and Average 1949-1958

	W	L	PCT.	ERA	IP	H	BB	Ratio	K
Totals	199	147	.575	3.26	2978	2836	565	10.3	1474
Average	20	15			298	284	57		147

Best 15-Year Run and Average 1949-1963

	W	L	PCT.	ERA	IP	H	BB	Ratio	K
Totals	251	212	.542	3.44	4023	3919	738	10.4	2013
Average	17	14			268	261	49		134

Career

W	L	PCT	G	GS	CG	SH	SV	IP	H	HR	BB	SO	Ratio
286	245	.539	676	609	305	45	25	4688	4582	505	902	2357	10.6

ERA	Opponent's Avg
3.41	.255

25
KID NICHOLS

Born: 9/14/1869 Madison, WI, Died: 4/11/53 Kansas City, MO
Played 15 years: 1890-1906 (missed 1902-1903)
1890-1901, Boston (NL); 1904-1905, St. Louis (NL);
1905-1906, Philadelphia (NL)

Charles Augustus Nichols, better known as "Kid" for his boyish face and lanky build, began pitching for the Boston Beaneaters in 1890 and in his first 10 years won 30 games seven times. Nichols pitched with the maturity of a veteran from the time he was 20. At the age of 30, with 10 seasons under his belt, he had won 327 games. He was the youngest pitcher ever to reach 300 wins. Above all else, he was resilient and consistently good.

Nichols debuted with Kansas City in 1887 in the Western League and made his mark two years later with Omaha of the Western Association, winning 36 games. He joined the Beaneaters when his manager Frank Selee went, winning 27 games in his rookie year.

He pitched more than 400 innings in each of his first five seasons and more than 375 in each of his first 10. He was relieved in only 24 of the 501 starts he made for Boston. In 1892, a year in which he won 35 games, he pitched complete game wins three days in a row. No pitcher ever posted more 30-game seasons than Nichols' seven.

He got the nickname "Nervy Nick" for topping the Orioles twice in three days to win the 1897 pennant. He held out for more than $2,400, the maximum allowable at the time, and, by some accounts, earned a top salary of $3,000. He drew a $285 bonus for winning the 1898 pennant. He was worth it: he led Boston to five pre-1900 pennants and became the youngest ever to win 300.

By the time he retired in 1906, the 37-year-old had 361 posted wins and 208 losses (.634), 48 shutouts and had compiled a 2.95 ERA. *Total Baseball* relates that Nichols was an especially vigorous man in his retirement, capturing the Kansas City bowling championship at age 64. He bowled competitively into his seventies.

He was elected to the Hall of Fame in 1949 and died four years later at 83 years old.

Best 5-Year Run and Average 1890-1894

	W	L	PCT.	ERA	IP	H	BB	Ratio	K
Totals	158	79	.667	3.13	2134	2105	575	11.3	861
Average	32	16				421	115		172

Best 10-Year Run and Average 1890-1899

	W	L	PCT.	ERA	IP	H	BB	Ratio	K
Totals	297	151	.663	2.98	3984	3913	991	11.1	1476
Average	30	15			398	391	99		148

Career Average 1890-1904 (entire career, missed 1902 and 1903)

	W	L	PCT.	ERA	IP	H	BB	Ratio	K
Totals	361	208	.634	2.95	5056	4912	1268	11.2	1873
Average	24	14			337	327	85		125

Career

W	L	PCT	G	GS	CG	SH	SV	IP	H	HR	BB	SO	Ratio
361	208	.634	620	561	531	48	17	5056	4912	156	1268	1973	11.2

ERA	Opponent's Avg
2.95	.250

Some deserving pitchers who just missed making the top 100:

Jim Bunning
Bert Blyleven
Bob Caruthers
Stan Coveleski
Dizzy Dean
Dennis Eckersley
Rollie Fingers
Ron Guidry
Catfish Hunter
Addie Joss
Phil Niekro
Amos Rusie
Don Sutton
Hoyt Wilhelm
Early Wynn

Up and Coming

In time, these pitchers may take their place among the all-time greats.

Randy Johnson
Pedro Martinez
Andy Pettitte
Mariano Rivera
John Smoltz